TEXTILE UNDER NEOLIBERALISM IN INDIA

Contents

Acknowledgements

During the course of this study, I have received encouragement, help, and inspiration from several personalities without whom I am sure this work would not have been completed. Let me take this opportunity to acknowledge their direct/indirect contribution to shape and finalize my idea of this thesis. At the outset, I am extremely thankful to my supervisor, Prof. Zoya Hasan. Without her inspiration, guidance and direction this study would not have reached this stage. On many occasions when I was confused and wondered how to proceed on certain issues, her meticulous explanations opened new windows. She has always extended support and helped understand my limitations. It was a tremendous opportunity to work under her and I wish to cherish those ideals I have learnt during my association with her.

I wish to thank the Chairperson of my center, Prof. Pralay Kanungo, who not only arranged a timely 9 (b) interview of mine but helped in adding clarity in my Ph.D structure at the initial stages. Prof. Valerian Rodriguse had not only shaped my thesis but throughout this journey he supported me to understand myself. I have always looked forward to meeting him for all kinds of help and support. I have found him always willing to understand my situation and help me. I have received encouragement from my teachers in the centre, like Prof. Gopal Guru, Prof. Vidhu Verma and Prof. Manindra Nath Thakur. Thakur sir has been very kind to me and once even approached me to discuss about the Banaras weavers' situation. I was moved by his humble gesture. Not only that, he offered me a chapter in his co-edited book as well. Thank you so much, sir. Special mention is also needed to Prof. Vidhu Verma. I still remember her interaction with me when she enquired about my background and encouraged me to achieve big. I am thankful to all my teachers at Centre for Political Studies for their support and inspiration behind this work. I owe thanks to the office bearers of the centre for extending technical support.

I express special thanks to CPS friends group, which we used to call CPS Republic. The proud members have been Moo, Simu, Tobu, Sumeet,

Pal, Butku. But, I am thankful that I have got such friends in life who are always ready to pull me up whenever I feel beaten and defeated. The list is very long in which everybody stands first. Thank you Adnan, Suchi, Harish, Parimal, DJ, DT, Rajiv, Aftab, all the friends from Mau. This is also time to specially mention my friends who edited my Ph.D in very short duration. Simantini, Suchi, Moo and Pooja Rangaprasad, thank you. I also acknowledge the help and support provided by the teachers from BHU, especially Mr. A. Mohanty, who helped find accommodation for my stay during my field visit. During my field work Mr. Sabir Ali too helped me a lot. The CPI (M), Banaras unit, had helped me by providing local contacts within Bajardiha locality and given relevant documents related to labour movements they conducted in and around the area.

I would also like to thank the staff of Central Library of Jawaharlal Nehru University, S.A.P. Library of Centre for Political Studies, Central Library of Banaras Hindu University, PVCHR office staff and Nehru Memorial Museum and library Teenmurti Bhawan, as without their cooperation this work would not have been possible.

This would remain incomplete unless I am grateful to my parents Noor Mohammad and Najiboon Nisha, my wife Khusboo and entire family who keep on praying Allah for the completion of my thesis. Without their affection, inspiration, moral and material support I would not have been able to reach this position. I am indebted to all my brothers and sisters and sisters-in-law for encouraging me during my Ph.D work. Finally, I am extremely thankful to the people of Banaras who gave their precious time and extended to me their generous hospitality when I interviewed them.

The responsibility for all the lapses and errors in this thesis remain mine alone.

MANJUR ALI

Abbreviation

ADI	: Additional Director of Industries
ANZ	: Australia and New Zealand Banking Group
BDAM	: Bunkar Dastkar Adhikar Manch
BDM	: *Bunkar Dastkar Morcha*
BMS	: Bhartiya Mazdoor Sangh
BPL	: Below Poverty Line
CEM	: Computer Embroidery Machine
CFC	: Common Facility Centre
CITI	: Confederation of Indian Textile Industry (CITI)
CPM	: Communist Party of India (Marxist)
CSS	: Centrally Sponsored Scheme
DFID	: Department for International Development
DHDS	: Diversified Handloom Development Schemes
DICCI	: Dalit Indian Chamber of Commerce and Industry
DOH	: Directorate of Handloom
EDII	: Entrepreneurship Development Institute of India
FICCI	: Federation of Indian Chambers of Commerce and Industry
GATT	: General Agreement on Tariffs and Trade
GCTI	: Government Central Textile Institute
GDP	: Gross Domestic Product
GSDP	: Gross State Domestic Product
GI	: Geographical Indication
HCL	: Hindustan Computers Limited
HIS	: Health Insurance scheme
HMS	: Hind Mazdoor Sabha

HNI	: High Net worth Individual
IHDS	: Integrated Handloom Development Schemes
IHWT	: Institute of Handloom Weaving Technology
INTUC	: Indian National Trade Union Congress
JDI	: Joint Director Industries
KPI	: Key Performance Indicators
KVIC	: Khadi and Village Industries Commission
LIC	: Life Insurance Corporation
MFA	: Multi Fibre Arrangment
MGBBY	: Mahatma Gandhi Bunkar Bima Yojana
MGPS	: Mill Gate Price Scheme
MSP	: Minimum Support Price
NHDC	: National Handloom Development Corporation
NITRA	: North India Textile Research Association
NTP	: New Textile Policy
OBC	: Other Backward Class
OGL	: Open General License
PDC	: Post-Dated Bearer Cheque
PSU	: Public Sector Unit
SCR	: Sachar Committee Report
SEZ	: Special Economic Zone
SGDP	: State Gross Domestic Product
TPDS	: Targeted Public Distribution System
UNCTAD	: United Nations Conference on Trade and Development
UPICA	: Uttar Pradesh Industrial Cooperative Association
UTUC	: United Trade Union Congress
WSC	: Weavers Service Centre

Glossary

Akta: It is advance money on interest rate paid by traders to the family head of a young boy in the beginning of job. To repay the amount boy works as a bonded labour.

Battedars: Persons who offer cash to recipients of Post-Dated bearer Cheque at a discount. The weavers bear the discount or interest rate.

Dharki Phekna: Throwing of shuttle carrying weft-yarn from one side of loom to another is called *Dharki phekna*.

Dharki: It is shuttle made of wooden or animal horn which is used to throw the weft-yarn from one side to another.

Gaddidar: It refers to large traders who are primarily selling finshed product to markets including export markets.

Ghat: The stone steps and platforms leading down to river which characterise the ancient sacred city of Banaras.

Grihastha: is the one who is small trader, mostly Muslims, gets saris woven by the weavers on contract, paying them wages, and also buys the finished saris woven by the self-employed weavers and master weavers.

Jamawar: The glory and colours of nature captured skilfully on cloth characterise the famous Jamawars of Kashmir. "*Jama*" means robe and "War" is yard. King and nobles bought the woven fabrics by the yard, wearing it as a gown or using it as a wrap or shawl.

Jangla: Running pattern of leaves and flowers all over the ground work and complex floral patterns consists of *bel* and *buti* and combinations thereof.

Karigars: The artisans/weavers.

Karkhana: Manufacturing workshop

Kimkhab: Persian word for brocades.

Nakshabands: The designers.

Nari Bharna: Yarn for the weft (*Bana*) is reeled on a small (few centimetres long) cylindrical object mostly by women and girl child.

Sattiwalas: He is a broker who intermediates between the seller and the buying trader and gets 3 per cent commission from the seller.

Tani Taanana: The process of reeling yarn on the wooden cylinder of the handloom for warp (*tana*).

Weaver: The one who sets and adjusts the looms, and operates them to weave textiles. The definition of weavers considered in the census (1995-96) was as follows: Weavers include persons who actually operated looms at least for a week during the last one-year. Individuals who operated the looms on a full-time basis have been classified as full-time weavers. There were weavers who operated the looms only during their leisure hours or when the regular weavers were out on lunch, tea, such weavers have been classified as part-time weavers.

GSDP: It is defined as the total market value of all final goods and services produced within the state's in a given period of time (usually a calendar year). It is also considered the sum of value added at every stage of production (the intermediate stages) of all final goods and services produced within a country in a given period of time, and it is given a money value.

List of Tables

List of Figures

Introduction

This research is an attempt to look at the dynamics governing the Muslim weavers of Banaras and contextualising their position in the structure of production while exploring their relationship with politics, society and economic structure. A weaver (*julaha*) is a lowest unit in the whole production chain. The chain contains many actors at various levels such as suppliers of yarn and other raw materials, designers and *gaddidar*, each having a unique relationship with weavers, which shall be discussed later. Hitherto all the research works, with rarity, on Indian Muslims has treated them either from 'communitarian' perspective or 'caste' point of view, which is a recent phenomenon and is going strong. In the communitarian perspective, scholars treat Muslims as a separate religious group, which is in minority vis-à-vis dominant Hindu religious group. So, the problems dealt with here are of their identity and security, which remain endangered from the rise of majoritarianism or 'silent majoritarianism'. It treats all the Muslims as one homogeneous category, so are their problems.

This hegemonic thought has been perpetuated by the ruling class and elites of the community itself since independence. The interaction between the western civilization in the form of colonial rule and vulnerable Islam in South Asia led to the foundation of misunderstood knowledge of homogenized identity of Muslims. Nonetheless, the then Muslim leaders too helped in creating an impression that they are different from the Hindu community. The major source of this inference came from the religiously inspired feeling of oneness among the Muslims of the world propagated by that time Muslim leader like Shah Wali Ullah, Shah Abdul Aziz, Jamalluddin Afghani and others. On the other sides, colonial masters used it for their colonial objectives to check the rising influence of the Congress party. All this was manifested in the form of separate electorate in 1909, which opened the gates of communal tension in Indian politics and society. It inevitably led to the creation of political camps organized against each other and teaches men to think as partisans and not citizen.

However, 1990s was a watershed in the politics of Muslim community when eighty-four out of hundred twenty seven castes got listed in the central list of Other Backward Classes (OBCs) category. This was for the first time that Indian State recognised the fact that Muslims are not a homogenous group, rather they are stratified on 'caste' basis. This brings forth the assertion of downtrodden '*Ajlaf*' (uncivil or unjust) and '*Arzal*' (impure) Muslims with the tilt in political agenda from communitarian to 'secular' and development of the community. There have been continuous efforts by various individuals in some regions of the country to unite the *Pasmanda* (backward) Muslims not only against the politics of *Ashraf* (noble) Muslim elites, but in favour of their due rights under the influence of general process of democratization and implementing Mandal Commission recommendation, in order to come out of the degrading socio-economic position. In Maharashtra, for instance, this movement originated before the implementation of Mandal Commission. Under the leadership of Shabbir Ahmed Ansari, national President of All-India Muslim OBC Organization, activists like Vilas Sonaware tried hard to organize Dalit and the Muslim OBCs. On February 5, 1984, Shabbir Ansari held a massive rally of Muslim OBCs and Dalits at Jalna in Maharashtra, where his organization received massive support from intellectuals, social activists and politicians. Similarly, in West Bengal, among various organizations working to raise the consciousness of OBC and Dalit Muslims, Uttar Bango Anagrasar Muslim Sangram Samity (UBAMSS) is the most active one. But, the activism of OBC Muslim organizations in Bihar has set-up a high standard in terms of influencing regional level politics. Coming up of various caste categories as one unit engendered a sense of unity and produces consciousness about their strength in terms of electoral politics. As, many OBC leaders like Ali Anwar, Ejaz Ali have worked tirelessly to consolidate these scattered and benign masses and transformed them into a political force.

Notwithstanding all these efforts, this movement has certain weaknesses. The movement is not fully democratic as they avoid discussing the unequal power structure between men and women of the community. Secondly, although, they have not abandoned the principle of secularism but sharing power with the political allies of Bhartiya Janta Party (BJP) stops them from questioning the rise of communal politics, as has been witnessed in Bihar. Brutal killing of Muslims in Forbesganj, Bihar, including a pregnant woman, was silently borne by the *Pasmanda* (backward) groups. However, if we take a look at the castes that belong to '*Ajlaf*' and '*Arzal*', most are occupational castes that are an important part of the economic structure of a society. These castes are the real producers as they apply their labour to add value to the available material and produce commodities for sale in the market. For example, ironsmith produces tool for various purposes, carpenters, oil presser, weavers, milkmen, farmers etc. In India, most of the Muslims are involved in skilled and unskilled occupation, but very less attention had been paid till now to treat these occupational castes as a working unit.[1] As this exercise has the potential to bring forth the commonality among workers of different religious group and develop the possibility of cooperation between the groups which ascriptive identity like caste and religion won't allow despite the common interest. It also explains the exploitative relationship between workers and owners of means of production, which similar caste or religious group factors do not allow for investigation. It further exposes the exploitative nature of ascriptive identities itself, which has been employed by rich/elite to garner the support of the group to push their own self-interest. In other words, the elite project their interest as the community's interest.

At the broader level, to comprehend this complex nature of relationship between the caste, class and religion, this research has taken weaver, an OBC by caste and Muslim by religion as the case study. The timeframe taken for this research is the first two decades of liberalization i.e. 1990-2010. Time period under scrutiny is vital as it has undergone substantial changes at the levels of production, marketing and technology. Apart from alteration in economy brought in by liberalization, changes at the level of culture, religion and communitarian behaviour of handloom weavers are also analysed. It is remarkable that in some cases handlooms have been wiped out in countries where modern textile industry has been established, while in India, it still occupies a strategic position in nation's socio-economic set up. N.G. Ranga, while analysing the status of handloom in early period of the twentieth century, had shown optimism for this sector. He noted that "Many people who have studied the decay of the handloom weavers of England because of their inability to stand before the competition of mills fear that the handloom weavers of any country must also fare the same fate…But they overlook the fact that what resulted in England may not happen in India and that conditions in India are different from those of England."[2] He further noted that though it is true that number of actual (male) workers in this industry has not risen to the same extent as the total population, the industry as a whole has not yet shown any serious sign of decay. He listed out a number of factors which helped handloom industry to sustain. These are the general inefficiency of the capitalists and entrepreneurs, the unskilled character of the managerial staff, the lack of initiative in the supervisors, the want of training in the workers and the insufficiency of capital, internal and external economies have limits the capacity of the mills; weavers are extraordinarily loyal to their caste occupation and they do not like to leave their profession; weavers were ever ready to change the mode of work in weaving; every centre of handloom weaving is specially dependent upon one or two particular specialities of its own and upon the demand coming from particular centre; the merchants of the consuming centres are prevented by lethargy and loyalty from abandoning their customary supplier of customary places and so they create a sort of stability of demand for the clothes of the handloom weavers; some of these handloom weaving centres specialise in particular kinds of cloths which have not yet been produced in the mills on a large scale; and the fashions in clothing do not change so quickly in India as they do in England.

The factors sustaining this growth were, on the demand side, an expansion in average cloth consumption partly as a result of fall in cloth prices, partly that of agricultural growth in some areas, and partly tariff protection to the textile industry from the mid-1920s. It is suggested that growing nationalist sentiments in the inter-war period, the ideology of 'Swadeshi', helped the handloom weaver. However, in the post-independence period, it is the wage 'advantage', when combined with reservation, duty concessions and rebates, which unfortunately have been poorly implemented, were the real factors accounting for the survival of the handloom industry.

Even today most of the weavers work at the handloom, thus, an introduction to this sector is important. Handloom is a part of unorganised sector of Indian textile industry. It is widespread to all regions of the country and their share in the apparel production is substantial. Further, the handloom sector is the largest economic activity after agriculture providing direct and indirect employment to more than 43.31 lakh weavers in India.[3] It is characterised by: (1) the coexistence of a broad spectrum of production techniques – hand-operated to sophisticated automated technology; (2) a dualistic manufacturing structure dominated by fast expending decentralised small-scale manufacturing segment and a declining vertically integrated, large scale "composite mills"; (3) a predominance of cotton as a primary raw material; (4) the existence of large public sector composed mainly of nationalised and sick mills taken over by the government; and (5) a predominantly small-scale apparel sector.

The textile industry is divided into organised and unorganised sectors. Organised sector consist of mills – spinning and composite. Spinning mills involved only in spinning activities whereas composite mills are vertically integrated mills covering the full array of textile processing operations – spinning, weaving, dyeing, printing and finishing. According to the annual report, 2011-12, of the Ministry of Textiles, currently, 470 spinning and 85 composite mills exist. On the other hand, the unorganised sector includes handloom, powerloom, hosiery, etc. Apart from handloom, powerlooms operated in households by family members themselves too are considered as cottage industry and part of the unorganised sector. The basic differences between handloom and powerloom of unorganised sector are: powerloom produces more, operates by the help of electricity, use mixed yarn against the pure silk yarn by handloom.

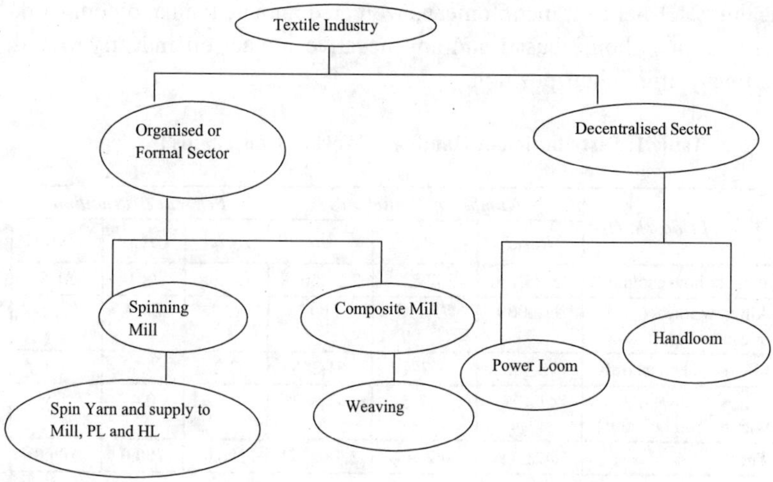

Figure 1: Structure of Textile Industry

There are several distinctions between the unorganised sector and organised sector in textile industry which are as follow:[4]

(a) This distinction is based primarily on the scale of operation and the nature of organisation.

(b) Often, the technology employed may also be different.

(c) In contrast to the organised or formal sector, units in unorganized sector may or may not be registered.

(d) Further, reliable statistics of employment and output in this sector are generally not available.

(e) In contrast with the organised mill sector, almost the entire requirement of working capital and fixed capital or powerlooms is met from non-bank sources obtained at higher than institutional lending rates of interest. One major source of labour for this sector is the migration from countryside. The other source could be workers from partially closed or fully closed mill.

(f) The working hours in the unorganized sector are relatively longer.

Apart from providing employment to large section of the population and acting as an important source of the rural economy, "this sector accounts for 13 per cent of the total cloth produced in the country, excluding clothes made of wool, silk and hand spun yarn".[5] The 3rd Handloom Census (2009-10) interestingly revealed that among adult (18 and above age) handloom workers women constitute 77.9 per cent against 21.1 per cent men. It means women dominate the handloom work force as it is home based and any negative impact on industry would seriously affect their position.

Table 1: Distribution of Handloom Worker Households by Type

Type of Households	*Number of Households*			*Per cent Distribution*		
	Rural	*Urban*	*Total*	*Rural*	*Urban*	*Total*
Weaver households	1,985,186	282,822	2,268,008	82.0	78.1	81.5
Allied workers households	316,009	75,116	391,125	13.1	20.7	14.1
Idle loom households	78,495	2,761	81,256	3.2	0.8	2.9
Others (households with no adult worker)	41,427	1,455	42,882	1.7	0.4	1.5
Total	**2,421,117**	**362,154**	**2,783,271**	**100.0**	**100.0**	**100.0**

Source: 3rd Handloom Census, 2009-10.

The data shows that handloom is still a rural phenomenon. Of the total handloom worker households, 87 per cent belong to rural area and 13 per cent to urban. Within rural handloom worker households, 82.0 per cent belong to weaver households, allied workers household (13.1), idle loom households (3.2), and others (1.7). Break-up of data social-group-wise reflects that OBCs (40.9) have the maximum presence in the handloom industry, followed by others (27.2), Scheduled Tribes (22.1), Scheduled Castes (9.8). Religion-wise data revealed that handloom in India is dominated by Hindus (77.6), followed by Muslims (15), Christians (5.9), Buddhists (0.9), others (0.5) and Sikhs (0.1). A religion-wise comparative study of handloom worker revealed that Muslim handloom households are mostly located in urban areas, while a comparatively higher proportion of households of other religions (including Christians) are located in rural areas. A state-wise distribution shows that Hindu households are the majority in most states with the exception of Uttar Pradesh (UP), where 85.4 per cent households are Muslims; West Bengal, where 36.6 per cent households are Muslims; and the group termed 'other states', where 44.2 per cent households are Muslim. The number of Handloom weavers and allied workers as per the Second Census of Handlooms of India (1995-96) and Third Handloom Census of India (2009-10) are:

Table 2: Number of Weavers and Allied Worker in Handloom

Sr. No.	*Census (Year)*	***Number of Handloom Weavers and Allied Workers (in lakhs)***
1.	Second Census (1995-96)	65.50
2.	Third Census (2009-10)	43.31

Source: 2nd and 3rd Handloom Census.

The census shows the decline of handloom weavers in the period of liberalization. With the onset of the liberalization process, Multi-Fibre Arrangement (MFA) came to an end in 2005. In 1974, MFA came into existence whereby industrialized countries, through bilateral agreements with individual trading partners, could establish quotas on textile and clothing imports from competitive developing countries. Initially, the MFA was supposed to remain in force for four years, but it was extended several times till 1994. In 1995, the MFA was integrated into General Agreement on Tariffs and Trade (GATT) via the Agreement on Textiles and Clothing (ATC). The principal objective of the ATC was to integrate the textile sector into the World Trade Organisation (WTO – the successor to GATT) in four stages over a transition period of 10 years ending January 1, 2005. Due to the termination of MFA, the handloom sector has been experiencing changes. As this sector is very different in terms of production, structure or organisational base, as well as in relations between actors within the production structure around the country and type of individuals or groups involved into it, the effect of liberalization is also varied. So to comprehend the nature of effects on the handloom sector at the micro level, this research aims to study the weavers of Banaras handloom, which is dominated by Muslims.

Banaras Weavers

Oriental scholars, British missionaries and administrators and several Indian writers have projected Banaras overtly as a 'Hindu' city through their writings.[6] The researchers disregard the fact that substantial presence of Muslims in and around the city has been there for centuries. When Macaulay wrote that "from Benares went forth the most delicate silks that adorned the balls of St. James's and of Versaille", in fact he was talking about the Muslim weavers involved in silk industry of Banaras. Before Macaulay, a British India administrator, James Phillips, recorded 31,248 Muslims of various castes present in Banaras. Ten thousand out of total strength of Muslims belonged to the *julaha* caste.[7] The other term used for them is "*nurbawf*"[8] (weaver of *Zari* cloth), used in Jahangir's *firmans* and some other formal government documents, which is no longer employed by them to refer to themselves. With the political mobilisation in Banaras under All India Jamiat ul-Ansar in 1930s, the title "*Ansari*" came to be used by weavers. However, Vasanti Raman, while tracing the history of the *julaha* in this area, believed that most of them are of Indian origin, and had humble origins. "The Momin Ansaris were formerly *julahas*, considered an occupational caste who converted over many centuries to Islam. The *julahas* were themselves quite differentiated. Economic differentiation (between the master weavers, independent weavers who worked their own looms, and those who worked on the looms of others) melded with differentiations based on "caste." Thus, there were the *Koli Julahas*, *Chamar Julahas*, *Mochi Julahas* and the *Ramdasi Julahas*; and it is probable that after a few generations, these men will drop the prefix which denotes their lowly origin and become *julahas* pure and simple."[9]

In 1951 and 1961, the district gazetteers of Varanasi estimated 194,890 and 243,253 Muslims population respectively.[10] According to 1991 census, Muslims were 29.5 per cent of the total populations, which was approximately 739,892.45. In 2001, Muslim population was 497,516 i.e. 15 per cent of the total population in the district.[11] But, it should be noted that majority of Muslims have been urban dwellers since the beginning. They live in urban areas i.e. in the vicinity of Banaras city as compared to rural. In 1951, a total of 107,605 Muslims were living in urban areas, as compared to rural population of 87,285. In 1961, a total of 137,920 Muslims were living in urban areas as compared to rural population of 105,333.[12] Today, Muslims constitutes 35.7 per cent of the 1.5 million of total population of Varanasi City and around 90 per cent of them belong to the weaver community, known as *Ansari/Julaha* involved in making

Banarasi saris,[13] mostly living in ghettoised areas of Alaipur, Jaitpur, Adampura, Lallapura and Madanpura areas of the city.[14] 30 per cent of rural weavers are Muslims.

They produce saris, stoles, mufflers, mats, dress materials, furnishings, wall hangings, scarves, cushion covers, napkins, table covers and leno fabrics. However, the estimated share of saris in the total value of output varies from 90 per cent to 95 per cent. Thus, saris continue to dominate as a production item in Banaras.[15] Different areas within Banaras produce different styles/designs of the sari. The two famous area-specific designs are Madanpura and Alaipura designs. The Madanpura design is highly sophisticated and is woven on light transparent materials. Fine cotton, *zari, jamdani*, organza, *dupattas* with *konia* of *kain*, the stylised mango pattern at each of the corners; and a big circular pattern called *chand*, moonshaped in the centre. The ground of this fabric is either woven with diagonal creepers called *ari-jhari*, or a variety of small flower patterns popularly known as *butis*. Alaipura design is not as sophisticated. Its pieces are considered coarser. Alaipura weavers adopted new design and weaving techniques, and were ready to experiment. In fact, the experimental nature of Alaipura weavers has helped the brocade industry of Banaras to survive even during that crucial period. In Banaras, according to 1995-96 'Joint Census of Handloom and Powerloom', 78.50 per cent weavers of all ranks belong to OBCs category and as mentioned earlier 90 per cent of Muslim population is weaver.[16]

Along with the commonality of occupation, the *Sardari* or *Mahto* system works as another factor that holds together the social structure of the *julaha*. In Banaras, *Sardari* system started around 1611 AD, which had its presence in other adjoining area. This system will be discussed at length in chapter five. Beneath these similarities, Muslim weavers of Banaras have complex and heterogeneous identity overlapping one-another, rather simplistic it appears. At present the Momin Ansari community of Banaras is spread in between three major residential areas, i.e., Madanpura-Rewari Talab area, Lallapura and Alaipura-Jaitpura area. These are *julaha* ghetto in Banaras city. L. Gayer and C. Jaffrelot argued that the incidence of violence have sustained dynamics of self-segregation among Muslims, who have been searching for safety in numbers. This process has been reinforced by the socio-economic marginalisation affecting Muslims. Ghettos have even been granted official recognition in the Sachar Committee Report (SCR), whose authors claim that 'Fearing for their security, Muslims are increasingly resorting to living in ghettos across the country'. And according to SCR this ubiquitous process of ghettoization would have severe effects on the community: 'inadequacy of infrastructure facilities, shrinking common spaces where different socio-religious categories can interact and reduction in livelihood options.[17]

As the population has increased over a period of time, new residential areas of weavers have developed on the outskirts of the city or in the near vicinity of the city. Lohata in the west, Saraiyya in north and Bajardiha in south are the newly developed and thickly populated weavers' settlements. The newly inhabited areas are simply extension of the earlier mentioned three areas.[18] These areas are mainly populated by Muslim weavers, but in ethnic origin, marital network and in production activities, these areas have distinctive features of their own. The Alaipura-Jaitpura segment in local parlance is known as '*Mauwale*' (People of Mau), by their racial characteristics, kinship network and the type of silk work produced. Lallapura are said to be rural migrants who at different points of time, came and settled in the area. Madanpura-Rewari Talab area is quite distinctive compared to the previous two groups. A legend of how Madanpura area became famous as the origin point of Banaras brocade said that seven Muslim families fled from central Asia of the western Iranian plateau and settled at Madanpura. They are later called *Sat Gharav*. They may have belonged to a group of *Kazzaz* weavers, who had migrated from west Asian weaving centres and were employed in the royal weaving workshops of the Sultanate King. It is believed that the weavers belonging to the seven families brought with them a special silk weaving technique for *Kazazi* and *Nassaji* fabrics from Khajistan in the western plateau of Iran.

However, local members of this area believe that their ancestors migrated from Afghanistan, Iran, Iraq, Arab and other places across Asia and settled in this area due to the conducive atmosphere for the growth of the silk industry. This group of Muslim weavers, by their appearance and other physical features appear to be of foreign origin. The weavers of this area have been further distinguished between '*Gurra*' which has fair complexion, handsome and seem to West-Asian origin and other known as '*Dumaon*' which is relatively dark and appears to be mongoloid origin, like Bengali weavers (*tati*) of West Bengal. The linguistic traces also attest to their migration. The Madanpura dialect is colloquial version of Urdu, which contains Arabic, Persian and Bengali.[19] The weavers of Madanpura-Rewari Talab preserve their ethnic identity by the mechanism of caste as well as territorial endogamy. Weavers rarely marry outside their caste and geographical boundary. Similarly, the weaver of other localities does prefer marital relation within their own area and caste.

Other than the caste and territorial segregation of *julaha*, sectarianism, further separates them. Weavers of different sects do not marry into other sects. Its root can be traced to the reform movement in the late 19th and early 20th century. The reform movement was focused on bringing social and ritual practices closer to pristine Islam, but met with little success. Most of the weavers follow Barelvi tradition; however, the situation began to change 1920s onwards, with a few master weavers experiencing economic mobility, combined with social reform campaign that led to their conversion from one sect to another in search of newer, and possible, superior identity. Weavers are divided into Deobandis[20], Barelvis[21], Ahl-e-Hadith.[22] By now, Madanpuri Muslims are well represented among the merchants and have even breached the upper levels. By becoming Ahl-e-Hadith, they differentiate themselves from other groups. This has had the effect of intensifying the pre-existing division between the localities of Madanpura, near the city centre, and the more prosperous neighbourhoods in which many Muslims live, in the older, northern wards. Even before 1940, Madanpuri Muslims married only within the locality, other wards being seen as poorer, inferior and less meticulous in Islamic observance. In doing so, they followed the general Indian practice of endogamy, of marrying only within the same status group, while at the same time maintaining Muslim customs so contrary to North Indian Hindu practice, of kinship and locality endogamy. But once the Madanpura weavers changed their sect, social divisions became deeper. Since 1950, Ahl-e-Hadith families in Madanpura have ceased arranging marriages with Deobandis and have become totally endogamous. This indicates that they no longer consider Deobandis to be of equal status or worth.[23] Similarly, a Barelwi does not prefer social relationship with weavers from other sect. The initial period of conversion from one sect to another has seen less effect on the individual relationship. However, with time, sectarianism became stronger among weavers with the help of 'hidden fatwa'[24] from each school of thought, asking their followers to refrain from marital links with other sects.[25] Social institutions, mainly schools and madrasas, controlled by various schools of thought furthered this sectarian division.

Since the second decade of 20th century, handloom industry of Banaras has been suffering from problems such as competition from powerloom, middlemen, shortage of raw material, no control over marketing, corruption inside the cooperative organisations meant for poor weavers etc. But, despite these hindrances, the handloom industry and weavers continued with their traditional occupation. According to Nita Kumar, success of the industry was based on the traditional skill weavers, the suitable climate of the place, and the virtues of Banaras as a market, both in its role as pilgrim centre and as favoured residential preference of the gentry from the 18th century onwards. To these may be added: the well-developed infrastructure of trade, a system not disturbed by the British; and the tremendous resilience and flexibility of the weavers in responding to changing markets. According to Tirthankar Roy "...in the twentieth century handlooms accounted for about 25 per cent of the cotton cloth produced annually in the first half of the 20th century. The market-share of handloom cotton cloth was roughly stable between the 1890s and the 1930s. The total production of cotton cloth has expanded by 30 per cent in between 1900-1939. Throughout this period, total cloth consumption was growing, and Indian cloth was steadily substituting imported cloth. In cloths made of silk and other fibres, handlooms dominated."

Banarasi weavers generally use pit loom. There are approximately 34,000 pit looms available in Banaras, which is most specific in construction, and the mode of operation of the loom differs from handlooms available in other parts of the country. The uniqueness of these looms is the production of specific design with 3/4 different weft thread and are popularly known as Varanasi design. These are outdated technologies used by Banaras weavers, which is one of the major factors for their impoverishment. Weavers were once proud artisans with a reputation worldwide. However, today enter any building now and they seem like poor houses for the malnourished and ill. This trend surfaced since the opening of the market, coinciding with the slump in the Banarasi silk market, the advent of power looms and the import of cheap Chinese silk. Weavers work 10-12 hours daily on the looms, but are paid about Rs. 50, less than the government's minimum wages of Rs. 58 for agricultural labour.[26] In the 1990s, powerlooms became very common, producing several saris in a day – the same time it takes for weavers to weave only the first yard of a classic six-metre sari on their wooden handlooms, thread by thread. Machine-made Chinese imitations have in recent years flooded the market, often sold by dishonest dealers as the real thing. Baranasi sari weavers say that they cannot compete, and so thousands of looms have fallen silent. "They started closing down slowly, one or two at a time," remembers Munni Devi, who lives in Gaurakala village, once home to about 100 handlooms.[27]

To restore the glory of handloom sector, UP government has also taken some State level policies, such as, new cluster scheme, up-gradation of skills and technology, marketing, District Industries Centres to help small industries in accessing information and latest technology etc. But, announcement of programmes, both at the Central and State level, has not been matched up with financial allocation made to this sector in the last decade. In the last ten years, budget allocation has been decreasing gradually and continuously. It is also interesting to see the overall budget for the Ministry (at the Union level) has been increasing. It has grown four times from 1997-98 to 2006-07 – from Rs.739.04 crores to Rs.3,045.75 crores. No positive programmes are being included in the Plans. Both the Ninth and Tenth Plans have failed the handloom weavers.

Review of Literature

Several studies are available on Banaras, handloom industry of Banaras and other places. These studies capture the journey of Banaras since its antiquity to its status in the current phase of development. While dealing with ancient Banaras, most studies focus on its cultural aspect, the city being a religious centre and a symbol of Hinduism. Vidyarthi, Jha and Saraswati (1979) describe the importance of Banaras in various religions in ancient period.[28] Kashi finds prominent mention in various sacred scriptures, such as the *Puran*, the *Smrits*, the *Nibandha*, the epics, and Buddhist and Jain literature. Of the *Puranas*, which have described Kashi at length, mention may be made of the *Agni Purana* (112), the *Padma Purana* (14.191), the *Kurma Purana* (1,31, 35), the *Matsya Purana* (191), the *Linga Purana* (92), the *Skanda Purana* (4) etc. The fourth chapter of the *Skanda Purana*, known as the '*Kashi khanda*', is exclusively devoted to the sacred shrines located in *Kashi-Kshetra* (area of Kashi).

"Of the *Nibandha* or the digests describing Kashi as the *tirhasthali*, mention may be made of the *Tirthakalpattaru* (particularly the *Tirthavivechankhanda*) written by Lakshmidhar; the *Tirthalisetu* of Narayana Bhatta; the *Chaturvarga Chintamani* of Vachaspati; the *Tirthayatra Vidhi Tattva* of Raghunandan; the *Tirtha-Prakash* by Mitra and Mishra, etc. In all these *Nibandhas* the authors have described the Kashi *tirthas* as the place where both this-worldly and the other-worldly desires are fulfilled. The modes of performing pilgrimages have also been indicated in these digests. Kashi is mentioned both in the Mahabharata and the Ramayana. The *'Anushasana Parva'* (108) and the *'Vinaya Parva'* (82) of the Mahabharata specially record the importance of the *tirtha yatra*, placing it even above the sacrifice. The Mahabharata mentions Varanasi as the *tirth* situated at the confluence of Ganges and the Gomati. The Ramayana (Chapter LVIII) describes Varanasi as the capital of Kashi. In the *Jataka* stories (3rd century B.C.), Brahmadatta frequently appears as the King of Kashi. The *Udalak Jataka* and the *Somanda Jataka* (532) refer to Kashi in connection with territorial disputes. Of the Jain works, special reference may be made of the *Kalpasutra* which records that Kashi is the birth place of the *Tirthankaras*."[29]

However, Hans Bakker (1996) contradicts the antiquity of Varanasi prevailing in Hindu community.[30] Hans doubts over the claim of antiquity of Varanasi and its rise as 'holy' city from time immemorial. He found no authentic record to substantiate the claim. Archaeological as well as literary testimony testified the rise of Banaras as a sacred to brahminical tradition only in first century A.D. The transformation of commercial, i.e. profane space into sacred space, which, incidentally, was by no means detrimental to commerce, took place in the fourth to sixth centuries of the Christian era, when North India was united under the Gupta dynasty.[31] Hans cites a number of books and evidence to make his point convincing. Later, Varanasi turned into the seat of political power by Gahadavalas. Hans Bakker argued that the reason for the move to Varanasi may be as part of the Gahadavalas' reaction to the challenge of Islam, a strategy to enhance prestige, boost morale and rally support. Already in their first known inscription, the Gahadavala kings proclaimed themselves as the 'protectors of the (North) Indian holy places' (*tirtha*), to begin with those in Kashi, and boasted of their own piety.

There are few studies which have tried to project Banaras as a commercial centre, especially in the context of tracking the genesis of weaving. Many authors felt that being a religious centre, Banaras has been attracting a lot of visitors and traders who buy the local product and sell it to the neighbourhood. Richard Lannoy in his study argued that since Vedic age, Banaras has been the centre of weaving.[32] Under the Mughal, it rose to its old glory with Persianized motifs. According to Lannoy, Ralph Fitch (1583-91) informs that Banaras was once a thriving centre of cotton textile industry and manufactured turbans in great numbers for the Mughals. Further, the author noted how the weaving motif changes during the British period. Concurring with Lannoy, Rana P.B. Singh reiterates the history of weaving in Banaras that existed even before the Vedic age.[33] Rajendra Panday discuss the economic life of Banaras in the ancient period. He found that Banaras had acquired great fame in ancient days for the special excellence of its ware – "Fine Kashi cloth, worth ten thousand pieces", had become a proverbial phrase. It may also be mentioned that Kashi's contemporary kingdoms like Gandhara and Kodumbara were also known for manufacturing woollen clothes of great value.[34]

When it comes to the weaving and its link with economic activities, the two prominent questions come forth. These are – intervention of Mughals in the field of weaving and cultural degeneration of Banaras. A.K.Narain and Lallanji (1970) take readers to a voyage of medieval and modern history of Varanasi in their book 'Introducing Varanasi'.[35] They argued that during the rule of the Delhi sultanate, Varanasi lost its political importance. The Muslim rule brought creative life to a standstill for a few centuries.[36] No important literary or philosophical works in Sanskrit were composed at Banaras during the period 1200-1500 A.D.[37] The natural outcome of the historical distortion of the fact is that whenever it comes to defining the Mughal or Muslim rule over Banaras, it is termed as the 'dark age'. The emotional bias continues to mould the social psyche of the city, with which this research deals in the last chapter. There are aberrations to the general understanding about Muslims. O.P. Kejriwal in a book dispels the popular belief that Banaras was attacked by Mahmood Ghazni.[38] The author argues of the lack of authentic written documents which can substantiate this claim. In fact, the UP District Gazetteers of 1965 claimed the lack of proof of the Ghazni attack on Banaras. Kejriwal argued that no mention of the conquest of Benares by Mahmood or his officers occurs in *Ferishta*, not in the authorities consulted by Colonel Stewart. From these, it appears that Mahmood's victories in this direction were limited to Kannauj. However, it is quite certain that Muhammad Ghori sent his general Qutub-ud-din against Benares and Kannauj, in which Raja Jaychand lost the battle. Thus, Benares came under the rule of Qutub-ud-din.

After the failure of Mughal rule, local rulers, who were at the forefront of challenging it in collaboration with British, captured power. Banaras has seen unequal partnership between local rulers and the British, as the British dictated policies. B.S.Cohn, in his article looks at the role of British in influencing the political system in India by using Banaras as a case study.[39] The new recruits from among upper castes Hindus later emerged as the new landed class due to change brought about by the British. Again, focusing on the history of Banaras, C.A.Bayly in his book documents how Banaras emerged as a significant commercial city under the British after the failure of Murshidabad, Bengal.[40] After the failure of Mughals, Banaras had seen the emergence of new pattern of production relation where Hindu classes controlled business and Muslim masses constituted actual artisan workers. This is an important point as this pattern continues to exist even today in Banaras.

Being geographically at the crossroad of east-north hinterland, it always remained a very important city for rulers. Influx of various races and their settlement make Banaras a complex city. The complexity has been captured by S.B.Freitag. Her study 'Culture and Power in Banaras: Community, performance and Environment, 1800-1980' focused on Banaras, one of the largest urban centres in India's eastern Gangetic plain, which is united by a common interest in examining everyday activities in order to learn about shared values and motivations, processes of identity formation, and self-conscious constructions of community.[41] Part one examines the performance genres that have drawn audiences from throughout the city. Part two focuses on the areas of neighbourhood, leisure, and work, examining the processes by which urban residents use a sense of identity to organize their activities and bring meaning to their lives. Part three links these experiences within Banaras to a series of "larger worlds", ranging from language movements and political protests to disease ecology and regional environmental impact. Banaras is a complex world, with differences in religion, caste, class, language, and popular culture; the diversity of these essays embraces those differences.

Despite so many complexities, Banaras stood up against the British. All the communities took an active part in the movement. However, sketching the movement against British, the biased reporting missed the role of others'. Thakur Prasad Singh recognised the role played by the citizens of Banaras in the freedom struggle.[42] Though this book has been very encouraging in documenting wide participation in the freedom movement, but it misses the role of the subaltern. The heroes of the freedom movement, according to this account, almost all belong to the upper castes. This could be seen as the fall out of the communal interpretation of the history as described by Vasudha Dalmiya, Nita Kumar, or Gyanendra Pandey. Not only the subalterns, but women too were restricted to the household, reflecting the patriarchal nature of Hindu society. Steve Derne argued how the Hindu male uses cultural ideas to bolster their power over women by restricting their movement inside and outside the households.[43]

On the contrary, Nita Kumar (chapter 13), in Abdul Wahid's 'Muslim artisans, Craftsmen and Traders: Issues in Entrepreneurship', 2006, talks about the contribution made by *Ansari biradari* in the process of nation building. This article focuses on the biases in writing history which so far tried to negate the role of *Ansaris* in the nation building process. However, the author does talk about the gender biases within the written history of *Ansaris*. In *Ansari* history, the role of women in nation building has been missing. Their role has been restricted to the home affairs. Whereas, *Ansari* women through their various roles as within the family as mothers, and outside the family as teachers, masters, has helped men become a good citizens and skilled weavers. The public place and involvement of men was to a great extent due to the efforts of women. In her study 'The Artisans of Banaras: Popular culture and Identity, 1880-1986', she portrayed rarely explored aspects of Hindu culture through her analysis of the way leisure time is used by Hindu and Muslim artisans of Banaras – the weavers, metalworkers, and woodworkers. The importance of going 'to the outer side', the place of physical culture, music, and festivals all are examined as Kumar looks at changes that have occurred in leisure-time activities over the last century. The discussion raises questions of the cultural and conceptual aspects of working-class life, the role of fun and play in Indian thought, the importance of public activities in terms of personal identity, and the meaning of an Indian city to its residents.

The indifferent attitude toward the Muslims, mainly weaver community, is not restricted to the cultural space but it percolates to the economic and political level. The socio-economic status of Muslims remained of no concern. Writing about the socio-economic condition of Banaras' weavers of late 1970s, Bhagwati Prasad Singh found the existence of a slavery-like situation.[44] "If they do not get job for one day, they would die of hunger. They do not have any vacation period for whole working year. If a worker is absent from work due to illness, he loses his pay", notes Bhagwati Prasad Singh.[45] Further, Abdul Bismillah in his novel "*Jhini Jhini Bini Chadaria*" presents a wretched picture of Banarasi weavers. "…the workers who put their heart and soul and a fair amount of sweat and blood into making beautiful patterns on these saris are forced to live a very hard life. They cannot have two proper meals a day; their children cannot receive education worth its name; there is no proper healthcare for them and most importantly they are not even fully recognised as weavers by government agencies. The lack of education forms a vicious cycle with poverty and destitution and is chiefly responsible for the ghettoisation of their life…"[46] How the current status of Muslim weavers is different from the one elaborated above is a matter of concern for this research.

There have been many studies focused around the globalisation and its impact on the handloom industry of Banaras. S.C.Rao, in his study

'Employment in Handloom Industry', observes that the employment in handloom industry is declining. In recent years, weavers are trying to change their profession. Due to inadequate financial support from the government, weavers are facing problems such as hike in the raw material price, scarcity of the necessary inputs, lack of proper production marketing, and financial facilities. K.C. Pant arguing in favour of globalisation in India mentioned that 'Globalisation and integration of the world economy is an inescapable reality'.[47] India's reforms in the 1990s have had good effect, as its growth rate was about 7 per cent during 1992-97. But, India needs to do more, if it wants maximum benefit of reform.

(a) Public sector reform: The failed PSU is liability to the scarce resource of nation. To make it efficient, disinvestment in PSU with retaining majority control is required.

(b) Agriculture sector reform: There has been stagnation in the growth of agriculture after green revolution. We should allow reform in this area too.

(c) Reforms in Financial sector: Such as in insurance sector.

(d) Investment in social sector.

Debroy and Bhandari (2005) argued that Small Scale Industries (SSI) is on the decline.[48] Authors recognized the growth potential and subsequent benefit of SSI, but continuous rise of sickness that is from 23,149 in 1980 to 304, 235 in 2000 has worried policy makers. As SSI provided huge employment and contributed towards exports, the authors appeal for strengthening this sector by opening it up to further competition. SSIs produced reserved items are not allowed to cross the investment limits. Handlooms fall under SSIs. This artificial cap on growth acts as a negative factor. Since policy environment prevents the successful units from growing, it acts as a dampener on entrepreneurship. In line with the WTO obligations, the import policy and tariff reforms are undergoing reforms, and the SSIs are to face competition from the imported goods. So the reservation policy is meaningless. On the contrary, removal of reservations would enable the large-scale sector to enter and the resulting outsourcing and sub-contracting arrangements would be instrumental in the growth of existing SSI units. If reservation policy is to continue, the investment limits for individual products should vary, reflecting the minimum economic scale of production. The reservations policy has benefited only a few sectors. De-reservation would as a whole promote technology upgradation, enhancement of productivity.[49]

Deepak Nayyar argued that market and democracy may not ensure prosperity for everyone but, in fact, exclude a significant proportion of people, particularly the poor, from the process of the development. The author goes against the orthodox liberal argument that "market and democracy cannot be separated."[50] The East Asian markets existing without democracy has been cited by author as an example. The author firmly argues that "Exclusion is inherent in the logic of markets. Markets may exclude people as consumers or producers or both." (p. 61). "In addition, markets exclude people both as buyers and sellers if they do not accept, or conform to, the values of a market system" (p. 62). Actually, markets favour or include people with money or capital, whereas a democracy operates on one-person-one-vote. There is clear mismatch between those whom the market favours, and those whom democracy favours. The state exists to manage this gap, but has however, tilted towards the market and on those who control it.

In the context of MFA and WTO, Prof. C.P.Chandrshekhar argued that the industry needed protectionist policy not due to purely labour welfare considerations, but as a strategy of industrialization itself. Another important study on the subject has been done by B.Nagaraju and S.C.Narayana. Their prime focus was to assess the performance of handlooms and powerlooms in the changed economic context. They revealed that although handloom performance remained almost stationary in absolute terms, but as a proportion, it declined substantially.[51] The data representing two phases of economic reforms for handlooms reveal that during the second phase (1995-96 to 1999-2000), membership under the cooperative fold declined from an average of 12,798 during the first phase (1990-91 to 1994-95) to 3,789 during the second phase, indicating a decrease of 9,009 member (70.4 per cent).[52] It seems, due to various reasons and adverse effects of reforms, the number of looms operating under the cooperative fold also declined by 2,901, indicating a 61.1 per cent decrease during the second phase as compared to the first phase.

Analysing the impact of economic reform on handloom in Andhra Pradesh, Asha Krishnakumar argued that Government policies, that focused on liberalization, modernization and globalization of the industry but ignored the livelihood issues pertaining to the lakhs of traditional handloom and powerloom weavers, are behind the tragedy that has overcome them. The current crisis in the handloom sector, unprecedented in the post-Independence period in terms of its scale, has been precipitated ironically by successive textile policies and the recommendations of various committees, pushing the weavers into a debt trap, starvation and death.[53] Dubakka once had over 1,500 looms producing traditional cotton saris. Now the figure has fallen to 700, as its products have become uncompetitive in the market.[54] According to one report, as per the 1987 Handloom Census, there were about 4.27 lakhs handlooms in Tamil Nadu. After reforms, the number was reduced to 2.83 lakh who are members of about 1,354 handloom Weavers Cooperative Societies in the State, leading to the worsening of living conditions of weavers. Similar situation also persists in handloom sector of Orissa. The handloom industry in Orissa, both in co-operative and private sector, with its vast rural work force, especially of weaver communities, is confronted with the challenge of competitive economic environment.[55] This has posed a serious threat to the socio-economic life of the traditional weaver communities, in general and to the socio-economic status of rural women of these weaver communities in particular. The effect has been more severe for those women working under the co-operative societies and production centers. Majority (98 per cent) of the women reported that modern textile items are available at relatively cheaper prices affecting market for handloom products. Nearly 87 per cent of women respondents reported that growing consumer preference and taste, in recent times, towards a variety of modern fabrics has severely affected the demand for handloom items.[56]

Another study on North-eastern States' handloom sector from the gender point of view found that with respect to raw materials, globalization has some negative effect in domestic market. The process of globalization of the industry, although generated economic gain from rapid growth of export, the negative aspects such as inadequate healthcare, education, training and credit facilities are a few important problems that deprived mostly women workers involved in the industry. Looking at the overall experience of liberalization and its impact on various sectors including handloom, it appears that the handloom industry was not ready for the competition. Like handloom industry across the country, market economy has influenced Banaras too. Seemanthini Niranjana, in her study 'Appraising the Indian Handloom Industry' pointed out that opening of economy has exacerbated crisis for handloom industry, although it is one of the many factors.[57]

Giving a glimpse of Banarasi sari, Thomas (1985) in a review article on 'Banaras textiles' reported that, Banaras brocade is India's fabric of dream; a cloth of gold. In olden days very fine and delicate gold and silver wires were interwoven instead of yarn. The sari ultimately glittered with a metallic sheen. However, the silk yarns used in weaving were purchased from Bangalore, Kashmir and Malda and *zari* from Surat. The varieties of Banaras silk saris are Brocades, Jangla, Tanchoi, Satin border, Organza, Resham butidar and Cutwork woven with a harmonious combination of plain, satin and twill weaves to create interesting floral, fruit, animal, bird, geometric patterns and human figures. Colours used were the shades of pink, red, blue, green, yellow and purple. Tondon (1997) performed a study on "Marketing of Banarasi silk goods" and stated that Banarasi silk saris are famous for their exquisite beauty, splendid and ethnic designs. The marketing of these silk saris is as complex and intricate as that of its production. The article deals with '*Satti*'- the traditional pattern and practice of buying and selling continuously is the backbone of the merchandising Banarasi silk saris.

These products are mainly produced by Muslim weavers. Giving a social profile of the weavers Pathak *et al.* (1993) in the survey on "Varanasi silk industry" found that, in Banaras, silk weavers were generally known as '*julahas*'. In general, all communities were involved but the share of Muslims (*Ansari*s) was prominently high. Silk weavers constitute 69.2 per cent of the population of weavers in the state. The silk industry was run by three levels of weavers; small independent weavers, master weavers and wage weavers of cooperative societies. Apart from these historical, cultural and political descriptions, there are studies focusing on the present situation of weavers. Nesar Ahmad focused on the condition of handloom industry and weavers in the globalized economy. Ahmad noticed the closure of many looms and starvation among the weavers community. In his interaction with the stakeholders – weavers, master weavers[58] and traders – each perceived the problems differently. Handloom weavers blamed powerlooms. However, traders felt that the import of Chinese fabrics, which is also used as a sari after embroidery and the Surat powerlooms-woven saris are the main reason for the declining demand of *Banarasi* saris.

Tarun Kanti Bose in his study 'Globalization pushes Varanasi weavers to hunger and Death', for ActionAid, PVCHR, argued the ill effects of economic reform. Bose observed that "demand of Banarasi saris has shown a downward trend over the years. Since the 1990s, when the economic boom has been sweeping the nation, the wages of the weavers are declining day-by-day. Though the quality of the sari has gone up but it is not commensurate with the wages of the weavers. Presently, weavers who toil for 12 to 16 hours get half the wages they received earlier. Moreover, power looms have wreaked havoc in the lives of the weavers by snatching their work and pushing them to starvation. The middlemen and Gaddidars are taking full advantage of their helplessness."[59] The economic reform not only worsened the prospects of Muslim weavers but other lower castes weavers in and around Banaras. Manuela Ciotti in her article 'Ethnohistories behind local and global bazaars: Chronicle of a Chamar weaving community in Banaras region' analyzes the history of weaving in a Chamar community on the outskirts of Banaras. Further, the author argued that the weaving era represented a historical moment of relative prosperity for the Chamar community, where strengthened ties with urban Muslim weavers enabled a progressive disentanglement from relationships of domination by rural landed elites. However, the "promotion of economic liberalization policies in India has swept aside the protective barriers that had sheltered the Banaras silk weaving industry. The opening of the handloom sector to competition from machine-manufactured textiles and the import of silk textiles from China led to the precipitate decline of the Banaras silk and sari industry. The Chamar weaving community began to experience a business slowdown which culminated in the almost total disappearance of their industry in the early 2000s."[60]

The slowdown not merely impacted economy but culture of weavers' too. Mary Searle-Chatterjee in her article focuses on one particular instance of 'Islamicization' among merchant weavers in the city of Varanasi, North India. She argues that despite the use of 'global' Islamic symbolism, the cultural changes in question are best viewed as an expression of social mobility in the local arena.[61] Though not a response to globalization, this instance of Islamicization is partly a consequence of changes in the world markets. This period also gave ample scope for communalism to chip-in as the struggle for survival became tougher. It is also linked with the deepening of democracy where political parties use every means to capture power. Caste, regionalism and religion have become tools for mobilisation. Jobless growth after the economic reform, unemployment, and poverty gives rooms for fissure between the communities. The economic and political elite of Banaras mobilise the masses for their individual interest. Vasanthi Raman takes us to a journey in the world of weavers, detailed account of community relations, of the search for a new identity by a community burdened by negative epi-thets, of craftspersons caught in the web of a changing world and a changing India.[62] The first part of the book explores how the identity question arose and was resolved differently for the Muslim weavers and the Hindu traders, both of whom are intrinsically involved in the production of the Banarasi sari. Starting with the ques-tion of how the projection of Banaras as a Hindu city came about, Raman takes us through the extensive literature that brings out how this was partly a colonial con-struction and partly a function of a Hindu resurgence, which was supported largely by the upper castes, for whom Sanskrit was the core of Hindu civilisation. The author has also explored the world of women, looking at how the distinction between the private and public spheres works itself out in the lives of the women. Taken together, they show how the Muslim women of Banaras, like women from any other community, have had to cope with the economic challenges by moving out of the relatively safe location of the home to take up outside work. Emily Christine Antze falling to communal propaganda about the Muslim mis(rule) over Banaras argued that the place no more remained centre of knowledge under Mughal rule. She pointed out that, although Banaras is now 'modernizing' (the first McDonalds opened in 2006, and the first shopping mall not long before that), compared to the opulence found in the cosmopolitan cities of Mumbai, Delhi, Bangalore or even the UP state capital of Lucknow, it is a conservative, "backward" provincial town.[63]

However, all previous studies have similar problems in their observance. Firstly, they treat handloom industry as a homogenized unit without noting the regional variation in the products, organizational base, as well as in relations between actors within the production structure. This diversity is not reflected in the aggregate data on the industry. And unfortunately, it is often such aggregate data, which form the basis, not only for people's impressions about the industry, but also in attempts to formulate policies for the sector. Secondly, they treat all the weavers as one category and so do their problems and approaches toward it; however there is no such thing as 'the' weaver, but rather, a diversity of conditions that characterize weavers and weaving. It is this heterogeneity and its responses to the challenges thrown up by the reform needs empirical elaboration. Third, most of the literature on Banaras weavers focused on cultural aspect, is quite dated, and does not deal with the impact of economic reforms on the weaver community.

Statement of the Problem

The *Banarasi* handloom products, especially the silk sari, has its genesis a century ago, evolved throughout the period, seen many ups and downs and survived till now despite technological change. The government, while adopting planned economy, also had plans for the handloom sector. The idea was to protect the handlooms of the throw-shuttle or fly-shuttle type manufacturing special fabrics with an intricate body design.

Government did introduce reservation to the items to be produced by mills, powerlooms and handlooms. However, gradually, many items were excluded from the list, restricting it now to only eleven. Under the compulsion to meet the demand of the growing population, the government took such steps. It prioritised powerloom production. But, opening up of India's economy under the compulsion of International Finance Institutions opened the Pandora box for the handloom sector. The already tattered handloom was put into competition with technologically advanced countries. But, this was not the only thing happened to handloom. Economic reform opens the domestic market for the cheap product from other countries which takes away secure market for the handloom. The weavers' troubles began way back in 1995-1998 when the Deve Gowda-led Central Government imposed a ban on Chinese silk yarns. The idea was that *Banarasi* saris would only be woven from silk yarns from Bangalore. Out of habit or because of its superior quality, some weavers started smuggling Chinese yarn into Banaras. Realizing that their need for Chinese yarn would only grow, the weavers demanded an Open General License (OGL). The decision of the Government to allow the free import of Chinese plain crepe fabrics brought the entire business to a standstill. Now most customers prefer crepe silk to the traditional *Banarasi* silk because of its smooth appearance and cheaper price. The flaws of *Banarasi* silk relating to its colour, texture and durability are not found in Chinese crepe since they are woven in automated looms.

The sick mills were closed down by the government. The government did not ensure its revitalisation as if it was actually preparing for the opening of this sector to private investment. The closure of mills affected the handloom sector. Whatever little yarn supply was there was stopped. The high inputs and low gain put weavers into a debt trap. Further, with the economic reforms, change in the taste of attire, people began choosing various fabrics. This slumped the demand of *Banarasi* product, sari. So, cumulatively, a number of factors have worsened the case of *Banarasi* sari. Due to shrinking demand of silk product since 1995, 60 per cent handlooms are now laying idle in Banaras.[64] The closure of handlooms in such a large scale has led to poverty, malnutrition, starvation death and suicide by weavers. More than 50 cases of suicide and starvation deaths have been reported in Banaras. The exploitation has reached its zenith, throwing skilled artisans from the sector and pushing them to obscure work profiles, such as pulling rickshaws, peeling and selling green chanas, making incense sticks, cleaning garbage heaps. Women have started working as domestic maids in middle class houses in their neighbourhood.

The scenario has become so bleak that weavers are forced to migrate to Surat. Surat provides better opportunities to *Banarasi* weavers', which has a demand for their products and provides them with better wages. In Surat, these weavers are in fact, pushed to such a paradoxical situation, that they are joining the 'duplicate' *Banarasi* sari manufacturing process, which has proved to be economically viable to them. With the abandoning of the *Banarasi* silk sector by rare skilled artisans with the influx of thousands of 'unskilled' hands into weaving from the rural hinterland due to problems in their areas, if left unchecked can sound the death knell of the sector. Out of desperation, hundreds of families have started migrating from the city; those left behind alternate between cursing the politicians and seeking divine help through special prayer meetings. "This is the biggest crisis that we have faced in our lifetime and unless the Government does something about it, we are doomed," says Rajan Behl, general secretary of the Banarasi Vastu Udyog Sangh.

The opening up of the Indian economy to world markets worsened the problems of handloom weaver of Banaras. Decline in the demand for silk saris and facing competition from the cheaper goods inflowing from the new entrant developing country has been pointed out in the recent past. Even the case of suicide by weavers in UP especially in Banaras has also been highlighted in the local newspapers. Local non-governmental organisations (NGOs) have also come out with reports on starvation and starvation deaths in the area.[65] Today in Banaras, there are more households with non-functional looms than functional ones. Weavers are compelled to resort to menial labor, pulling rickshaws and doing construction work to survive. The collected literature and reports makes the case that liberalization is worsening the situation for weaver. However, one must also analyse the role of the State and its policy towards the weavers in current crisis.

Research Objective

Indian government in 1991 had introduced new reform measures in various key economic sectors characterizes greater privatization and deregulation for efficiency and accountability, poverty reduction, and to overcome the immediate financial crisis were the major objectives of the reform. Many social scientists are engaged in decoding the impact of reform in various sectors, such as, food and social security, poverty, on organized labour, industries, employment and overall development process. Similar approach has been taken by researchers and academician to study the effect of Indian economic integration with world economy on various deprived social groups such as Dalit, Tribals and Women. Various Human Development Index indicators have been used to understand what globalization meant for them. Likewise, this research aims to study the impact of liberalization on the weavers of Banaras, who happened to be low-status sections of Muslim community, traditionally called *julaha* and disturbance of any magnitude in handloom market may wean away bread and butter from large and vulnerable population. Some key questions that this research would like to focus upon are as follow:

1. How do economic reform and international trade agreement casting impact on the Indian Textile industry in general, handloom industry in particular?
2. What are the major points of differences between pre-reform and post-reform handloom industry of Banaras?
3. How is the Banaras handloom industry, with complex production relations, is evolving as a whole after the economic reform?
4. Why is the vast majority of labour class i.e. weavers till now not been able to organize themselves?
5. What measures State and Central government have taken to redress the weavers' problems and critical evaluation of various welfare programs undertaken by them?
6. How are weavers laden with multiple identities (class/caste/religions/sects/regional) are responding to the challenges thrown up by market?
7. How has economic reform influenced the life of women and children of Banaras weavers' families, who were once the very active participants of the weaving process?
8. How have various identities of Muslim weaver groups negotiated within the broader debate of minority perspective on globalisation?

This research is focused on three borad issues around which the study was conducted. First, the impact of liberalization and whether it has had a deleterious impact on Handloom Industry in India. Second, how has liberalization affected livelihoods of weavers in Banaras Handloom industry, forcing significant section of them into non-traditional informal sector. Third, has there been a significant shift from community to class among Muslim Handloom weavers after liberalization.

Methodology

To examine the effect of economic reform on the weaver community, Banaras Muslim weavers/*julaha* community has been selected as the case study. The three fundamental reasons for this selection are; this area has a large population of Muslim weavers; secondly, the weavers of Banaras have been worst effected by economic reforms; thirdly, some localities like Madanpura consist of master weavers and has economically advanced population which have been be used for the comparative analysis. To further the comparative analysis, this research would like to focus on the textile centres like Mau in Eastern UP and Andhra Pradesh.

To gather the data about the economic and social problem in the post-1990, the survey method was used in Banaras and Mau. Various tools such as questionnaire, personal and group discussion have been used. However, secondary materials have been used in the case of Andhra Pradesh. To testify the hypothetical questions such as what jobs weavers are involved in after leaving loom's work; are they aware of the government programmes meant for the weavers; income before and after leaving handloom work et al will be asked. To make this survey more representative and precise, the stratified sampling of Banaras' weavers has been done. For this purpose, weavers of all the localities categorised into different units based on occupational criteria. So, in this way weavers are stratified into four occupational categories i.e. loom less weaver, cooperative weavers, self-employed weavers and contract weavers. A total of six hundred interviewees, three hundred each from Mau and Banaras, are asked to feel the questionnaire. All the respondents were male, which act as a limitation for this study. However, being a male researcher I was not allowed to meet the women as they observed purdah. All the respondents were *julahas* and follower of Islam. The literacy rate among Banaras weavers' was low as compared to Mau. This reflected the better economic condition of Mau weavers which came after their shift from handloom to powerloom. Further on the issue of social and economic conditions of weavers, literature, various State and Central government agencies, NGOs, weavers' organizations, website were used as the secondary sources. These are as follows:

(1) Diagnostic Study of Handloom Silk Cluster, Varanasi

(2) Weaver Service Centre's Varanasi

(3) Central Silk Board's (CSB) Certification Centre, Varanasi

(4) Ministry of Textile, Government of India

(5) Department of Industry, Government of Uttar Pradesh
(6) Department of Planning, U.P
(7) Entrepreneurship Development Institute of India (EDI)
(8) NABARD and SIDBI
(9) Directorate of Handloom, U.P
(10) National Handloom Development Corporation (NHDC)

NGOs - Dastakar-Bunkar Adhikar Manch (Weaver-Artisan Rights Front); Craft Council of India; Craft Revival Trust; Craftmark; CRY and ASHA; PVCHR and FWRA

Website – www.action.org; www.craftmark.org; www.aiacaonline.org; www.udai.org

Journal – Statistical Patrika, Varanasi

References

1. This research does not intend to treat caste as a class as it carries other distinct features along with it. It decides individual dignity and humiliation; stands in social hierarchy, nature of job, place of living etc. However, as they primarily are a producer, this research tries to understand the economy of the castes.
2. N.G.Ranga, *The Economies of Handloom*, Taraporewala Sons, Bombay, 1930, p. 71.
3. 3rd Handloom Census, Ministry of Textile, Government of India, 2009-10.
4. Sanjay Mishra, *India's Textile Sector: A Policy Analysis*, Sage Publication, New Delhi, 1993.
5. Handloom Industry, 'Annual Report 2002-03', Ministry of Textile, Government of India.
6. James Prinsep, (Benares Illustrated: 1829); M.A. Sherring, (The Sacred City of Hindu – An account of Benares in Ancient and Modern Times: 1868); F.B Havell, Benares the Sacred City – Sketches of Hindu Life and Religion: 1905); Rev. Arthur Parkar, (A Handbook on Benares: 1895); E. Greaves, (Kashi – The City Illustrious or Benares: 1909); C. Phillips Cape, (Benares - The Stronghold of Hinduism:1910).
7. James Phillips, *Benares Illustrious*, Pilgrims Publishing, Delhi, 2009, pp 191-92. The list of castes is given in Annexure of this research.
8. Rumi had used "*Parchabaf*" i.e. the term has no reference to lineage or community, but only to the work of weaving; in fact, as is known, Islam opposed differentiation based on descent and family.
9. V.Raman, The Julaha – Momin Ansaris of Banaras: A Socio-historical Trajectory, *Voice of Dalit*, 3(2), 2010, pp. 253-264.
10. Uttar Pradesh District Gazetteer, Varanasi, Government of Uttar Pradesh, Allahabad, 1965.

11. Number of Muslims in the district had gone down as three new districts carved out of Banaras.
12. *Ibid;* p. 85.
13. Singh and Rana, *Banaras Region: Cultural and Spiritual Guide*, Banaras, 2002.
14. According to 2001 census, Banaras as a district has the total population of 3,147,927 of which 1,650,138 and 1,497,789 are male and female respectively.
15. According to the Joint Census of Handloom and Powerloom (1995-96) Banaras was producing 3483090 (in Linear meters) of sari i.e. 82.98 per cent of the total handloom product (i.e. 4197038) much ahead of Mau.
16. Of the total Muslim population 90 per cent belongs to Sunni sect. For further details please see; Singh and Rana (2002).
17. Laurent Gayer and Christophe Jaffrelot, *Muslim in Indian Cities: Trajectory of Marginalisation*, Columbia University Press, New York, 2011.
18. Mahfooz Alam, 'Continuity and Change among the Muslims', Ph.D.Thesis, BHU, 2001.
19. *Ibid.*
20. Followers of Deoband school of thought. It is used for a revivalist movement in Sunni Islam under the Hanafi School. The movement was ispired by the spirit of scholar Shah Waliullah. The sect is against many practices common in the Indian subcontinenet such as building over tombs, celebrating *Milad al-Nabi*, and calling on the prophets and saints for assistance.
21. It is a term used for a movement of Sunni Islam originating in South Asia. The name derives from the north Indian town of Bareilly where its founder Ahmed Raza Khan shaped the movement by his writings. The followers of movement often prefer to be known by the title of *Ahle Sunnat Wal Jamat*. The movement is much influenced by Sufism and defends the traditional Sufi practices from the criticisms of Islamic movement like the Deobandi, Wahabi and *Ahl al-Hadith*.
22. Its literary meaning is 'The People of *hadith'*. It refers to the adherent's belief that they are not bound by *taqlid* (means to follow), but consider themselves free to seek guidance in matters of religious faith and practices from the authentic hadith which, together with the Quran, are in their view the principal worthy guide for Muslims. In the Indian subcontinent, the followers of the Salafi movement are known as Ahl al-Hadith.
23. Mary Searle-Chatterjee, "Wahabi" Sectarianism among Muslim of Banaras, *Contemporary South Asia*, 3(2), 1994.
24. It should be read as rational decision of any sect's followers not to have social relationship in general and marital relationship in particular with followers of other sect due to consistent propaganda of all the school of thought. And if any one dares to cross the sectoral boundaries he/she should be ready to face the social boycott with immediate effect.
25. This aspect had come up during an interview with Barelwi followers in my fieldwork.
26. NDTV.Com, Weavers in Distress, April 30, 2007.

27. Samar, 'Varanasi's Silk Sari-Weavers face bleak, hungry future', *Hindustan Times*, July 04, 2007.
28. Lalita Prasad Vidyarthi, Makhan Jha and B.N.Saraswati, '*The Sacred Complex of Kashi: A Microcosm on Indian Civilisation*', Concept Publishing Company, 1979.
29. *Ibid.* p. 25.
30. Hans. T Bakker, '*Construction and Reconstruction of Scared Space in Varanasi*';, Numen, Vol. 43, No. 1, pp. 32-55.
31. *Ibid.*
32. Richard Lannoy, Benares: A World within a World. The Microcosm of Kashi Yesterday and Tommorrow, India Books, Varanasi, 2002.
33. Rana P.B. Singh, *Where Cultural Symbol Meet: Literary Images of Varanasi*, Tara book Agency, Varanasi, 1989.
34. Rajendra Pandey, *Kashi through the Ages*, Sundeep Prakashan, New Delhi, 1979.
35. A.K. Narain and Gopal Lallanji, *Introducing Varanasi*, BHU, Varanasi, 1969.
36. *Ibid.*
37. *Ibid.*
38. O.P.Kejriwal, *Benares Illustated: With James Prinsep*, Pilgrims Book House, Benaras, 2009.
39. Bernard S. Kohn, 'The Initial British Impact on India: A Case Study of Benars Region', *Journal of Asian Study*, Vol. 19, No. 4, 1960.
40. C.A. Bayly, Rulers, *Townsmen and Bazars: North Indian Society in the Age of British Expansion, 1770-1870*, Cambridge University Press, Cambridge, 1983.
41. Sandria B. Freitag, *Culture and Power in Banaras: Community, Performance and Environment, 1800-1980*, University of California, Berkley, 1989.
42. Thakur Prasad Singh, *Swantantra Andolan aur Banaras*, Banras, 1990.
43. Steve Derne, *Culture in Action: Family Life, Emotion, and Male Dominance in Banaras*, State University of New York Press, New York, 1995.
44. Bhagwati Prasad Singh, *Banaras ke Vwaysayi*, Laxmi Narayan Press, Varanasi, 1977, p - 6.
45. *Ibid;* pp. 8-9.
46. Mohd Asim Siddiqui, The Wretched of the Earth: A Representation of the Life of the Weavers of Banaras in Abdul Bismillah's Jhini Jhini Bini Chadria, in Adbul Waheed (ed.), *Muslim Artisans, Craftmen and Traders: Issues in Entrepreneurship*, Icon Publication, New Delhi, 2006.
47. K.C.Pant, *India's Development Scenario: Next Decade and Beyond*, Academic Foundation, New Delhi, 2003.
48. Bibek Debroy and Laveesh Bhandari, *Small Scale Industries in India: Large Scale Exit Problems*, Academic Foundaiton, New Delhi, 2005.
49. *Ibid.*
50. Deepak Nayyar, *Globalisation: What Does it Mean for Higher Education*?', Economic and Political Weekly, 2007.

51. B. Nagaraju and S.C.Narayana, 'Impact of Reforms on Handlooms and Powerlooms: A Case Study of Chitoot District, Andhra Pradesh', *Journal of Rural Development*, Vol. 22, No. 3, pp. 345-362.
52. *Ibid.*
53. Asha Krishnakumar, 'Weavers in Distress', *Frontline*, Vol. 18, No. 8, 2001.
54. *Ibid.*
55. Narayan Sahoo, '*Impact of Globalisation of Textile Industry on Position of Rural Women in Handloom Sector in Orissa*, Development Innovator, Orissa, 2004.
56. *Ibid.*
57. Seemanthini Niranjana, 'Appraising the Indian Handloom Industru', *EPW*, Vol. 36, No. 45, 2001.
58. Santosh Kumar Rai, 'Becoming a Grihasta – Hierarchies of work among Handloom Weavers in Early Twentieth Century United Provinces, India', in Rana Behal, Alice Mah and Babacar Fall, (ed.) '*Rethinking Work: Global Historical and Sociological Perspectives*', Tulika, Delhi, pp. 73-82. Their position at top was the result of reconfiguration of the internal spaces of 'community', 'work' and 'forms of labour' that took place after colonial encounter in 18th and 19th century. By the late 19th century Muslim master weavers or *karkhanadars* (*karkhana* lossely means a factory, so *karkhanadar* refers to 'one who ran/owned a factory' but at the cottage industry level) had started employing the term *grihasta* to refer to a senior master weaver who had extra resources, and who was a mediator between the community, and traders and merchants. But, this grihasta was unlike the English or European Guild system. European guilds were characterized by centralization of production and trade under a single 'master'. However, Indian *Grihasta* was far more than an economic category of 'master trainer'. He was the hierarchical head of the production process. He connected the producer and the marketing network by participating in both production and marketing. In this process, *Grihasta* used community as social capital to form new relations of production and maintain control over labour. *Grihasta* occupied the space left by British appointed *gumashta*, who acted as an interface between the native producers and the procurement network of the East India Company. By the second decade of the nineteenth century grihastas had begun to emphasize controlling production more as a business concern. Hence a hierarchy among labourers and weavers emerges. These were:

    1. Unpaid household labour: women and children
    2. Paid weavers without their own means of production, including low caste Hindu weavers.
    3. Weavers who had looms but were dependent on the master weaver or grihasta for raw material.
    4. Self-Employed weavers who had loo and other means of production.
    5. The master weaver or *grihasta*: the interface between the production and marketing.

    For Muslim weavers the relationship with the *grihasta* had a stronger sense of solidarity, as the *grihasta*, being a Muslim, generally did not practice usury, which is prohibited by Islam.

59. Tarun Kanti Bose, '*Globalisation Pushes Varanasi Weavers to Hunger and Death*', PVCHR, ActionAid, Banaras, 2009.
60. Manuela Ciotti, 'Ethnohistories Behind local and global bazaars: Chronicle of a Chamar Weaving community in Banaras region', *Contribution to Indian Sociology*, Vol. 41, No. 3, 2007.
61. Mary Searle-Chatterjee, "Wahabi' Sectarianism among Muslims of Banaras', *Contemporary South Asia*, Vol. 3, No. 2, 1994.
62. Vasanthi Raman, *The Warp and the Weft: Community and Gender Identity Among Banaras Weavers*, Routledge, New Delhi, 2010.
63. Emily Christine Antze, "They Should Stand on their Own Feet": Mothers' Account of Education School Choice and their Children's Uncertain Futures in Varanasi, India, Ph.D Thesis, Toronto, 2011.
64. Rahul Kodkani, *Varanasi Weavers in Crisis*, 2007. (www.udai.org)
65. Francis and Lenin (ed.) "Handloom has become live grave for weavers" published by Jan Mitra, Varanasi and Voice of Voiceless Weavers, by PVCHR and FWRA, Varanasi, 2005.

Chapter - 1

Liberalization and its Contextualization in India

Theory of Liberalization

At the academic, socio-political and economic levels, the previous two decades have been dominated by the debate about liberalization/ globalisation. Scholars and leaders from diverse background have endowed their much valued time to understanding what the word globalisation meant, its origin, its attributes, assess the range of its impact etc. The answers are as varied as it could be. There is no consensus around any one particular aspect of it. However, the overall position in relation with liberalization can be broadly categorised into two – those who favours and those who do not. Between these two extreme points on the continuum lie a wide ranges of positions vis-à-vis liberalization.

Fundamentally, it is the closer integration of the countries and the peoples of the world which has been brought about by breaking down of artificial barriers to the flows of goods, services, capital, knowledge and (to lesser extent) people across borders. It is very clear from the vague understanding about liberalization that it isn't merely about economic integration. Liberalization requires not only the opening of the border for trade and goods, but it also expects State to play minimum role of maintaining fiscals balance and law and orders situation. Another thing which set globalisation apart from economic liberalism is that it convinces us that market has potential to lead stable and faster growth with minimal State. In the backdrop of failed Soviet Union[1] and slow growth rate in many countries following Keynesian model of development,[2] the pro-market forces used globalisation as an instrument to justify the greater role of market. Jagdish Bhagwati, Anne Krueger and Ian Little in early 1980s, argued that outward-oriented trade policies is far more likely than protectionism to lead to economic growth. Thomas Frank argued that markets as mediums of consent are more democratic than popularly elected governments, and entrepreneurs, such as Bill Gates and Richard Branson are the champions of the common people.[3]

Yet, the word globalisation suffers from the problem of definitional clarity. Jan Aart Scholte, while defining the term, found the existing definitions i.e. globalisation as internationalisation, liberalization, universalization and westernisation as *cul-de-sac*.[4] He exhausted another category of transplanetary (supra-territorial – connections between people) to identify globalisation. Amiya Kumar Bagchi[5] has drawn a vast canvass to capture the varied aspect of globalisation through nine sub-aspects, which is attributed with globalisation. First, there is a spread of international trade in goods and 'commodities'. Secondly, people migrate from one country or region to another, temporarily or permanently. Thirdly, money or means of payment are exchanged on an increasing scale between different regions within the same country have different media of exchange. Fourthly, capital flows from one country to another to help produce goods and services. Fifthly, finance – not necessarily linked to the production of goods and services – flows between different countries. Sixthly, Transnational companies arise which increasingly engage in the activities listed above. Seventhly, technology is traded as between different countries. Increasingly, with the spread of the patent regimes governed by the Paris Convention as modified by the provision of the World Trade Organisation, frontier technologies take an increasingly proprietary form. The eight aspect of globalisation is the spread of print and electronic media. The ninth aspect is the growth in international trade and production of services of all kinds – shipping, insurance, banking, healthcare and finance.

The on-going phase of globalisation became buzz word once third world countries and erstwhile communist States opened up their economies to integrate with global one under the conditionality trap. However, many scholars find its origin much before one can presumes. Kevin O' Rourke and J.Williamson, James Petras and Chronis Polychroniou, P.Bardhan et al. argued that globalisation is not a new phenomenon. Petras and Polychroniou argued that "it is a gross conceptual error to treat globalisation as a new phenomenon, an inevitable process, or as the 'ultimate' phase of capitalism. Globalisation is a 'cyclical' phenomenon alternating with periods of national development, a product of state policies linked to international economic institutions. The rise of globalism is intimately related to the growth of class conflict and the squeeze of profits during the limited globalisation period associated with the 'welfare state'.[6] On the exaggeration of integration of economies to world economy, Pranab Bardhan argued that "...many economic historians actually tell us that, by most indicators, trade and capital markets are no more globalised today than they were at the end of the 19th century.... The indicators of long-term market integration (like ratios of trade or long-term capital flows to GDP) are not higher today than they were at the end of the 19th century."[7] Further, highlighting the economic aspect of globalisation, B.R.Nayyar traces "its origin in the development of a regional international market in Europe as foreign trade increased following the commercialisation of agriculture and national specialisation in agriculture activities after the Middle Ages....thus, the origins of economic globalisation lie in the rise of capitalism in Europe and the penetration by capitalism from that economic core into the regional economies of the periphery around the world."[8] But, there are noted differences in the earlier and contemporary forms of economic globalisation. As for Nayar, the earlier economic globalisation was 'extensive' or 'widening', which linked the entire world economically, whereas, contemporary form of globalisation is rather 'intensive' or 'deepening'. Bardhan too noted the distinction between the two. He argued that "compared to the end of the 19th century, when international trade was concentrated in generic products (one country sold, say, wheat and bought textiles), today a country quite often imports as well as exports the same product, whether it is cars or computer parts. Economists call this intra-industry trade. It has made transaction more competitive today. Further, in 19th century along with capital mobility, labour as well was mobile, unlike today. There was huge European migration to the US, Australia and New Zealand."[9] Nevertheless, Bardhan has not taken into account the unequal terms of trade between the industrially developed country and non/less developed country in the past.

The second phase of intensive or deepening globalisation begins after the Second World War with US came out as a new centre of capitalist power. It reorganized the world's economic institutions, chiefly in the form of GATT and the Bretton Woods system, to establish what has been characterised as a liberal international economic order, but one that was clearly designed to serve the interests of the advanced industrial powers, more particularly the United State (US). However, scholars like Joseph Stiglitz argued differently about these world financial institutions. According to Stiglitz, World Bank and International Monetary Fund came into existence with the realisation that markets often did not work well, thus a collective action at the global level was required for economic stability. But, narrowly-defined economic aspect of globalisation by these institutions to the serve the interests of the G-7 countries has diverted from its ideal. If one is forced to ingest this argument, the fact would be that the ideal of economic stability was meant for developed nations only. These institutions, who denied help to Third World Countries in its nascent phase, started using their economic and political instability to push Multi-National Corporations (MNCs) inside with strict loan conditionality such as structural adjustment. These MNCs, in turn, became the key agents in intensification of economic globalisation in Third World countries like India.

Liberalization in India

The year 1991 is often referred to as the real start of the economic reform process in India. A new government, headed by P.V. Narasimha Rao and Manmohan Singh as Finance Minister, announced its first reform measures almost immediately after it took office in June 1991. It continued to introduce new reform measures in various key economic sectors during its term. The first measures were aimed at stabilisation, and included a large devaluation of the currency and deflationary measures. This was followed by structural adjustment reforms, including removal of controls on private industrial investment, opening the economy to foreign trade and investment, a reduction of price controls, and reforms of the banking system.[10] However, there have been attempts on the part of the Indian government to bond with the world economy, which was experiencing economic globalisation since Second World War. Either India was forced under critical circumstance to go for liberalization or government willingly decided to do so.

The failure of second and third plan due to the capital and foreign exchange constraints, and resource constraint and the imbalanced nature of the economic strategy with its relative neglect of agriculture and consumer goods respectively, led US to successfully pressurize India to devaluate the rupee as part of liberalization in 1966. According to Nayar, this is for the first time that India experienced liberalization, though for a short duration. After that, Indira Gandhi went on a spree of socialism, nationalizing everything, what Nayar called it 'reign of ideology'. But, that policy threw two major challenges: soaring inflation amidst widespread scarcities and a sudden and severe deterioration in the balance of payments position. The manufacturing industry saw a decline in production due to limits set on big business houses, a drought in 1972-74 led to food scarcity in the country. Massive demonstrations and violence occurred in the streets. The State attempted to crush the opposition. On the external front, the government obtained no-conditionality or low conditionality loans from the International Monetary Fund (IMF) in 1974, while overt devaluation was avoided, covert devaluation was sustained. India thus began the long process of reintegration with the world economy.

"After returning to power in 1980, Indira Gandhi was clearly determined to get back to the firm foundations of economic reform",[11] and the Economic and Political Weekly also reported in an editorial entitled 'All for Production', Review of Management', that the prime minister in her various meetings with industrialists had clarified that "what the government was most concerned about just now was higher production."[12] The three components of the new model of development that Indira Gandhi adopted from 1980 on – and that has pretty well been pursued by subsequent governments – were: prioritisation of economic growth as a State goal; supporting big business to achieve this goal; and taming labour as a necessary aspect of this strategy.[13]

On the other hand, scholars put forth numbers of factor, responsible for economic reform in the year 1991. Atul Kohli, focusing on the external factors, pointed out that the collapse of Soviet Union and changed circumstances divides Indian capital, whose major faction was willing to open the market. As Soviet Union was a major trading partner of India, it decline to pressurize for liberalization. A second important global change that occurred over the 1980s was the growing availability of investible resources – in foreign exchange, to boot – in the form of portfolio investments. And, finally, it must have been clear to Indian decision-makers (government, big business house etc.) that WTO was going to happen.[14] Amiya K. Bagchi argued that the immediate reason to introduce the economic reforms in India was the aggregating debt amount, which government has borrowed on very onerous terms. In June-July 1991, in order to restore confidence among India's debtors and in the rupee, the government entered into an agreement with the IMF for a stand-by first tranche credit of SDR 551.93 million (about US $ 754 million) and drawings under the compensatory and contingency financing facility totalling the equivalent of SDR 1352 million (about US $ 1,847 million). Later in the year, the IMF granted another standby credit authorizing drawings up to the equivalent of SDR 1,656 million (about US $ 2,262 million). In accordance with the memorandum of understanding reached with the IMF, the government of India carried out a series of policy reforms. The rupee was devalued by about 24 per cent.[15]

According to B.R.Nayar, the economic crisis triggered by oil price hikes and collapse of commodity prices which led to the balance of payments crisis, combined with previous economic policies of the State, pressurised India to liberalize. While substantiating the Haggard and Kaufman's view on economic adjustment, Nayar notes that external economic elements were undoubtedly present as immediate precipitants, the proximate causes of the crisis lay principally at home, fundamentally in the persistent fiscal deficits budgeted by the State year after year for more than a decade. The crisis was thus basically the consequence of earlier economic policies, not of external shocks.[16] Nonetheless, internal factors apart from economics were at work, rationalising the efforts for economic reform.

The presence of a sizeable Indian middle class and their overall changing perception about India was a major variable influencing the decision. The traditional Indian middle class developed aspirations of integrating into the globalized world and visions for a powerful State. They crave to be at par with their western counterpart. They wanted to reflect their distinctiveness from the rest of Indians and imitate western lifestyles, culture and consumption patterns. These aspirations of 150-200 million[17] strong middle class, i.e., 15-20 per cent of the total population, and their economic strength gave the necessary impetus for economic reform. "The consumerist thirst of the middle class became an asset, a sign of the dynamism of the Indian market. The votaries of pro-market reforms revealed that 'urban India itself is the world's 3rd largest country'."[18] This is a significant section of the population, providing a considerable market, following a policy that is concomitant with the global corporate structure, and can provide a more unified framework for development and participation and involvement in development. Thus, one of the main agendas of liberalization was to liberate the middle class from any restraint in the unchecked pursuit of its becoming global.

According to Prabhat Patnaik and C.P. Chandrasekhar, India's transition in 1991 to a program of "structural adjustment", was due to changed international conjuncture on the one hand and an accentuation of the contradictions of the *dirigiste*[19] regime on the other. Three contradiction of the *dirigiste* regime noted down by Patnaik and Chandrasekhar are as follow:

(a) Unlocking from the hand of metropolitan capital and metropolitan commodities, Indian bourgeoisie state tried to strengthen domestic market by increasing in investment expenditure. Thus, lending help in primary accumulation of Indian capitalism at the cost of people's money.

(b) Inability of the state to impose a minimum discipline and respect for law among the capitalists.

(c) The third contradiction had its root in the cultural ambience. Post-independence development had put lots of purchasing power in the hands of a narrow section of society, whose growing consumerism made them vocal supporters of liberalization.

As has been earlier said that globalisation at the universal level was used as a justifying ideology, especially with the failure of the communist regimes. The advocates of the market argued it as 'end of history', where there will be no contradiction. Many commentators termed it as the final victory of the market over the interventionist State. Australia and New Zealand Banking Group (ANZ) chief economist Saul Eslake argued that "market is irresistible and globalisation is simply the logical extension of the tendency toward specialization and trade has been going on almost since mankind first walked on the surface of the earth."[20] Thomas Friedman exclaimed that "globalisation as not just about trade but about the triumph of market forces, technology and open and democratic forces throughout the world."[21] The idea that markets are the only righteous entity derived its theoretical and philosophical support from libertarianism. Charles Murray – a libertarian – argued for a reduced role for government, particularly at the federal level. "For example, Murray identifies the following federal programs and functions to be eliminated entirely: Social Security, Medicare, welfare, agriculture, housing, training and employment, energy, and the Post Office. He advocates the repeal of most consumer and product safety laws leaving redress to traditional tort and contract remedies. He would also repeal civil rights laws in favour of a constitutional amendment to the effect that:

(1) No administration at any level shall pass any law that requires bias by ethnicity, race, religion, or creed;

(2) No government shall pass any law limiting freedom of association for private individuals and group."[22]

Robert Nozik, another libertarian, vehemently defended the minimal role of state against market. State is to protect people against force, scam, and burglary, and enforces contracts. Thus it exists to safeguard rights, and the state itself violates people's rights if it attempts to do any more than this. His 'Entitlement Theory' is based on the idea that only free market exchanges respect people as equals. The theory consists of three principles, which are as follow:

(1) Transfer principle: Holdings (actually) freely acquired from others who acquired them in a just way are justly acquired.
(2) Acquisition principle: Persons are allowed to hold initially acquired in a just way (according to the Lockean Proviso).
(3) Rectification principle: Rectify violations of 1 or 2 by restoring holdings to their rightful owners, or "one time" redistribution according to the Difference Principle.

"Murray Rothbard believed that the monopoly power of government over the issuance and distribution of money was inherently destructive. The belief derived from Ludwig von Mises and Hayek's theory of the business cycle, which holds that undue credit expansion inevitably leads to a gross misallocation of capital resources, triggering unsustainable credit bubbles and eventually, economic depressions. He, therefore, strongly opposed central banking and fractional reserve banking under a fiat money system and supported full reserve banking and free banking, which he also called 'free market money', as an alternative".[23]

The world financial institutions controlled by developed nation use various argument ranging from poverty reduction to efficient uses of industrial strength to push economic reform in third world countries. As Patnaik and Chandrasekhar note, "in the late fifties and early sixties the Bank used a macro argument to push its line: substantial unutilized capacity in the industrial sector existed because of a scarcity of foreign exchange; a combination of import liberalization and exchange rate devaluation therefore would set up a virtuous circle of 'more imports – more capacity utilization – more exports – still more imports' and so on, which would unshackle the economy from the clutches of *dirigisme*. In the Robert McNamara years the emphasis shifted to poverty. The argument was expressed in terms of domestic inter-sectoral trade, which were more unfavourable for agriculture vis-à-vis industry, so that removing trade restriction and thereby preventing state-sponsored industrialization would benefit the agricultural sector, which is the repository of mass poverty…More recently, the Bank has shifted to the well-known micro theoretic 'marketist' argument that focuses on the allegedly interrelated phenomenon of 'inward orientation', 'price-distortion', and 'inefficiency'.[24]

Pro-market forces in India borrowed the line of argument forwarded by those international institutions. Arvind Virmani mentioned while arguing in favour of structural adjustment that "the heavy hand of government in the form of incentive-distorting laws, rules, regulations, procedures and red tape have corrupted industry and business and other organised interest groups. These must be removed so as to release the energy of the people. The state should confine itself to managing the economy so as to accelerate employment and income growth in a self-sustaining manner, ensure that all citizens receive their basic entitlements of basic public goods and services and empower the poor so that they have equal rights (and responsibilities) with the better off citizens."[25] Y.V.Reddy noticed that despite State led development to fulfil this high aim, India didn't perform well at the levels of income, health, literacy, poverty etc. However, the post-reform period recorded high rate of growth with space for improvement through more systematic opening of economy.[26] Bhagwati, while analysing the developmental policies adopted by India (1950-90), argued that "India has long suffered from a mindless commitment to policies that were advertised in the public policy domain as solutions to poverty and destitution but that tragically accentuated instead these tragic phenomena over decades...."[27] He found that economic reform has taken out India from the garb of poverty. Bimal Jalan justifies the decision to open up Indian economy, while looking at the inefficient performance of economy driven by socialist ideology. Jalan noted that "in 30 out of 35 years between 1956 and 1991, India had balance of payment problems of varying intensity....However, the most conspicuous failure, in his view, for which there is no alibi, and the responsibility for which lies squarely and indisputably at our doors, is the erosion in public savings and the inability of the public sector to generate resources for investment or provision of public services."[28]

While summing up the on-going debate, on the record, both external and internal factors contributed to the reforms. Yet, the decision to go ahead with the reforms was a 'minority' choice. Rob Jenkins argued that "India's shift to a market-oriented development strategy during the 1990s was made possible by the political skill of elites operating within established, yet flexible, state and non-state institutions. This often showcased the less democratic elements of the liberal parliamentary tradition – what has been called 'reform by stealth'. Underhanded tactics, aided by propitious international circumstances during most of the 1990s, may well have sufficed to promote the initial stages of India's process of marketisation..."[29] Atul Kohli concurred with above proposition and noted that "When the policy shift was announced, the main forces supporting such a shift included the narrow political leadership, the technocratic policy elite, a segment of Indian capital, and external actors, expressing their preferences mainly in the form of policy conditionality set by the IMF. It was a minority decision."[30]

An overall assessment of its impact in India

Before dealing with the liberalization at the micro level – UP and Banaras – a succinct evaluation of the phenomenon should be done. Two decades of reform is enough to trace the trajectory of development initiated by economic reforms in India. The debate around development is following almost similar line as it was categorized during the initiation of the reform: one, who finds that globalisation, which has inherent potential of common goods, really triggered off the Indian growth rate, whereas, another group thinks that economic reforms has created havoc on large section of population by deepening poverty, rising inequalities, joblessness, cutting back of social security and so on. In between, there are third group, who are not averse to the idea of globalisation, but notice down the negative effects of globalisation, thus asking for perceptive policy draft. Scholars like J. Bhagwati, A. Virmani, IMD Little, V. Joshi, Srinivasan, Suresh Tendulkar, V.N.Mishra, M.G.Rao, N.R.Bhanumuthy, A.Mitra et al argued that globalisation has really benefited India. Bhagwati exclaimed that post-reform growth has helped to reduce poverty because of three central reasons:

(1) It creates jobs that 'pull up' the poor into gainful employment by providing more economic opportunity;
(2) It provides the revenues with which we can build more schools and provide more health facilities for the poor; and
(3) It creates the incentives that enable the poor to access these facilities and also for the advancement of progressive social agendas generally.[31]

Virmani claimed that "the growth rate of the economy increased further to 6.5 per cent per annum during 1993-94 to 1999-2000. As a result the real wages of agricultural labour increased by about 3 per cent per annum during this period and the proportion of people below the poverty line fell from 36 per cent in 1993-94 to about 26.1 per cent in 1999-2000."[32] Mishra and Rao analyzing the reform's impact on agriculture argue that "aggregate crop output in 1993-94 prices is 3.08 per cent per annum as 2.94 per cent of eighties. This is because of addition of values crop in 1990s. Public investment in 1990s was higher than 1980s. During the nineties agricultural exports increased at 8.96 per cent per annum as compared to only 2.43 per cent during the eighties."[33] Bhanumurthy and

Mitra looks into the effect on poverty after the introduction of economic reform, while comparing pre/post decade of liberalization. The research found that at the all-India level the fall in the incidence of poverty in the nineties (1993/94 through 1999/00, period 2 hereafter) seems to be higher than during 1983 to 1993/94 (period 1 hereafter). The rural-urban differences are noteworthy: rural poverty dropped by a little more than 10 percentage point in the second period, whereas it was around 8.3 percentage point in the first period, and urban poverty fell by 8.38 and 8.74 percentage points in periods 1 and 2, respectively. At the state level, except for Assam and Haryana all the other states registered a fall in the incidence of rural poverty in the eighties and in the nineties each of the major states recorded a decline. In the case of urban areas excepting Andhra Pradesh and Orissa in the eighties and nineties, respectively all the other states show a decline in the incidence of poverty.

However, the extent of decline varies considerably across states though in the rural areas it seems to have fallen in the nineties compared to the eighties: the coefficient of variation of the change in rural poverty dropped from 98.75 per cent in the first period to 51.03 per cent in the second period. On the other hand, the coefficient of variation increased from 61.58 per cent to 70.21 per cent in the urban areas of the states during the same period indicating a rise in the inter-state variations of change in the incidence of urban poverty in the post-reform period.[34] Assessing the impact of reform on social sector expenditure, Seema Joshi argued that "a proportion of aggregate expenditure, i.e., the share of social sector expenditure in the combined expenditures of the central and state governments has registered an increase during the reform period. In case of central plan and non-plan expenditure, the social sector spending (as a per cent of aggregate expenditure) increased significantly from 10.59 per cent in the pre-reform period (1986-87 to 1990-91) to 13.87 per cent in the post-reform period (1991-92 to 2002-03).[35] K.C. Pant looking at the overall growth rate argued that "India's reforms in the 1990s have had good effect, as its growth rate was about 7 per cent during 1992-97."[36] Ghose (2000) shows that "in case of industrialised countries, growth of manufactured imports from developing countries has a small adverse effect on manufacturing employment but virtually no effect on wages. But, in case of developing countries that have emerged as important exporters of manufactures to industrialised countries a growth in trade has a large positive effect on manufacturing employment and wages. On the other side, those who are opposed to economic reforms policy visualize it as a 'capitalist manifesto."[37] A.K.Bagchi argued that "the neoliberal regime in

India, has failed to improve the macro-economic management of the economy and to attain a better level of 'macro-economic capability."[38]

Commenting on poverty vis-à-vis liberalization, Utsa Patnaik asserted that it has failed to reduce poverty. According to Patnaik, Planning Commission except for 1971 never used nutritious diet as a parameter to define poverty. By making 1973-94 as a base year, Planning Commission brings forth price indices to define poverty. Thus, for the year 1999-2000, those who earned Rs. 328 p/m is not poor. It means Rs. 11 per day at the national level, as this is up to Rs. 7 and Rs. 8 in many states. But, with this amount a rural poor access 1890 calories against the required 2400 calories. The conclusion that 'poverty has declined in the 1990s' is solely the result of this clandestine lowering of the consumption standard over time, a lowering which is inherent in the official price-index adjusted estimation method.[39] The steep fall in foodgrains availability per head is a highly abnormal trend which we do not expect to see in an economy where average per capita income is rising, nor has it been observed for any length of time in the past in this country after Independence: it is consistent only with worsening income distribution of a particular type, involving an *absolute decline* in incomes and purchasing power for a major part of the population. The foodgrains absorption figures are calculated following the official definition, from physical net output in tones, adjusted for change in stocks and trade, and have to meet all final uses in the economy – direct consumption as food, use as feed for producing animal products (a part of this is exported), and industrial use. The present level is one of the lowest in the world and only the Sub-Saharan African countries and the least developed countries have a lower level than India.

To sum up, macroeconomic policies of expenditure deflation is the key to understanding the agrarian crisis, and the resulting loss of purchasing power or, in Keynesian terms, a severe squeeze on aggregate effective demand of the majority of the population, the key to understanding why such abnormal levels of public foodgrains stocks of 64 million tonnes, 40 million tonnes in excess of buffer norms, had built up by July 2002. These stocks were coming out of more and more empty stomachs. Subsequent analysis of expenditure trends from the thin-sample rounds of NSS data confirm this analysis they show that the lowest 40 per cent of persons ranked by expenditure levels had absolutely lower per capita total real expenditure by 2001-2 compared to 1995-6 while the next 40 per cent had stagnant real expenditure. In fact the situation is worse because asset adjustments have been taking place to maintain the consumption flow – for the lowest deciles even reduced real expenditure and reduced food intake, is seen after they have incurred un-repayable debts and liquidated part of their assets including land. The latest 60th Round (2004) data show an even bleaker picture – without any adjustment for prices, the per capita expenditure on food in current prices at official poverty lines, shows an absolute decline between 2000 and 2004.

The government and the majority of economists have put forward a totally incorrect analysis of the rising stocks and falling availability. They closed their eyes to the falling purchasing power deliberately brought about by public deflationary policies and instead they put the blame on allegedly 'too high ' minimum support price (MSP) which they claimed gave the 'wrong signals' to the farmers who therefore produced more than the market required, and they advocated reduction of MSP. This fallacious argument ignored the fact that food grains growth rates had virtually halved, so that output per capita has been declining (owing to the investment and development expenditure cuts), and this should have led to the need for imports had demand been maintained at normal levels. The freeze on procurement price which followed this wrong analysis, when input prices have been rising, has generalized deflation further to include more farmers and added to the problem of deficient demand. Rather than restoring lost purchasing power and boosting aggregate demand by using food stocks for food-for-work programmes, the government exported 22 million tonnes of grains out of public stocks at a subsidized price during 2002 and 2003, which apparently was mainly used as animal feed abroad.

"The growth rates in the labour force and work force have recorded a marginal decline. Whereas, the unemployment rate has shown an increase during the reference period. It has decreased from 8.3 per cent to 5.99 per cent between 1983 and 1993-94 and subsequently increased to 7.32 per cent by 1999-2000. This observation holds well in both rural and urban areas."[40] While the total employment in absolute terms showed an increase over time, the growth rates have shown a declining trend. In the sectors such as agriculture, mining and quarrying, electricity, gas and water, and services, the growth rates in the employment have recorded negative trends. Chadha and Sahu show absolute decrease in the rural employment during 1993-94 to 1999-00. In post-reform period there is decline in labour force participation ratio (LFPR) occurred both for rural males and rural females in as many as 11 states, namely, Andhra Pradesh, Bihar, Himachal Pradesh, Karnataka, Madhya Pradesh, Maharashtra, Orissa, Rajasthan, Tamil Nadu, UP and West Bengal."[41] According to the 2001 Census

Scheduled Castes (SCs) has strength of 16.20 per cent of total population. Thus, it becomes imperative to diagnosis the effect of economic reform that followed after liberalization. It also acts as litmus test to the defender of 'invisible hands of market' and its trickledown effect on the downtrodden section of society.

The whole debate surrounding the impact of liberalization on Dalits is divided into two broader theoretical lines: one who thinks that liberalization works for Dalits and other who thinks otherwise. Gail Omvedt argued that "Globalisation is inevitable and has some good aspect. It is better to be exploited by capital than not to be so exploited."[42] Following Omvedt's defence of globalisation A. Ramaiah too argued that the phenomenon can possibly benefit the Dalits and other marginalized section of India. "A due share to the marginalised can be achieved also by way of moving from higher growth rate to further higher growth rate, which is considered possible through globalisation, and investing the surplus so generated in social welfare sectors. Globalisation brings in for achieving higher and rapid economic growth rate. And with the advantage of higher growth rate, it may not be difficult for the State to invest more on social and social welfare sectors. What is lacking for investing in social welfare or social justice is the State's will."[43] Ramaiah believed that globalisation is inevitable so Dalits should participate in the process to grab the opportunity it is throwing. He does not care about depletion public sector. According to the author it has recruited Dalits in jobs of scavengers and sweeper

The establishment of Dalit Indian Chamber of Commerce and Industry (DICCI) emulating Federation of Indian Chambers of Commerce and Industry (FICCI) highlighted as the trickledown effect of globalisation on poor section of the society. Dalit capitalists, though much less in number, is trying to flag the idea that in the current economic system Dalit is no more dependent on reservation policy. The defender of globalisation from deprived section also point out that State has failed in its agenda of egalitarian society. Thus, not much improvement can be seen in the socio-economic condition of Dalits.

Hence, globalisation is defended by some Dalit intellectuals for new opportunity and turns. According to Dhananjay Rai "New turn is offshoot of globalization and encompasses 'caste withering thereby escaping "hunger and humiliation"; opportunity to possess material goods thus entering into middle class basket and challenging Upper Caste Consumer Club and replacement of caste capitalism. The Bhopal Document echoes similar resonances (The Bhopal Document, 2002). The Bhopal Document categorically praises the American democracy: "American society is now an enthusiastic advocate and practitioner of equal opportunity, affirmative action and diverse policies in every sphere of life, from the government sector to the private sector to arts, media and in sharing the national prosperity." The aforesaid process has received accolade and depicted as…In Search of a Bourgeoisie: Dalit Politics Enters a New Phase, "Rashtravadi Chintan Se Pare" (beyond the nationalist thinking) and "New Economies of Desire." New turn is justified because 'Dalits are not very much hurt due to the weakening of the nation state; Dalits are not worried about globalization per se but share therein. They are afraid that in the name of unity for the struggle against globalization, their own struggle could be asked to be suspended'. [T]he new economies of desire include the explosion of a series of new aspirations: the celebration of capitalism by sections of the most oppressed, especially by [d]alits" …The initial years of the neo-liberal regimes were thus spent by [d]alit intellectuals in mobilizing for defending the public sector and opposing globalization."[44]

However, the opposition to globlisation argued that globalisation, has, on the whole, resulted in the contraction of public sector and ascendancy of the private sector which in turn has begun to dismantle the limited protection being granted to the marginalised sections such as the SCs and STs in the sphere of employment. They fear that such a process is bound to worsen their plight further in the second-generation reforms. Such scholars fear that globalisation will drastically narrow down Dalits' access to basic means of sustenance and development such as education and employment, and health care facilities. With globalisation, they fear, there will be no statutory mechanism to redress grievances of Dalits especially when the exploitation or victimisation is by the organizations or companies from outside India. They theorise their position vis-à-vis economic reform by invoking Ambedkar argument about capital and capitalism. Ambedkar throughout his life was anti-capitalism, argued Anand Teltumbde. "In 1938, Ambedkar, while addressing railway workers in Manmad, had famously declared that the Untoucha-bles had two enemies: brahmanism and capitalism…The "States and Minorities", a memorandum submitted to the Constituent Assembly in 1947 on behalf of the Scheduled Castes Federation (SCF) had proposed a radical model of state socialism, to guard against unbridled grid of capitalists. As an abiding lover of democracy, he termed capitalism "a dictatorship of private employer." Elsewhere he rationalised his choice saying that "capitalism appeals to the rich and does not appeal to the poor. On the contrary socialism appeals to the poor but does not appeal to the rich." In fact, even at the very fag end of his life, while explaining why he embraced Buddhism, his love for socialism (and hence hate for capitalism) comes out starkly. In his "Buddha or Karl Marx" Ambedkar comes closer to accept Marx but for his methods, which according to him were overcome in Buddhism."[45]

A careful analysis of the economic reform exhibit that poor has become poorer and rich is getting richer. Obviously, this poor comprises large number of Dalits as well. After fierce struggle against Brahminism, Ambedkar was able to earn the safeguards for Dalits and adivasi in the Constitution. The Constitution viz. Article15, 16, 38, 46, 164, 275, 330, 332, 334, 335, 338, 340, 341, 342 and 366 gives democratic rights to SCs/ STs. It underpins to build various institutions for their welfare. With the withdrawal of the State from social sector investment these safeguards provided by the Constitution will tumble upon, feared many scholars.

The STs (adivasi) population of our country is badly hit by economic reform, started since 1991. For developmental project to the big MNCs government has begun to displace tribals as their inhabitants are rich in mineral and other resources. Valuable iron ore, bauxite, coal, stone quarries and so on can be found in areas under the Fifth Schedule or in other adivasi dominated areas. Lure of profiteering without much or no responsibility is attractive to the MNCs. Government too play its role in facilitating the valuable land in the clout of development. According to Brinda Karat "between 1980 and 2006 11.33 lakh hectares of forest land, including in Fifth Schedule areas has been "diverted" for non-forestry purposes. Of these as much as 5.7 lakh hectares was "diverted" between 2001 and 2006 – a joint project clearly of the National Democratic Alliance (NDA) and United Progressive Alliance (UPA) Governments. The term "diversion" is of course a euphemism for the legal sanction given for land grab by corporate, mining companies, power companies and also for Government projects like building dams, roads etc."[46] This has tremendously disturbed the communitarian form of tribals' life. Their culture – language, religions and social values – is under attack. Due to market intervention in tribal area new class categorization can be seen as:

(1) poor and marginal peasants with small unproductive landholdings (2) as landless agricultural workers (3) as workers in plantations, mines, quarries (4) as workers in the unorganized sector with no rights such as construction workers or daily waged or contract workers in nonagricultural work like coolies, as domestic workers in towns and cities. A large section

of adivasis are migrant workers (5) Those sections who have had access to education facilities have been able to avail of the reserved quotas and get Government or public sector jobs and therefore been able to achieve a better standard of living through which there is a developing, though still comparatively small middle class among adivasi communities. However these sections still face different forms of discrimination. (6) The traditional chiefs, the "royal" families, who have diminished power and wealth.[47] Tribal women are the worst among the effected. Apart from their economic and social exploitation along with their male counterparts they are sexually exploited by the forest guards, corporations, government office, et al. According to 2010-11 report of Home Ministry shows that tribal women are subjected various form of crime.

As per the 2001 census, the total work force in our country is 402 million, of which 313 million are main workers and 89 million are marginal workers. Out of the 313 million main workers, about 285 million is in the unorganised sector, accounting 91 per cent (Government of India, Economic Survey: 2005-06). When the labour absorption in the organised sector declines during the period of reforms, it would naturally push the additional labour force to the unorganised sector leading to further swelling of unorganised workers.

Table 3: Trends in Employment in Organised and Unorganised Sectors in India (in lakhs)[48]

Year	*Organised*	*Unorganised*	*Total Workforce*
1983	240.10 (8.33)	2640.00 (91.67)	2880.00
1987-88	257.00 (8.75)	2680.00 (91.25)	2937.00
1991-92	267.33 (8.27)	2966.22 (91.73)	3233.55
1992-93	270.56 (8.20)	3027.42 (91.80)	3297.98
1993-94	271.77 (8.09)	3089.14 (91.91)	3360.91
1994-95	273.75 (7.98)	3157.21 (92.02)	3430.96
1995-96	275.25 (7.97)	3224.26 (92.03)	3499.51
1999-2000	277.89 (7.65)	3355.41(92.35)	3633.30

Source: Alternative Economic Survey: 1991-98 and Economic Survey 2002-03.

As a large number of labour forces are pushed into the unorganised category of workers, the excess labour supply creates disequilibrium or imbalance in the labour market that leads to several adjustments in the unorganised labour economy. The surplus or excess labour supply into the unorganised category leads to partial or casual employment at low wages and without job or social security of any kind. Jeemol Unni based on the study conducted in Ahmedabad highlighted the differential benefit between a regular and casual employee. It revealed that the casual labourers are highly exploited in terms of assurance of employment, contract procedures, paid leave, provident fund/ pension, medical and other benefit and notice for termination.[49] Her analysis clearly indicated the disadvantageous position realised by the unorganised workers in terms of their earnings in the recent years. In fact, this trend could be attributed to the negative impact of globalisation on the unorganised workers. Aseema Sinha through data analysis argued that the nature of economic reform has exacerbated rural-urban, regional and sectoral inequalities. The wage difference is contributing to the insecurity of those who are already poor. If we further, disaggregate the category poor, it is India's Scheduled Castes and Minorities, especially Muslims are most affected.

Shrinking government jobs due to the privatization has forced poor into self-employment, as 57.4 per cent of the total Muslim workers engaged in this act. An indirect implication of rising intra-urban, rural-urban and inter-state inequalities is that impoverishment, and economic insecurities afflict some sections, social groups, and regions more than others. Sinha further argued that the economic problems and impoverishment of these sections gives impetus to the rise of regionalism and communalism. The decline of the textile industry in Gujarat and Mumbai has led to massive insecurities among the population in these industries creating the potential for deep social unrest utilized by Shiv Sena and the BJP. Many Muslims stressed that the neo-liberal economic policies being followed by successive governments in the last two decades or so had hit Muslim artisan communities, such as potters, weavers, craftsmen etc. particularly badly. "They had resulted in further economic marginalization of these communities. Linked to this, the cutting down of subsidies and the privatisation of education had made quality education even more difficult for these communities to access. Yet, the government had done little to address the situation."[50]

Liberalization in Uttar Pradesh

Somehow, at the Union level, government was able to sell the idea of liberalization, but States like UP had to face varied range of problems. Hence, U.P started off comparatively later than other States. For instance, Andhra Pradesh prepared its 'Vision 2020' in mid-nineties, which documented the goals to be achieved through economic reform. The aims can be summarised as "per capita income higher by ten times; rate of growth of employment higher than the rate of growth of population, suggesting that the level of unemployment in the state would decline; improved urban and rural amenities, suggesting significantly better standards of living; and all this made accessible to a progressively larger proportion of the population. In order to translate this vision into reality, the document aimed to identify the strengths of the state so that all available resources could be directed towards facilitating development along a path based on these strengths. By reducing the risks and associated costs for the private entrepreneur in these priority areas, it was expected that private investment would get effectively channelized into these programmes. This would allow the state to benefit from the underlying economies of scale in production/R and D activity/commerce in these areas."[51] Gujarat has been leading the pack of States who have opened their border for foreign capitals. The State government only facilitated the growth of private enterprise since its strategy was already consistent with the changes in the policy reforms at the Centre. But the story of UP was a bit turbulent and inconsistent with regard to economic reform.

Uttar Pradesh has 199 million populations i.e. 16.49 per cent of India's population spread across seventy one districts. The State is divided into three hundred twelve tehsils and has 1.08 lakh villages. The sex ratio has shown increase from 898 in 2001 to 908 in 2011.[52] The total literacy rate in the state recorded in census 2011 is 69.72 per cent. The State is classified into four economic regions, western, central, eastern and Bundelkhand. "The western UP has 5 divisions and 26 districts, the central covers two divisions and 10 districts, Bundelkhand has two divisions and seven districts, and the eastern encompasses eight divisions and 27 districts."[53] It is an agriculture-dominated state as 2/3rd of the workforce is dependent on agriculture for their livelihood. However, census 2011 indicate that though a large part of the state's working population still remains affiliated to the farm sector, the number of farm labourers has increased as against individual farmers. While Census 2011 categorises farmers in the "other workers" segment, cultivators and agricultural labourers are recognised as other than those persons engaged in plantation activities. It stands first in food grain and sugarcane production in 2011.

Table 4: Gross State Domestic Product and its Composition in Uttar Pradesh

Sectoral contribution in GSDP in Current Price (per cent)			
Component	*FY 2006*	*FY 2008*	*FY 2011*
Primary	30.1	27.9	27.6
Secondary	23.2	25.2	23.7
Tertiary	46.7	47.0	48.6

Source: PHD Research Bureau, compiled from Directorate of Economics and Statistics, Government of Uttar Pradesh.

This table shows that the tertiary sector contributes a significant share of around 49 per cent in the Gross State Domestice Product (GSDP) followed by primary and secondary sector at around 28 per cent and 24 per cent respectively during FY2011. It may be noted that the share of primary sector has declined marginally from around 30 per cent during FY2006 to around 28 per cent in FY2011, while the share of secondary sector has remained stagnant at around 24 per cent during the same period. The employment in farm sector has shown decrease which also marks the shift to non-farm jobs. Non-farm workers in UP registered a rise to 30.1 per cent in 2004-05 from 18.0 per cent in 1983.[54] "The western region of UP has the highest number of workers in the secondary sector followed by the southern region at 18.3 per cent. This high share of southern region in total employment is attributable to the considerable size of construction activities. These activities accounted for 13.9 per cent of employment in the southern region. In contrast with this, the western, eastern and central regions have substantial employment in manufacturing activities to the tune of 12.1 per cent, 9.2 per cent and 8.6 per cent, respectively. Second, the proportion of employment in the tertiary sector in the western, eastern and central regions was 18 per cent, 15.1 per cent and 11.9 per cent, respectively, but in the southern region it was 6 per cent. Trade and other services sectors provided the highest proportion of employment while transport and communications provided the least in all the regions."[55]

The data above shows the intra-regional disparities within the State. The intra-regional distribution suggests that the highest incidence of poverty among casual labour was in the eastern region, followed by Bundelkhand. The distribution of poverty by ownership of land suggests the highest concentration of poor was among the marginal landholders, followed by the landless.

Table 5: Intra-Regional Distribution of poor households by Sector and Religion in UP

Region	*Rural*				*Urban*			
	Hindu	*Muslim*	*Others*	*Total*	*Hindu*	*Muslim*	*Others*	*Total*
Western	25.04	23.51	15.95	24.68	24.72	45.1	37.75	30.92
Central	27.25	33.21	0	27.76	29.24	35.44	32.01	30.55
Eastern	37.91	38.32	44.09	37.97	36.72	58.08	14.28	41.68
Bundelkhand	17.07	12.63	17.18	16.83	28.48	23.38	13.17	27.28
Total	30.91	30.01	20.88	30.74	28.6	44.95	32.85	32.88

Source: D.M.Diwakar (2009).

The table above shows that poverty by religion suggests that there was no difference in the distribution of poverty with respect to religion in rural areas. However, intra-regional variations were different. In the eastern region, other minorities were poorer than Hindus and Muslims, and in the central region, Muslims were poorer than Hindus. Unlike rural areas, in urban areas, a higher degree of poverty was found among Muslim households, followed by other minorities. Again, poverty among Muslims in urban areas was highest in the eastern region, followed by the western region. Apart from the intra-regional variation in development, UP as a whole has some other imbalance which are as follow: imbalance in population and state's land area, state rich in natural resources, but low in industrial development; large food grain output, but a large number of marginal operational holdings (that is, farm holdings below 1 hectare); large population (a potential human resource), but a high level of illiteracy; large development needs, but political apathy. Though the condition of the peasantry remains by and large poor, UP has not witnessed farmers' suicides on a scale visible in other states like Maharashtra or Andhra Pradesh. Ajit Kumar Singh argued that this is so because "as compared to Maharashtra or AP, where rain-fed agriculture is dominant, in UP over 70 per cent of the cultivated area is irrigated. Thus, agriculture is less prone to fluctuations due to adverse monsoon conditions. Moreover, agriculture in UP is dominated by food grains and is less commercialised. The level of indebtedness is also relatively low. Recent NSS surveys on farmers' conditions reveal that only 40 per cent of farming household in UP are indebted as compared to the figure of 55 per cent in Maharashtra and 82 per cent in Andhra Pradesh."[56] However, the State has been politically important, given number of prime ministers, but it was not able to reap its benefit.

Only between 1974 till the end of 1990 the general rate of economic growth was above the national average both in agriculture and industry. The table given below also points out that during the period 1975 to 1990, the growth performance of U.P. compared well with the national level growth. However, UP has not been able to maintain the pace of growth with the onset of economic reforms. Thus, it is regarded as one of the BIMARU States. The State has come to be regarded as poor and backward, suffering from political instability, poor governance and as a drag on the national economy. Overall, the State is characterized by low levels of per capita income, high incidence of poverty, sluggish economic growth, high population pressure with mortality and death rates and low life expectancy. In many ways its position is comparable to some of the poorest countries of sub-Saharan Africa. In terms of most human development indicators, UP ranks 13th or 14th out of the 15 major States of the country, while in terms of poverty ratio, it ranks 11th. There are many theories which points out the reasons for the inter-state inequality after the economic reform. M.S. Ahluwalia argued that coverage and quality of infrastructure may be affecting the growth of poorer States. Rodrik and Subramanian argued that "weakness in manufacturing sector and absolute slowdown in Agriculture might effects the poorer states to use the benefit of reform."[57] Virmani proposed that public (roads, electricity, railway) and quasi-public (dam, canal) goods that affect investment are likely to be more important determinants of inter-State variation in growth than other infrastructure goods and services. 12th Five Year Plan pointed out that unequal access to social and physical infrastructure by States; quality of human capital, which in turn depends on the level of education and health of the population, and regions with better law and order and governance benefit in the form of higher and sustained growth.

Table 6: Growth in UP during Five Year Plan (FYP)

Plan Period	*Annual Growth Rate in Total Income*		*Annual Growth Rate in Per Capita Income*	
	India	*UP*	*India*	*UP*
1st FYP (1951-56)	3.6	2.0	1.7	0.5
2nd FYP (1956-61)	4.2	1.9	1.9	0.3
3rd FYP (1961-66)	2.8	1.6	0.0	-0.2
4th FYP (1969-74)	3.3	2.3	1.1	0.4

(Contd...)

5th FYP (1974-79)	4.7	5.7	2.9	3.3
6th FYP (1981-85)	5.7	3.9	2.7	1.5
7th FYP (1985-90)	5.8	5.7	3.6	3.3
8th FYP (1992-97)	6.8	3.2	4.9	1.4
9th FYP (1997-02)	5.5	2.3	3.6	0.0
10th FYP (2002-07)*	7.7	5.3	6.0	3.3

Source: Government of UP (2002).

* Figure taken from Annual Plan 2007-08, UP.

Almost all the factors have contributed to the slow economic growth of UP. But, the most important reason pointed out by many experts is the political instability in and competitive politics which stops successive government from taking decisive policy measures to attract capital. R. U. Arora argued that inter-states barrier in trade and political factors such as different regional political parties and their interests, have limited the effect of development. Sudha Pai pointed out that political instability, weak leadership, and decline in governance during nineties were together responsible for the slow reform in UP. M.K.Agarwal underlines that political instability and coalition government dare not to take much-needed policy fearing political backlash from the voters. Consequently, among 17 major States of the country, U.P. ranked 15 in 2001 and 16 in 2005 in Human Development Ranking (HDR). During 2001-2011, literacy in UP has increased by 13.4 per cent which is more than the national average literacy increase of 9.24 per cent but it is still lagging behind the national average. Health and nutrition status of the state is not satisfactory. At the end of 11th FYP Infant Mortality Rate (IMR) is 61 as compare to 47 at all India. Maternal Mortality Rate and sex ratio in the State is not encouraging.

As political weaknesses of regional political parties stop them from taking any difficult decisions, the State's internal resource mobilisation deepens. It plunged into the vicious circle of debt trap. Kripa Shankar argued that UP is not making sufficient effort to mobilise the internal resource through taxation like Tamil Nadu, Andhra Pradesh etc. "Many other states which are at the middle level are making greater efforts at internal resource mobilisation. Per capita state tax revenue in Tamil Nadu in 2000-2001 was Rs. 2,014 as against Rs. 665 in UP. In Kerala, the same stood at Rs. 1,988 and in Karnataka and Andhra Pradesh the same was Rs. 1,745 and Rs. 1,415 respectively. In other words, if UP could achieve the same taxation level as that of Tamil Nadu, it could increase its tax revenue by Rs. 22,000 crores more, i.e., it could almost double its own tax revenue."[58] The incapability of the State to manage its fiscal deficit makes it revenue deficit from revenue surplus in 1980s.

When each State was designing policy to prepare the ground for structural adjustment UP was dealing with three important issues – *mandal* (reservation to OBCs), *mandir* (Ayodhya issue), and *mandi* (economic slump). The assertion of backward classes and Dalits into the Indian politics was like never before. They were looking for their share in the system. This gave rise to Samajwadi party (SP) and Bahujan Samaj Party (BSP) who were representing the interest of majority in UP. They had to delay the process of reform as its conditionalities were not in favour of nascent emerging classes. The efficient financial management was to be done by curtailing the permanent recruitment process and subsidies. However, during the reign of SP and BSP welfare measures for the backward classes and Dalit took place. The recruitment drive during the SP government has been termed as 'Yadavisation' of UP. During his earlier tenure (2003-07), Mulayam Singh recruited more than 18,000 police constables and many of them were allegedly Yadavs.[59] "The BSP launched social policies, especially related to health, education, housing, employment and social welfare, targeting Dalits and other oppressed people. For instance, in 1995, scholarships were provided for Dalit students up to standard eight. This was expected to have benefited about 7,200,000 students, and for that the government arranged Rs 1,110 million. As many as 53 new student hostels were to be constructed and several old student hostels to be renovated. The BSP government also arranged coaching centres for Scheduled Castes and Scheduled Tribes students who wished to appear for civil services examinations at the State and Central levels. Mayawati started the Ambedkar Rojgar Yojana (Ambedkar Employment Scheme) for Dalit women with an outlay of Rs 600 million. The outlay for family health/planning programmes was increased and 50 per cent of the beneficiaries were Dalits. In 1997, Rs 700 million was allocated for setting up schools on the *ashram* model for the children of the *Balmiki* (SC) caste. Scholarships were increased during this period. Marriage support money for SC girls was increased from Rs. 5,000 to Rs. 10,000. A sum of Rs. 1,000 was provided for medical expenses. The allocation of funds for the Indira Awaas Yojana [Indira Housing Scheme (IAY)] was increased four-fold."[60]

Scholars argued that these competitive politics keeping in mind the social support push UP in economic debt trap. Hence, they suggest "cutting down of non-developmental and wasteful expenditure, introduction of efficiency, and redeployment of resources towards social sectors and infrastructure to encourage investment and growth. It also suggested a 'socially equitious and politically acceptable' resource mobilisation strategy using tax/non-tax measures, involving broadening of the tax-base and modernisation of the collection machinery."[61] It is an undeniable facts that this assertion has threaten the social, political and economic position of brahminical forces in UP. Upper castes domination was absolute and perpetuated until the assertion of these forces. They were not going to recruit OBCs and dalits. But, it is also true that social movement which had wider scope of social transformation failed to capitalize the opportunity and succumbed to undemocratic principles like family rule, one-caste domination, one man party and more importantly compromise with the capitalist and brahminical forces in UP. After initial commitment both the parties, SP and BSP, have gone for liberalization which was about to hurt their social base most. "The SP responded to the onslaught of the market in a very cool and calculated manner. It adapted itself easily to the requirements of LPG without creating a fuss. The party does retain its agenda of equalitarianism, ruralism, and socialism along with its ability to adapt pragmatically to the demands of LPG. Mulayam Singh had constituted the State Industrial Development Council, with Amar Singh as chairman. Other members of the council were Anil Ambani, M.S. Banga of Hindustan Lever, K.V.Kamath of ICICI Bank, Shishir Bajaj (Bajaj group), N.M. Nilekani (Infosys), Ramdas Pai (Manipal Academy), P.C.Reddy (Apollo Hospitals) and Subrata Roy (Sahara group)."[62] Again in 1995, efforts for economic reform were undertaken by the coalition government of SP-BSP. 13 out of 50 public enterprises were shut down and 24 spinning mills were leased out on the condition that no workers would be retrenched.

But due to structural weaknesses, the reform could not rise to its fullest capacity. A diagnostic appraisal, following the CM's Conference of 1997, brought out the following weaknesses in UP: Weak governance that manifested itself in poor service delivery; excessive regulation and uncoordinated and wasteful public spending; inadequate transparency accountability and integrity of public services; high fiscal deficits forcing the State to resort to debt financing; low level of human development; over stretched public sector that was unable to discharge responsibilities effectively and infrastructure bottlenecks especially in power sector. In the same year, BJP chief minister Ram Prakash Gupta promised to cut down 2 per cent of government staff annually and abolish the posts that are vacant for more than a year. But this was not achieved due to the short tenure of Ram Prakash Gupta. Rajnath Singh decided not to implement the report of 5th Pay Commission and bring down fiscal deficit. Revenue deficit came down to 40.32 billion in 2001 from 72.53 billion in 2000. In 1999, Rajnath Singh introduced the Electricity Reform Bill which was supported by World Bank with US $ 150 million. The analysis of electricity reform in UP proves that it was a hasty decision by the then government. There were a number of shortcoming in the power sector reform in UP – "inadequate ground work before recommendation of the reforms model; major sabotage-prone gaps in the proposed model' in terms of jettisoning of the social agenda of equity of distribution; ad hoc handling of implementation of the model' as reflected in the undemocratic manner in which the state government and the Board's top management acted before, during and after the employees' strike."[63] Agriculture and industry were ready for adjustment. Agricultural reforms meant diversification of output like horticulture, fisheries etc. It required increased government expenditure. However, if we look at the post-reform state's expenditure on agriculture, it has gone down.

Despite political instability between 1999 and 2004, the State government following new Governance Policy, 2000, introduced too many changes in the line of economic reform. The few initiatives were as follows: "a ban on recruitment of government staff was put in place so as to move towards right-sizing through the normal attrition process; high level bodies for divestment, deregulation and expenditure efficiencies were constituted; several PSUs were wound up; efforts also began to privatise others; state initiated the 'UP Fiscal Reform and Public Sector Restructuring Programme'; in the transport sector private participation was invited and transport development was sought to be linked with a massive programme of strengthening the road network with World Bank support; A Special Economic Zone legislation (SEZ) was put in place and four new SEZs were planned for Agra , Kanpur, Badohi and Baranas."[64]

UP introduced combined industrial and service sector policy in 2004. It is expected that with the announcement of the policy, it would be possible to generate the envisaged investment and employment during the Tenth Plan period, The policy aimed at expediting the process of industrial development in the state with the promotion of private sector participation, development of village and small industries, promotion of export, and greater capital investment by attracting Non-Resident-Indians (NRIs) and Foreign Direct Investment (FDI). Also, the policy highlights ways and means of promoting export, comprising master plan for export oriented cities, strengthening the offices of Export Commissioner, and freight subsidy etc. The policy has special package for small scale and tiny industries, handloom industries, Khadi and Village industries, information technology, bio-technology, service sector lays emphasis on developments of hospitals. Information Technology training centres, cinema halls and multiplex, development of high-tech townships and so on is also important. As such, the industrial policy is quite ambitious and aims at the rationalisation and development of almost all aspects required for rapid industrial development.

Table 7: Expenditure of the Government of Uttar Pradesh on Agriculture

Years	Agriculture			
	Plan	Non-Plan	AG/TE	AG/DE
1990-91	55.1	44.9	6.4	10.0
1991-92	40.5	59.5	3.3	8.7
1992-93	51.0	49.0	5.5	9.4
1993-94	39.1	60.9	4.7	10.5
1994-95	37.9	68.0	3.2	8.4
1995-96	37.1	62.9	3.5	8.8
1996-97	38.1	61.9	3.1	8.5
1997-98	24.5	75.5	4.1	8.6
1998-99	31.1	68.9	3.7	8.4
1999-00	49.5	50.5	6.3	10.8
2000-01*	44.9	55.1	4.9	6.6
2001-02*	50.6	49.4	6.4	8.4
2002-03*	37.0	63.0	4.7	11.4
2003-04*	36.5	63.5	3.0	13.0
2000-01**	46.8	53.2	5.1	7.3
2001-02**	52.2	47.8	7.0	7.7
2002-03**	32.8	67.2	5.3	10.1
2003-04**	30.1	69.9	3.4	9.9

Source: RBI (2003), * Including Uttranchal. ** Excluding Uttranchal. AG – Expenditure on Agriculture; TE – Total Expenditure including revenue and capital. DE – Development Expenditure.

The policy has special package for small scale and tiny industries, handloom industries, Khadi and Village industries, information technology, bio-technology, service sector lays emphasis on developments of hospitals. Information Technology training centres, cinema halls and multiplex, development of high-tech townships and so on is also important. As such, the industrial policy is quite ambitious and aims at the rationalisation and development of almost all aspects required for rapid industrial development.

More investment from public and private sectors into the industry could be marker for the success of Industrial policy. "Total FDI of Rs.1.02 billion that is, a share of merely 1.5 per cent in the country's total, had gone to UP."[65] Thus it is understood that despite the reforms initiated by the UP government in the industrial sector, the performance of large-scale industry in the state has not been impressive. The total investment intentions filed through Industrial Entrepreneurs Memorandum (IEM) during the period April 2003-March 2004 constituted only 1.4 per cent of all India's share of total investment intentions. After first decade of hiccups, now the government of any parties, either regional or national, are ready to take all measures to put the economy in place. That means downsizing of the government, no permanent recruitment, giving the private sector a vital role in development etc. It would be interesting to observe how economic reform unfold in UP. 2012 election gave thumping majority to SP in Assembly and the first thing it did was to support the Union government over the Foreign Direct Investment (FDI) in retail sector. Now, if we look at the social base of the Samajwadi party in 2012 assembly election, 36 per cent of Muslim voted in its favour.[66] Most of them are into the retail sector.[67]

Infrastructure and Industrial Investment policy, 2012 declared that government of UP want integrated development of whole State. It aims for 11.2 per cent industrial growth rate along with 10 per cent SGDP. It has prioritized development of infrastructure. It promised to provide suitable conditions for the participation of private sector in the development of infrastructure. To have suitable conditions for industrial growth, the state has promised to give 100 per cent exemption from stamp duty to the units that are coming up in Eastern, Central and Bundelkhand region. These exemption are extended to the food processing unit, food park, agro-industry, BPO, IT, Bio-Tech, solar etc. But, government has shown no energy to rejuvenate handloom industry. In a passing reference, policy draft has mentioned the better implementation of the on-going schemes. Although, at least twice, the policy draft mentions the presence of traditional industries, but there has been no analysis of the problems faced by the handloom industry. This approach reflects a lack of seriousness.

Situating Banaras in the Debate

The background of Banaras weavers (*julaha*) has been given in the introduction. This section deals with the socio-political and economic background of Banaras. Its antiquity renders mysterious clout over its origin and name. It keeps travellers, scholars of various discipline and archaeologists guessing. This is perhaps due to the insensitivity of British archaeologists while excavating in and around Banaras. Rev. M. A. Sherring noted the chief reasons why Banares has been neglected were attributable partly to its great extent, and partly to the general ignorance as to the position of its ancient portions.[68] He had recorded the archaeological blunder to an extent in his book Benares: The Sacred City of the Hindus in Ancient and Modern Times. He wrote that 'Mr. James Prinsep, the great Indian archaeologists, was a resident in the city for about ten years; but it does not appear that he made any important discoveries in it. His "Views of Benares" are chiefly of a popular cast and do not give evidence of any extensive observation or research of this nature. Major Kittoe, the late Government archaeologists, and the architect of the Government college, , although interesting himself in the excavations of Sarnath, some three miles to the north of Benares, did not, so far as is known the city itself. Indeed, so inattentive was he to its claims to antiquity, that he removed many cart-loads of heavy stones, some of which were curiously carved, from Bakariya's kund, on the confines of the city and not more than a mile from the college which he was erecting, without reflecting that they might possibly be relics of ancient buildings formerly situated on that site… A third archaeologist, Mr. Thomas, late Judge of Benares, and a distinguished numismatist, trod in the same footsteps, only taking interest in the coins discovered in the city and in the Sarnath explorations. As instances of ruthless spoliation, I may here remark, that, in the erection of one of the bridges over the river Barna (Varna), forty-eight statues and other sculptured stones were removed from Sarnath and thrown into the river, to serve as a breakwater to the piers; and that, in the erection of the second bridge, the iron one, from fifty to sixty cart-loads of stones from the Sarnath buildings were employed…'[69]

Economically, ancient Banaras had three layers of society: artisans belonging to lower caste and class; merchants and bankers belong to *dwij* (born twice) caste and incurred profits; the king, generally Kshatriya, guided with the responsibility to maintain this system. However, the most important fact was the manufacturing of silk items in ancient times. It proves that Muslim rule had given new thrust to the silk industry in Banaras, but, certainly was not the originator of the industry. Reference of manufacturing of silk cloth can be noted down in the ancient Sanskrit and Buddhist texts. *Divyavadana*, a Buddhist Sanskrit text of the Gupta period, refers to *Kasikavastra* and *Kasikamu* and says that the fabrics were calendared in *kundi*. Patanjali's *Mahabhasya* refers to the Kasika textile which was better in quality and more expensive than similar material of Mathura. The trade continued to flourish even during the medieval period in vigorous manner. *Ukti-Vyakti Prakarana* [70] refers to the thriving textile industry of Banaras. The *zari* and brocades revived in the Sharqui period.[71] During the 16th century, the Mughals had introduced Persian motifs with emphasis on floral design by replacing the old one with animal and bird motifs. It became very popular and royal patronage enhanced the silk industry. Thus, Dr. Moti Chand in 'Kashi ka Itihaas', said that 'Since mahajanpad age to Mughal period Banaras has seen many political and cultural ups and down, but its business/trade never came down'.

With the fall of Mughal Empire the political power went into the hands of local/regional zamindar who claimed independence from the Mughals. However, that political instability did not last long. Slowly and gradually, all the local areas fallen to East India Company, which was transferred under direct control of British rule after 1857 revolt. Banaras was the first city of north India to become the part of British rule. Nonetheless, the transfer of power from Mughal to the British was not very easy. It took almost fifty-seven long years since the foundation of Banaras Raj i.e. year 1738, when Mansa Ram, a Bhumihar zamindar of Gangapur in the Banaras district and a subordinate of *Nazim* Rustam Ali,[72] managed to replace his overlord and employer and obtain from the Nawab of Awadh the right to collect for him the revenue of the district of Banaras, Jaunpur and Mirzapur, as his vassal and revenue intermediary.

The British intervention had tremendous affect in the Banaras region. The legal, judicial and revenue power shifted from Mughal to British. The three political systems which had existed juxtaposed to each other in the middle of the eighteenth century had been reduced to two. The main and all-powerful one, the British government, had replaced the Mughal and regional governments with a salaried civil administration controlled from the provincial capital in Agra, the Governor General's staff in Calcutta, the Secretary of State for India, and the Parliament in London. This political structure was rapidly destroying the third or local system.[73]

However, the power shift in favour of British changes many things vis-à-vis way of trading, items of trade, emergence of new class due to English education and government job etc. But it kept middleman and banker not merely unaffected but further strengthened their position in Banaras. This research found continued dominance of *dwija* (twice born) over the banking system in Banaras. They were the people mostly from the upper castes such as Vaishyas, Agarwal and Khatri followed by Gosains and Brahmans with high social status. In reference to their original homes, many of the Banaras bankers appear to have come from Gujarat, Rajasthan and the Western region of the present state of UP.[74] K.P. Mishra noted that "The banking business of Banaras was pursued within the framework of the Indian social system and so was monopolised by members of a few mercantile castes, knowledge of and skill in business being handed down from father to son. The bankers had their organised guilds and worked in cooperation settling their internal matters through arbitration within themselves…"[75]

The socio-economic position of artisans in general and weavers in particular, focus of this study, never ever changed. They remained at the bottom of social layer throughout the history. Most of the weavers were drawn from the low castes Hindu who later on converted to Islam.[76] The shift in occupation was intended to avoid the low social status and untouchability. However, conversion did not lead to upward social mobility of the weavers. Their caste '*julaha*' continued to be associated with illiteracy, stupidity and social backwardness and is supposed to refer to a particular *Biradari* or *quam* that is towards the bottom of the pure-polluted hierarchy.[77] Geo W. Briggs noted down that today's *julaha* (weaver) is collectivisation of *Chamar-Julaha, Koli-Julaha, Mohemmadan-Julaha* and *Rai Das-Julaha*.[78]

Table 8: Population of various Muslim castes in Banaras in 1820

Professions	***Number***	***On whose authority***	
Rais, Sheikh, Seid, Mughal, Patan, and C.	10,000	By estimation	Persons of independent fortune
Julaha	10,000	Wali Sah Mohammed (confirmed by enquiry)	weavers
Ghalla wala Trilochani	1000	Muradan	Grain merchants of Trilochan
Mali	62	Kinga	Gardeners
Kunjra	325	Ramzani Chaudri	Green grocers
Darzi	700	Sahay	Tailors
Dhobi (dilewal)	80	Imam Baksh	Washermen
(Benaresi)	100	Budhu Chaudri	,,
Kasbi (khangi)	1212	Enquiry	Courtesans
Ghungruband	500	,,	Dancing Girls
Jarrah	225	,,	Surgeons
Dafali	200	Bakhshu	Musiciana
Hijra	50	Enquiry	Eunuchs
Atashbaz	200	Babu Khan and Sera Ch.	Fire-Work Makers
Rangrez	475	Bakshan Chudri	Dyers
Halal Khor	900	,,	Scavengers
Hakak	112	Karman	Gem Polishers

(*Contd...*)

Moharkhand	25	Rajab	Engravers
Sikligar	71	Imambaksh	Metal Polishers
Kundigar	75	Miran	Wire flatteners
Kalabatun wale	28	Enquiry	Gold and Silver lace makers
Lohar	50	Rajab Ali Mukarband	Blacksmiths
Kherandi	50	,,	Turners
Churi Wale	300	Zia Ullah	Cutlers
Mochi (Jindaz)	105	Madar Baksh	Saddlers
Mochi (Jutiwala)	212	Behadur Chaudri	Shoe makers
Kasai (Bara)	354	Mihter Bhanger	Butchers
Kasai (Chhota)	250	Titu and Benaresi	,,
Nan Bai	130	Pir Mohammad Ch.	Bakers
Sabon wale	41	Subhani Chaudri	Soap sellers
Satrinji wale	63	Ramzani	Makers of Setrinjis
Bhatteara	381	Khanu and Jumani	Servants in Serais
Galicha wale	52	Bechan Chaudri	Carpet makers
Bihisti	180	Chhedi Chaudri	Water Carriers
Intpaz	173	Gausi and Madari	Brick-makers
Nycha band	32	Nur Mohammed	Hookah-Snake makers
Dhunia	100	Enquiry	Cotton Spinners
Madari	20	,,	Snake catchers
Rafugar	233	Mir Fazl Ali	Shawl menders
Trake Chhate wale	18	Phenku Badkash	Umbrella makers
Chylodar	9	Parasahi	
Niaria	125	Karm Khan	Refiners
Chabuk Sawar	200	Enquiry	Grooms
Raj	300	,,	Bricklayers
Kahar	200	,,	Bearers
Fakirs -	500	Enquiry at each takia	
Chandal	700	Madari Chaudri	Outcasts

Source: James Phillips, *Benares Illustrated*, Pilgrims Publishing, Delhi, 2009, pp. 191-192.

Though, silk trade flourished until the introduction of British cloth in Indian market, the weavers has had awful experiences. The situation of *karkhana* workers was also dismal. According to Eugenia Vanina "the position of *karkhana* workmen was thus rather secure, but not at all rosy. Apart from physical punishment, *karkhana* workmen cheated by its officials who pay them low wages with much delay or appropriated parts of it."[79] Hence, the situation of weavers in different political set-ups such as kingship, feudalism and industrial society governed by British was not good enough. The head of the political structure along with the intermediaries became over-rich by exploitation of one particular class, which led to their alienation. This particular situation fit to what Marx had argued while explaining about the situation of worker in his Economic and Philosophic Manuscripts of 1844. He said that "In a declining state of society – increasing misery of the worker; in an advancing state – misery with complications; and in a fully developed state of society – static misery. This alienation forced weavers and artisan class to revolt against the ruling classes."[80] Despite communal riots between Hindus and Muslims in major cloth producing centres of eastern Uttar Pradesh like Mau, Mubarakpur and Banaras,[81] weavers united against the common exploiter in revolt.

Post-independent, Banaras came to be officially known as Varanasi due to the efforts of Dr. Sarpurnanand. The Government of Uttar Pradesh has, in consultation with the Government of India, decided to change the name of Banaras to Varanasi with effect from May 24, 1957 when the 2,500th Buddha Jayanthi was due to be celebrated. It was pronounced as Benares by British. This city also known as Kashi, which is most favoured by the indigenous Hindus, is considered to mean 'splendid'. It is derived from the Sanskrit root '*Kaste*' or '*Kas*', which means 'one which shines' or 'one which is luminous'. Banaras Urban Area which has seven urban sub-units spread in 112.26 km. Being located in the Gangetic plains of North India, the land is very fertile because low level floods in the Ganges continually replenish the soil. It is located on a higher ground between rivers Ganga and Varuna. Total population of the district is 3.68 million i.e. 1.84 per cent of total population of the State in 2011. It ranked 18th. Percentage decadal growth rate of district population during 1991-2001 was 25.14 per cent whereas for 2001-2011 it is 17.32 per cent. In term of sex-ratio Banaras has ranked 24th with 909 which is better than State's average i.e. 908. In 2001 it was 903. It is one of most densely populated district in the State with 2,399. It ranked 2nd following Ghaziabad. Literacy rate of the district is 77.05 per cent, according to census 2011 which is better than State's average. Banaras ranked 9th. The male literacy rate is 85.12 per cent and female literacy rate is 68.20 per cent.

Table 9: District-wise and Caste-wise weavers in Uttar Pradesh

Zone	*SC*	*ST*	*OBC*	*Others*	*Total*
Lucknow	1.28	0.89	92.37	5.45	100
Kanpur	8.76	2.25	73.33	15.65	100
Etawah	32.34	13.17	51.55	2.94	100
Aligarh	51.79	2.80	37.42	7.99	100

Meerut	19.18	1.58	74.84	4.40	100
Jhansi	91.39	2.06	4.49	2.06	100
Moradabad	1.66	0.82	95.61	1.91	100
Allahabad	19.32	0.85	79.66	0.17	100
Faizabad	24.53	2.13	59.26	14.08	100
Mau	21.75	1.59	74.38	2.28	100
Varanasi	15.36	1.75	78.50	4.39	100
Gorakhpur	0.36	0.32	97.92	1.40	100
Bareily	4.51	1.04	92.28	2.17	100
Uttar Pradesh	15.25	1.59	79.06	4.10	100

Source: Compiled from *Joint Census of Handlooms and Powerlooms, 1995-96*.

Table given above shows the most of the weavers belongs to OBCs in Banaras. As this study is focus on *julaha* who are mostly situated in the city as said earlier the city profile is much needed. Varanasi town shows a constant increase in the population with varying rate of increase from decade to decade. In last seven decades the population has grown almost six folds, with increase in population from 207,650 in 1931 to 1,202,443 in year 2001. The growth of the population can be seen from the table below.

Table 10: Population of Varanasi city

Year	*Population*	*Increase*	*% Increase*
1931	207,650	–	–
1941	266,002	58,769	34
1951	355,771	89,769	34
1961	489,864	134,093	38
1971	671,934	182,070	26
1981	773,865	101,931	25
1991	1,030,863	256,998	33
2001	1,202,443	171,580	17

Source: Census of India, 2001.

Today, according to the census 2011, the urban agglomeration has total population of 1.43 million. Male population is 0.76 million whereas female has 0.67 million. Out of total population of the city, 0.15 million populations are of the 0-6 age group. Sex ratio in the city is 886 which are lower than district and state average. 0-6 age group sex ratio is even lower i.e. 877 in the city. The city of Varanasi is broadly divided into two zones:

the Cis Varuna and the Trans Varuna zone. Most part of the city is presently confined within the Cis Varuna area but with the provision of infrastructure facilities. According to the census 2001, the population density of the city is 15,070 pop/sq km i.e. 150 person/ha. Main economic base of the city is tourism and manufacturing.

Table 11: Varanasi Urban Agglomeration (UA): Population Characteristics, 2001[82]

Urban Unit	*Population (2001)*	*Decadal Growth Rate (per cent)*			
		1961-71	*1971-81*	*1981-91*	*1991-01*
Varanasi U.A. (Varanasi Dist)	1,203,961	23.85	25.50	29.48	16.69
1. Varanasi	1,092,445	23.04	22.45	28.95	17.58
(i) Varanasi (MC)	1,059,961	23.89	22.45	28.57	14.47
(ii) Lahartara (OG)	5,223	-	-	-	67.03
(iii) Lohta	19,706	-	-	-	-
(iv) Kandwa	7,555	-	-	-	-
2. Varanasi Cantt.	17,259	81.99	65.73	1.64	18.03
3. Maruadih Railway Settlement	18,739	-	85.38	17.56	-23.45
4. Ramanagar (MB)	40,619	7.17	35.13	28.26	34.87
5. Sheodaspur (CT)	11,420	-	-	85.43	50.08
6. Phulwaria (CT)	11,971	-	-	61.87	22.60
7. BHU (NA)	7,788	40.90	26.12	-6.63	-32.3

Source: S.N.Singh, S.KSingh, Pandey and Giri (2011).

According to ICRA report, around 11 per cent (10.69 per cent) of the total population is engaged across different manufacturing activities whereas the tertiary sector accounts for 6.80 per cent of the total employment. The report also mentioned that in city only 26.60 per cent of population registered as employed whereas 73.40 per cent were unemployed. Amongst manufacturing units, spinning and weaving alone accounts for 50.70 per cent of the existing employment in Varanasi followed by metal and metal products industry, accounting for almost 15 per cent of the manufacturing employment of the city. These two activities account for over 2/3rd of the total manufacturing employment of the city.

Table 12: Number of Employee in Different Industries in Banaras

Category	No. of Employees	Percentage to total
Spinning and weaving	65368	50.70
Metal and metal manufacturing	19223	14.91
Food and food processing	4938	3.83
Timber and wood workers	4487	3.48
Printing and publishing	7981	6.19
Manufacturing machinery	4435	3.44
Textile	1354	1.05
Zarda and tobacco	1147	0.89
Chemical production	2669	2.07
Transport equipments	1405	1.09
Electric machinery	6472	5.02
Miscellaneous	9451	7.33
Total	**128930**	**100.00**

Source: Varanasi 2025, Draft Final Report, ICRA 2006, p. 31.

The effects of liberalization have begun shaping the social pattern of economy of Banaras. However, it is at nascent stage which is also a sight of confrontation between traditional values that this city has adhered to and modern culture. For instances, wearing of jeans and carrying mobile was opposed in Banaras. Administration of Varanasi's Udai Pratap College passed the order to keep tight jeans and mobile out of the classrooms. "Gulab Singh, principal of the college, said 'They (students) can bring a mobile phone, but cannot carry it in classrooms. They are expected to deposit it at counters opened in the library and proctor's office. They are also expected to wear decent dresses on the college premises. "Although we have not prohibited jeans altogether on the campus, we expect them to wear decent dresses. Jeans shouldn't be skin-tight or with many pockets. This rule would be binding not only on students, but also on teachers,' he added.The problem is that some students wear vulgar dresses. They also misuse mobile phones. So we have taken a preventive measure."[83] Students, both girls and boys, protested this move of administration. Thus, a sort of dialectic is going on. A compromise between the two has been already worked out. One can see the girls are driving bike, wearing jeans, visit the malls but with face covered with their scarf.[84] They are trying to be in public sphere with a negotiation. Perhaps, that is the reason Emily Christine Antze argued that "Although it is now 'modernizing' (the first McDonalds opened in 2006, and the first shopping mall not long before that), compared to the opulence found in the cosmopolitan cities of Mumbai, Delhi, Bangalore or even the Uttar Pradesh state capital of Lucknow, Varanasi is a conservative, "backward" provincial town."[85]

The intervention of modern culture is not welcomed by many as they think that material world will crash the spirituality beholden by Banaras. They claim the material culture is full of hollowness. "Every Indian city is undergoing transformation. Beyond the dells of blue and saffron walls of old Banaras, there lies the hollowness of spatial modernity. This is where the malls brandish their angular existence. Fast foods, burgers, and denims, everything which we survive on is available. Banaras is prosperous and louder here. Business requires lights and generators. The edge in contrast between the old and new surprised me."[86] Many fears that if Banaras' spirituality would vanish the "evil paradise" (malls and shopping complexes) will not remain intact. The longevity of modernity is linked with the future of religion in the city. Hence, many wish to protect the antiquity, religiosity and spirituality of Banaras against modernity. "There are a number of shopping spaces that have a western fell. Some of the shopping spaces that Varanasi has are the Spice KCM Cinema, and the IP 3 Mall, both have a Cinema as a main outlet. These areas have such western stores such as Sony, Baskin Robbins, and Globus, to name a few. Some of the Shopping areas are in the Cantonment Area but there are also places like IP 3 Mall that are near the downtown area. Both of these buildings are also built by the same company. Here are many pressures to develop in the older parts of the Varanasi, especially with the massive amounts of tourist every year there. It will be hard to develop the inner city to build more vernacular buildings since the inner city has a density estimated to be from "500 to 700 person/ha." Though, the city is always being "reconstructed in various ways, it retains its function and significance as long as there are human beings who are willing to believe." If Varanasi ever loses the religious building or the religion dies then it would not exist and most of these "evil paradises" would not exist for there would be no reason for them."[87]

Conclusion

There has been a continuum of reaction to the liberalization, both at the Union and State level. At the State level it has been said that due to non-responsiveness of the government Uttar Pradesh was not able to reap the benefit of the economic reform for long. However, with the political stability since August 29, 2003 gave Uttar Pradesh ample opportunity for tougher policy decision. Respective government designed policies to boost the confident of the investors. Today, preparing the state profile Confederation of Indian Industry (CII) argued that "A series of recent policy initiatives and focus on infrastructure development, supported by availability of skilled manpower, good resource base and a large consumer market all makes Uttar Pradesh an attractive investment destination."[88] PHD Chamber of Commerce too boasts the current economic growth of the Uttar Pradesh and potential for further growth. Sector-wise decadal growth rate in UP is given below in table. The average real GSDP of the State has grown at around 6 per cent during FY2002 2011.

Table 13: Decadal Growth Rate of Sectors in Uttar Pradesh

(in per cent)

Period	*Decadal Growth of Sectors*			*State Income*
	Agriculture	*Manufacturing*	*Services*	
1950-51 to 1970-71	1.5	3.5	2.8	2.2
1970-71 to 1980-81	2.0	5.0	3.6	3.0
1980-81 to 1990-91	3.2	9.6	6.4	5.0
1990-91 to 1997-98	2.5	6.9	5.4	4.0
1993-94 to 2002-03	2.3	2.6	4.7	3.8

Source: Government of Uttar Pradesh (2002).

But, State ranked 14th in per capita income with Rs. 26,355 which is much below than national average i.e. Rs. 53,331. It has ranked 13th in per capita electricity consumption. According to the census 2011, UP is ranked 14th in term of literacy. These are some of the indicators which push the State into the backward category. But, in term of percentage of main worker in household industry Uttar Pradesh ranked second. According to Census 2011, 5.3 per cent of main work force of the State works in the household factory. Handloom is one of such an industry on which this research is focused upon. In introduction chapter it has been pointed out that in UP most of the handloom is situated in rural area and dominated by Hindu. But, Banaras city is one among many cities where household industry is dominated by Muslims. And, as we know that urban Muslim of Eastern part of the State are very poor this research would like to analysis the impact of liberalization on them.[89]

References

1. It was guided by the communist ideology and followed state-led development model.
2. Keynes sought to develop a theory that would explain determinants of saving, consumption, investment and production. In that theory, the interaction of aggregate demand and aggregate supply determines the level of output and employment in the economy. Because of what he considered the failure of the 'Classical Theory' in the 1930s, the Keynes firmly opposes its main theory –

adjustment in prices would automatically make demand tend to the full employment level.

3. Thomas Frank, *One Market under God: Extreme Capitalism, Market Populism and the End of Economic Democracy*, Secker and Warburg, London, 2001.
4. Jan Aart Scholte, 'What is globalisation? The Definitional Issue – Again', CSGR, Working Paper, University of Warwick, UK, 2002.
5. Amiya Kr. Bagchi, 'Globalisation, Liberalization and Vulnerability: India and Third World', *Economic and Political Weekly*, Nov. 6, 1999.
6. James Petras and C.Polycroniou, 'Critical Reflection on Globalisation', *Economic and Political Weekly*, Sept.6, 1997.
7. Pranab Bardhan, 'Social Justice in the Global Economy', *Economic and Political Weekly*, Feb. 3-10, 2001.
8. Baldev Raj Nayar, 'Globalisation, Nationalism and Economic Policy Reform', *Economic and Political Weekly*, Vol.32, No.30, Jul.26-Aug.1, 1997.
9. Bardhan, *op. cit.*
10. Joshi and Little, *India's Economic Reforms 1991-2001*, Oxford University Press, Delhi, 1997.
11. Arjun Sengupta, *Reform, Equity and IMF*, Har-Anand Publication, Delhi, 2001.
12. Editorial, 'All for Production, Review of Management', *Economic and Political Weekly*, 1980.
13. Atul Kohli, 'Politics of Economic Growth in India: 1980-2006', *Economic and Political Weekly*, April 6, 2006.
14. *Op. cit.*
15. A.K.Bagchi, 'Globalisation, Liberalization and Vulnerability: India and Third World', *Economic and Political Weekly*, Nov. 6, 1999.
16. B.R.Nayar, 'Political Structure and India's Economic Reforms of the 1990s', *Pacific Affairs*, Vol. 71, No. 3, 1998.
17. Rajni Kothari, Class and Communalism, *EPW*, Vol. 23, No. 49, 1988.
18. Pawan Kumar Varma, *The Great Indian Middle Class*, Viking, New Delhi, 1998, p. 171.
19. *Dirigiste* means state-led development.
20. Saul Eslake, *The Driver of Globalisation*, ANZ Banking Group, Melboune, 2002.
21. Thomas Friedman, *The Lexus and the Olive Tree*, Strauss and Giroux, New York, 1998.
22. Charles Murray, *What it means to be a Libertarian*, Broadway Books, New York, 1997.
23. Murray Rothnard, *The Mystery of Banking*, Mises Institute, 2008, p. 111.
24. D. Baker, G. Epstein and Robert Pollin (ed.), *Globalisation and Progressive Economic Policy*, CUP, 1998.
25. Arvind Virmani, 'A New Development Paradigm – Employment, Entitlement and Empowerment', *Economic and Political Weekly*, June 1, 2002, p. 2151.
26. Raj Kapila and Uma Kapila, *India's Economy in the 21st Century*, Academic Foundation, New Delhi, 2002, pp. 55-82.

27. Jagdish Bhagwati, 'Growth, Poverty and Reforms', *Economic and Political Weekly*, March 10, 2001, p. 843.
28. Kapila and Kapila, *op. cit.*
29. Rob Jenkins, *The Ideologically Embedded Market: Political Legitimation and Economic Reform in India*, Unpublished work, 2002.
30. Atul Kohli, *op. cit.* Sentence in *Italic* is mine.
31. Bhagwati, *op. cit.*
32. A. Virmani, *op. cit.*
33. Mishra and Rao, 'Trade Policy, Agricultural Growth, Rural Poor: 1978-79 to 2000', *Economic and Political Weekly*, 2003.
34. Bhanumurthy and Mitra, *Economic Growth, Poverty and Reforms in Indian States*, Institute of Economic Growth, 2002.
35. Seema Joshi, 'Impact of Economic Reforms on Social Sector Expenditure in India', *Economic and Political Weekly*, Jan. 28, 2006.
36. K.C.Pant, *India's Development Scenario: Next Decade and Beyond..*, Academic Foundation, New Delhi, 2003.
37. H.K.Paranjape, 'New Industrial Policy – A Capitalist Manifesto', *Economic and Political Weekly*, Vol.26, No.43, Oct. 26, 1991.
38. A.K.Bagchi, *Op. Cit.*
39. Utsa Patnaik, 'Poverty and Neo-Liberalism in India', Lecture delivered at Gokhale Institute of Politics and Economics, Pune, 2006.
40. A.C. Dhas and M.J. Helen, 'Impact of Globalisation and Economic Reforms on Employment in India', MPRA, Paper No. 9597, 2008, p. 9.
41. G.K.Chadha and P.P.Sahu, 'Post-Reform setbacks in Rural Employment: Issues that need further scrutiny', *Economic and Political Weekly*, May 25, 2002.
42. Gail Omvedt, 'Capitalism and Globalisation and Dalits and Adivasis', *Economic and Political Weekly,* Nov. 19, 2005.
43. A. Ramaiah, *Dalits to accept Globalisation: Lesson from past and present*, Tata Institute of Social Sciences, 2004.
44. Dhananjay Rai, 'Dalits, Globalisation and Economism', *Think India Quaterly*, Vol. 13, No. 3, 2010, p. 221.
45. Anand Teltumbde, 'Dalit Capitalism and Pseudo Dalitism', *Economic and Political Weekly*, Vol. XLVI, No. 10, 2011, p. 11.
46. Brinda Karat, 'Towards Intensified Struggles for Adivasi Rights', *The Marxists*, XXVI, 3, July-September, 2010, pp. 30-31.
47. *Ibid.,* pp. 22.
48. Alternative Economic Survey: 1991-98 and Economic Survey 2002-03, Government of India.
49. Alternative Economic Survey: 1991-98 and Economic Survey 2002-03, Government of India.
50. Report, *Socio-Economic Condition of Muslims in India*, Indian Social Institute, New Delhi, 2006.

51. R. Kavita Rao, 'Reform in Andhra Pradesh: Is Mid-Course correction called for?', *Economic and Political Weekly*, September 24, 2004.
52. Census 2011 data has registered a steep decline of 14 point in the state's child sex ratio in the State. According to the final population totals released by UP's Directorate of Census Operations in reference to the number of girls between the age of 0 and 6 years for every 1,000 boys, UP's numbers have dipped from 916 to 902 between the 2001-2011 census period. Though the abysmal drop has been felt markedly in rural areas, dipping by 15 points from 921 to 906, urban regions have also seen a downward slide, with the child sex ratio reducing by 5 points from 890 to 885, over the last decade. The lopsided sex ratio among children has been felt most keenly in the western districts of UP, with Baghpat registering the lowest sex ratio in the state at 841 girls to 1,000 boys, Gautam Budh Nagar at 826 girls to 1,000 boys in the rural segment and Meerut at 848 among urban areas. With none of UP's 71 census districts registering an equal number of girls and boys, the highest child sex ratio was found in Balrampur, where there were 950 girls to 1,000 boys. For more detail see http://articles.timesofindia.indiatimes.com/2013-05-30/india/39627603_1_census-2011-census-operations-farm-sector./
53. B. Srivastava, chapter 5(http://shodhganga.inflibnet.ac.in/bitstream/10603/44141/8/chapter-5.pdf)
54. Sharad Ranjan, 'Growth of Rural Non-Farm Employment in Uttar Pradesh: Reflections from Recent Data', *Economic and Political Weekly*, January 24, 2009, p. 64.
55. *Ibid.,* p. 65.
56. Ajit Kumar Singh, 'Signs of Economic Change', *Seminar*, 2007.
57. Rodrik and Subramanian, 'From "Hindu Growth" to Productivity Surge: The Mystery of the Indian Growth Transition, Working Paper, International Monetary Fund, 2004.
58. Kripa Shankar, 'Deeper into the Debt Trap', *Economic and Political Weekly*, December 7, 2002.
59. A.K.Verma, 'Formation of Muslim Political Front', *Economic and Political Weekly*, Vol. XLI, No. 40, 2006, pp. 4241-43.
60. Shyam Singh and V.Anil Kumar, 'Politics and Public Policies: Politics of Human Development in Uttar Pradesh, India', Working Paper, The Institute for Social and Economic Change, Bangalore, 2012, p. 6.
61. Sudha Pai, Pradeep Sharma, Pralay Kanungo, and Rahul Mukherji, 'Uttar Pradesh in 1990s', *Economic and Political Weekly*, 2005.
62. A.K. Verma, Backward Caste Politics in Uttar Pradesh: An Analysis of Samajwadi party, Chapter 8 in Sudha Pai (ed.) *Political Process in Uttar Pradesh: Identity, Economic Reform and Governance*, Pearson Longman, New Delhi, 2007.
63. Anjula Guroo and Rahul Pandey, Power Sector in Uttar Pradesh: Past Problems and Initial Phase of Reform, *Economic and Political Weekly*, 2001, p. 2950.
64. D.M.Diwakar and Snatan Nayak (ed.), *Development Challenges: Afflicting Uttar Pradesh*, Manak Publication, New Delhi, 2007, pp. 362-366.

65. Centre for Monitoring Indian Economy, 2004.
66. In 2007 Assembly election SP got 45 per cent of Muslim vote.
67. States have choice not to open the retail sector for FDI but how long it will avoid.
68. M.A. Sherring, *Benares: The Sacred City of Hindus in Ancient and Modern Times, 1868*, South Asia Book, 1996.
69. *Ibid.*
70. It was authored by Damodara during the period of Jayachandra in 12th century.
71. Malik Sarwar, who received the title *Malik-us-Sharq* (ruler of the East) from the Sultan Muhammad Shah IV Tughluq was the founder of Sharqui dynasty with its capital at Jaunpur. Malik Sarwar declared Jaunpur as independent State after Delhi sultanate weakened by the attack of Taimur. During the Sharqui period, Jaunpur, was a strong military power in Northern India, and on several occasions threatened the Delhi Sultanate. The Sharqui sultanate continued from 1394-1479.
72. *Nazim* means the governor of the province. When Saadat Khan (the first nawab of Awadh) became the subedar of Awadh in 1722, he allowed Mir Rustam Ali Khan to retain the management of the Jagir with himself on payments of Rs. 8 lakhs yearly. The arrangement lasted up to 1738 when the relations with Saadat Khan became strained. Saadat Khan deputed his son-in-laws, Safdar Jung (2nd nawab of Awadh), to demand accounts from Rustam Ali, who sent his deputy Mansa Ram to negotiate the settlement of the case. This case shows the failure of Rustam Ali and rise of Mansa Ram.
73. B.S.Cohn, 'The Initial British Impact on India: A Case Study of Benares Region, *The Journal of Asian Studies*, Vol. 19, Issue. 4, 1960, pp. 418-431.
74. This emigration of mercantile communities to Banaras from various regions was effected through a gradual process extending over centuries. For instance, the ancestor of Sahu Gopal Das, a leading banker of Banaras in 1780s, had come from Amroha, a town between Agra and Karnal at some time in seventeenth century.
75. K.P.Mishra, *Benares in Transition, 1738-95: A Socio-Economic Survey*, Munishram Manoharlal, Delhi, 1975.
76. As noted by Al-Beruni that weavers were part of *Antyaja* followed by Sudra caste. *Antyaja* render various kinds of services, who are not reckoned amongst any caste, but only as members of a certain craft or profession. There were eight classes of them, who freely intermarry with each other, except the fuller, shoemaker, and weaver. These eight guilds are the fuller, shoemakers, juggler, the basket and shield maker, the sailor, fisherman, the hunter of wild animals and of birds, and the weaver. These guilds live near the villages and towns of the four castes, but outside them.
77. Nita Kumar, 1987.
78. G. W. Riggs, 1920.
79. Eugina Vanina, 2004.
80. Irfan Habib quoting Sir S. Ahmad Khan argued that "…rest… was just cotton-carder and weaver, who had handled yarn, but never a sword. The official

ethnologist William Crooke was to recall later that weavers played a fanatical role in the revolt in 1857. It must be remembered that this was the time when the mass of town weavers were being deprived of their employment by competition from Lancashire.

81. Communal riot started in 1809 in Banaras; 1806 in Mau and 1813, 1834 and 1842 in Mubarakpur before the mutiny took place in 1857. The reasons of riots could be the hinge around the economic deprivation of weavers, which might was wrongly channelised to communalism.
82. S.N.Singh, S.K.Singh, V.C.Pandey and A.K.Giri, 'Fading Colours of a Glorious Past: A Discourse on the Socio-Economic dimensions of marginalised Banarasi Sari Weaving Community', *Indiastat.Com*, Dec. 2011-Jan. 2012, p. 4.
83. Mail Today, 'Ban mobile phones and jeans, it's the new fad in villages and colleges across India', *India Today*, Lucknow, July 19, 2012.
84. Author experienced it during field work.
85. Emily Christine Antze, "They Should Stand on their own feet: Mothers' Accounts of Education, School choice and their children's uncertain futures in Varanasi, India", Ph.D Thesis, University of Toronto, 2011.
86. Prateek Dubey, 'Many Moods of Banaras', *The Pioneer*, February 3, 13.
87. Source: http://varanasi.jimdo.com
88. Confederation of Indian Industry, 'Investment Climate in Uttar Pradesh', New Delhi, 2012.
89. Muslims are more urbanized than other communities, but urban Muslims are comparatively poorer than rural Muslims, in contrast to the situation prevailing among most other communities. In 1999-2000, the share of urban Muslims living below the poverty line according to the NSS (36.92 per cent) was more than fifteen percentage points higher than the share of urban Hindus living below the poverty line (21.66 per cent) and almost ten points higher than the share of rural Muslims living below the poverty line (27.22 per cent). For detail see Gayer and C. Jaffrelot (2012).

Chapter - 2

Textile Policy under Liberalization and its Impact on the Handloom Industry

Textile Policies in India under Liberalization

The New Textile Policy (NTP), 1985, marked a changed attitude of the government vis-à-vis handlooms. It could be considered as the preparatory stage for the handloom industry for oncoming reform in the sector. NTP (1985) sought to change the structure of textile industry. The textile industry has, so far, been viewed in a compartmentalised manner either in terms of various sectors namely, cotton textiles, woollen textiles, man-made textiles and silk textiles. According to the government, this had led to fossilisation. Thus, it sought to eliminate the existing "structural rigidities" and to create a more integrated view of the textile industry. Henceforth, "the textile industry was viewed in terms of the stages of its manufacturing process, namely, spinning, weaving and processing and provided with fuller flexibility in the use of various fibres."[1] Thus, NTP (1985) singularly aimed at increasing cloth production without looking into the basic questions of credit and raw material requirements.

Researchers, scholars and individuals associated with this industry found that New Textile Policy of 1985 brought ill fate to this industry. For instance, L.C. Jain, former Chairman of All-India Handicrafts Board, way back in 1985 claimed that NTP (1985) meant the end of Handloom Industry. He mentioned that "...Handlooms being killed by powerlooms gradually, behind the camouflage provided by the 'Handloom-first' Textile Policy. Now the killing will be in the open, accelerated and will no longer be even an offence."[2] Further, Ruddar Datt made a concurring analysis of NTP (1985) as the government's surrender to big mill owners in the name of modernization, upgradation of technology and rationalization of labour in sick units. The policy, therefore, was pro-capitalist.[3] The policy, however, still recognised the unique place of textile in the economy of our country. In order to improve the working conditions of the handloom weavers and to provide the direct benefit to them, the following schemes, amongst others would be introduced:[4]

1. Intensification of development efforts of handlooms through cooperatives and corporations.
2. Greater emphasis on modernization and provision of technological inputs for improving productivity, quality and finish.
3. Special efforts to ensure the availability of yarn and other raw materials through the operations of National Handloom Development Corporation (NHDC).
4. Encouraging production of mixed and blended fabrics.
5. Protection of handloom sector under the Handloom Reservation Act.
6. Removal of cost handicap of handloom vis-à-vis power loom products through suitable measures.
7. Improve marketing of handloom products, strengthen the infrastructure of marketing complexes, organize the training of marketing personnel and intensive publicity.
8. Strengthen the database and better planning in the handloom sector for better planning and execution of handloom development programmes, a census of handlooms shall be undertaken. The machinery for implementation, supervision and evaluation of handloom programmes shall be strengthened.
9. A Contributory Thrift-Fund scheme to provide assistance to the handloom weavers during times of need;
10. A workshed-cum-housing scheme to provide better place for work and living to the handloom weavers.

Central Assistance was given to nine State governments to set up an Enforcement Machinery in the State to ensure that there is no violation of the Handlooms (Reservation of Articles for Production) Act, 1985. These nine States were namely Andhra Pradesh, West Bengal, Gujarat, Rajasthan, Madhya Pradesh, Haryana, Tamil Nadu, Uttar Pradesh and Kerala. The Enforcement office also mandated inspection stalls at various National/1 to ensure sale of genuine handloom products in handloom exhibitions.

Table 14: Financial Assistance released during the last three years

Sr. No.	*Year*	*Power loom Inspections conducted*	*Financial Assistance Released (Rs. in Lakh)*
1.	2008-09	237,111	350.00
2.	2009-10	251,896	350.00
3.	2010-11	261,071	350.00
4.	As on Nov. 11	154,409	139.00

Source: Minister of State for Textile reply in Lok Sabha, 2011.

But, the welfare measures announced for the protection of handloom were never implemented. Reservation Act for handloom, which was introduced in 1985, was challenged by the powerful lobbies of powerloom and mill owners soon after its enactment and helped by the disinterested response, rather the complicity, of the officialdom, the act remained *sub judice* for eight long years. "When the Supreme Court finally upheld the reservation of articles to the handlooms in February 1993 the observations it made in its historic judgment (Parvej Akhtar V Union of India) while setting aside the objections deserve to be noted [(1993) 2 Supreme Court Cases 221, p 237]. Two major grounds on which this act was challenged were: (a) that the act would lead to the monopoly of the handloom industry; (b) that the act violated the equality clause (Article 14 of the Fundamental Rights) of the Constitution."[5] The virtual non-implementation of the Reservation Act is revealed by the number of cases of violations. According to Vasanthi Raman, "a mere 656 First Information Reports (FIRs) were lodged following the inspection of 72,553 powerlooms inspected till January 1995. These figures fly in the face of the fact that violations of the Act were more the norm than the exception."[6] Further, Raman argued that these details regarding the implementation of the Reservation Act only demonstrate the powerful interests and lobbies that the hapless handloom weaver had to contend with in his/her struggle for survival.

Meanwhile, the Government of India had appointed the Abid Hussain Committee in the year 1988 with the main aim being to analyse the problems arisen in the industry after the announcement. The committee submitted its report in the year January 1990. The basic conclusion of the committee was that 1985 Textile policy was anchored on the right principles and identified many problems facing the textile industry. In general, the committee felt that the 1985 textile policy did not address itself adequately to the institutional and financial to achieve the objectives it has set itself. "The basic issue facing the textile industry is to achieve the objectives it has to undertake by the turn of the century."[7] The committee argued that the handloom sector has suffered since the promises made in the 1985 textile policy have not been implemented. The committee had recognised that the labour employed in handloom, powerloom and factory will face serious dislocation as a result of any restructuring or modernisation process. "The most serious dislocation being suffered in this on-going process of adjustment is by the labour employed in the industry – be they handloom workers, powerloom workers, or factory workers. The problems faced by them, looming unemployment, underemployment, or redeployment, are not of their own creation. They result from the modernisation process that the industry is going through. These problems must be attacked directly. The accent of restricting policy in the textile industry must specially focus on the problems of the weavers. The restructuring and modernisation that the industry has to go through must have a human face."[8] The data shows the decline in cloth production both by the handloom and mills. The powerloom gained from the favourable condition the NTP (1985) had generated as we can observe from table 15.

Table 15: Growth of cloth production in Mills, Handloom, Powerlooms and Hosiery Sectors (in Million Sq. Metres)

Year	*Mill*	*Handloom (HL)*	*Powerloom (PL)*	*Hosiery (H)*	*All Sectors*	*Percentage shares*			
						Mill	*HL*	*PL*	*H*
1980-81	4533	3109	4802	-	12444	36.43	24.98	38.59	-
1985-86	3544	4135	9534	-	17213	20.59	24.02	55.39	-
1990-91	2589	4295	13348	2696	22928	11.29	18.73	58.22	11.76

Source: (Jayanta Bagchi, 2004: 7).

To solve the problems of handlooms Abid Hussain Committee charted out a number of recommendations. It speaks about the change in approach to handlooms. Committee recommended that greater emphasis should be on the interest and dignity of the weavers rather than on the activity. A new approach for handlooms should have the following elements: differentiate the requirements of different types of weavers on the basis of earning capacities and skills. This in itself will be related to fabric types, construction types and technology level; the requirements of weavers may be classified into three types of support – modernisation and technological up-gradation infrastructural improvement, and welfare measures. Different types of weavers would need a different mix of these three elements of support; support for handloom weavers should be universal and not based on membership of corporate or cooperative bodies.

On the one hand, government committee was sympathetic to the handloom and making recommendations to protect it and on the other hand, Supreme Court upholds its decision and ground was cleared for the execution of the Handloom Reservation Act. But, the act was yet to be implemented as liberalization came knocking on the door. Instead of implementing the act by creating a proper institutional mechanism to effectively control any further damage to the handloom sector, a multi-member committee was constituted to go into the very question of handloom reservations. Till 1994 the Indian textile industry was working on MFA, which was replaced by Agreement on Textiles and Clothing (ATC). Basically, MFA is a framework for bilateral agreement that proposes quota-limiting imports into countries whose domestic industries face serious damage from rapidly increasing imports. Since its inception i.e. 1974, MFA dealt with textile exports originating mainly from developing countries. It was as a short-term measure intended to allow developed countries to adjust to imports from the developing world. Developing countries have a natural advantage in textile production because it is labour intensive and they have low labour costs. Initially, the MFA was supposed to remain in force for four years, but it was extended several times till 1994. In 1995, the MFA was integrated into GATT via the ATC. On the other hand, ATC provides a blueprint for removal of restrictions on textile exports originating mainly from developing nations. The integration process was to be carried out in four stages. The integration process is represented schematically below in Table 16.[9]

Table 16: Integration process in Post-MFA period

Steps	*% of products to be brought under GATT (including removal of any quota)*	*How Fast Remaining Quotas should open Up, (if 1994 rate was 6 per cent)*
Steps 1 1 Jan. 1995 (to 31 Dec. 1997)	16 (minimum, taking 1990 imports as base)	6.96 per cent annum
Step 2 1 Jan. 1998 (to 31 Dec. 2001)	17 per cent	8.7 per cent per annum
Step 3 1 Jan. 2002 (to 31 Dec. 2004)	18 per cent	11.05 per cent
Step 4 1 Jan. 2005 (Full integration into GATT and final elimination of quotas)	49 per cent (maximum)	No Quotas left

Source: Bandyopadhyay and T. Sengupta (2006, 146).

Most of the economic commentators and advocates of WTO thought that the end of quota-regime after the Uruguay round of WTO in 1994 would bring ample opportunities for the exporters as they have advantage over many competing countries. A study carried out by Martin and Supachalasai showed that developing nations incur a loss of US $2 billion or 10 per cent the value of their total clothing exports as a result of quota restriction. Therefore, lifting quota restrictions is supposed to benefit India in those markets in which it has a binding export function. Sengupta, Chakraborty and Banerjee also estimated that except for certain products, namely cotton, other woven textile fabrics, and knitted fabrics, in all other categories (Cotton fabric Woven, Woven man-made Fibre Fabrics, Textile articles not elsewhere classified) competitiveness has increased for Indian products. Now, if we look at the claim and estimation made by D. Sengupta, Chakraborty and Banerjee, they have tried to project the positives and avoided the negative aspects of ATC.[10] Out of seven categories that D. Sengupta has carved out, three categories have shown the negative sign and one was stagnant. Only three were positive. The analysts were overlooking many facts like suicide by weavers in different parts of the country as early as 1991, as a sign of ruining of textile industry. They did not consider the fact that our handloom industry was somewhat "existing" because of government protection. Opening the textile industry for international competition was like sheep in front of a tiger, a hungry one. The decision was taken, in fact, on behalf of those exporters who were imagining the maximum profit from the export and missing the voices of marginalized ones. This was the sign of typical capitalist nature of Indian state.

Prior to NTP (1985) and economic reform it was not the case. "Earlier policies stressed the employment potential of the handloom industry and sought to strengthen it with appropriate measures such as the provision of adequate yarn, reservation of products, etc., considerations such as production of cloth of acceptable quality at reasonable prices to meet the clothing requirement of a growing population."[11] Emphasis on cottage industries was put on in Industrial Resolution Policy, which government published in April 1948. Although Small Scale Industries (SSI) fell within the provincial sphere, Government of India agreed to investigate how far and in what manner these industries could be coordinated and integrated with large-scale industries; for example, how the textile mill industry can be made complementary rather than competitive, to the handloom industry. The creation of Cottage Industry Board at the centre as well as of a Cottage and Small Scale Industries Directorate was envisaged. The encouragement to these industries by means of industrial co-operatives was suggested. Five Year Plans, too, was concerned about the industry's prospect in the coming future. First plan was designed by Planning Commission to remove social and economic inequality. Document called for prudent use of un/underutilization of potential Human and natural resource. During first five years of plan, government spent Rs. 11.1 crore for handloom and Rs. 1.3 crore for silk and sericulture. These investments goes up by third Five Year Plan and Rs. 25.37 crore was spent on Handloom whereas Rs. 4.39 crore for sericulture.

Table 17: Plan Expenditure on Handloom and Silk and Sericulture during 1st FYP (Rs. in crore)

Industry	*1951-55*	*1955-56*	*1951-56*
Handloom	6.5	4.6	11.1
Silk and Sericulture	0.8	0.5	1.3

Source: 2nd Five Year Plan, Planning Commission, GoI.

Apart from the employment concern, ideology and politics of pressure group also contributed in the formulation of textile industrial policy. Ideology was unquestionably the prime mover of economic policy in the first decades after independence from colonial rule. Since the mid-1950s, planners in India had opted for autarkic development strategies which give emphasis on investments in heavy industry for achieving growth objectives and small-scale, labour intensive manufacture of essential consumer goods for providing employment to the rapidly growing labour force. This came to be known as Mahalanobis model of development which tried to combine essentially antithetical elements of the Soviet model of development with its emphasis on comprehensive state planning and rapid industrialisation with Gandhian economic beliefs.[12] The pressure from the large and vocal body of cotton growers has been a major factor in the manifest policy in the favour of Industries. The existence of trade union resisted the move of government to favour the synthetic fibres. Under pressure, Government of India in 1950 and onward took some major steps to protect handloom and small scale industries (SSI). It reserved certain areas of production, comprising a wide variety of items of common use, for exclusive manufacture by the handlooms – mills being legally prohibited from producing these items. Despite the concern shown, the handloom was showing the sign of decline as the policy was much on the paper rather than real. In fact, government began to hide the real production capacity of the handloom. For instance, cotton handloom production was closer to

1,600 million metres against 2,520 million metres claimed.[13] In sharp contrast, the actual production of cotton cloth by powerlooms is much higher than revealed by official estimates. In 1981 it was an estimated 3,293 million metres and not 2,453 million metres acknowledged officially.[14]

However, the negative effects do not deter researchers to take a pro-ATC stand. Asiya Chaudhary argued that "After the MFA phased out the world T and C export had grown from US$ 272.43 billion in 1994 to US$ 530 bn in 2006, registering almost a two-fold rise. World textile and clothing trade rose by 9.7 % to US$530 bn in 2006, by 10.6 % to US$583 bn in 2007. In the post-quota period, India has emerged as a major sourcing destination for new buyers. As a measure of increasing interest in the Indian textile and clothing sector a number of buyers have opened their sourcing/liaison office in India. Commercially, the buoyant retailers across the world are looking for options of increasing their sourcing from the Indian markets. Indian manufacturers are also pro-actively working towards enhancing their capacities to fulfil this increased demand. India's textiles and clothing (T and C) export registered robust growth of 25 % in 2005-06, recording a growth of US$ 3.5 billion in value terms thereby reaching a level of US$ 17.52 billion and the growth continued in 2006-07 as T and C exports were US$19.15 billion recording an increase of 9.28 % over previous year. Though India's TandC exports in 2007-08 at US$ 22.13 billion were badly affected by strong appreciation of the Indian rupee against the US dollar, it still managed to record a healthy growth of 15.59 % in US dollar terms (in rupee terms, the growth was about 2.76 %). After the MFA phase out the textiles exports grew from US$693.28 million in 2005-06 to US$705.95 in 2006-07. During 2007-08 the silk exports have amounted to US$ 657.40 million, recording a decline of 6.88 % over the exports during the previous year. During the period of 2008-09 the Silk Textiles exports have amounted to US$ 675.53 million, recording a growth of 2.71% over the exports during the corresponding period of 2007."[15]

None other than Indian Prime Minister Manmohan Singh "saw the big opportunities for India in the dismantling of Multi-Fibre Arrangement... There are immense opportunities. The quota regimes everywhere are going to end or have ended but there are also immense challenges that we have. Countries in the East Asia, South Asia and countries like China are aggressively planning to take full advantage of these new opportunities. We don't have to be afraid of this competition. I think that the people of India want to hear that we can compete with China." It seems that for Indian Prime Minister the capitalists and medium entrepreneurs are "the people." He further added that "We have to meet the challenges of competition, our standards of performance can't be "*chalta hai*" attitude but we must aspire to meet the challenge of competition head on whether it is from China or any other quarters in the world. Government and industry must be active partners in making this future happen. That's the destiny of India to be great power and nothing can stop us from realizing that ambition." He added on that "With such a rich tradition in textiles, the desire to become a great global leader in textiles is a legitimate ambition which all of us you must have... We have now the opportunity with the dismantling of the Multi-Fibre Arrangement to make up for the lost time. We must take full advantage of the opportunities that are now on the horizon."[16] While mentioning about the Indian ambition to become a great global leader in textile Prime Minister forgot the fact that till December 2004 textile sector had amassed accumulated losses of Rs. 19,065.18 crore. This amount was piled up by 957 small, medium and large companies spread across the country. The sector had also rendered most of the 6, 61,967 of its employees jobless or under-employed.[17] The immediate record after the abolition of quota in toto in 2005 shows the steep decline in the textile export earnings. The Director General of Commercial Intelligence and Statistics (DGCI and S) data revealed that spun yarn was down by 15.9 per cent in the first seven months of the year and fabric exports down by 22.7 per cent.[18]

To make textile industry more competitive and of international standards Union government came with National Textile Policy, 2000, to further open the market. The thrust of the Textile Policy of 2000, based on the Sathyam Committee Report, is to make India a global player in textile production and exports, particularly of garments. It seeks to re-orient the handloom sector to the globalisation process – this, according to the policy, is the principal strategy to ensure its survival. To aid this process further, the government is to assist the private sector in specialised financial arrangements and to set up a venture capital fund. The policy permits 100 per cent FDI in the textiles sector against the earlier limit of 24 per cent. The new policy would also encourage the private sector to set up world class, environment-friendly, integrated textile complexes and textile processing units in different parts of the country and would review and revitalize the working of the Textile Research Associations (TRAs) to focus research on industry needs. Policies related with textile (clothing, Weaving, Spinning sectors) are as follow:

"Clothing: The role of this sector is poised for radical change in view of the transformation in the international trading environment brought about by the rules and regulations of the WTO. The industry will be restructured as follows:

(1) Garment industry will be taken out of the SSI reservation list.

(2) Joint ventures and strategic alliances with leading world manufacturers will be promoted.

(3) Schemes with required infrastructural facilities for the organization of textile/apparel parks will be designed with the active participation of state governments, financial institutions and the private sector.

Weaving Sector: In spite of 58 per cent global share of looms consisting of 3.5 million handlooms and 1.8 million powerlooms India's technology has remained backward. This sector, critical to the survival of the Indian textile industry and its export thrust, will be rapidly modernised. Clustering of production facilities in the decentralised sector will be encouraged to achieve optimum size and adopt appropriate technology. The Government will facilitate harmonious development of all the segments of the fabric manufacturing sector. The balanced growth of these sectors will be achieved based on their intrinsic strengths and capacity to meet the demands and requirements of the domestic as well as international markets. Spinning Sector: The NTP seeks to continue efforts to modernize and upgrade technology to international levels, and proposes to take the following steps, in cotton spinning as well as in the worsted woollen sectors:

(1) Encourage the spinning sector to continue to modernize.

(2) Liberalize and encourage export of cotton yarn.

(3) Review from time to time the hank yarn obligation while ensuring supply of adequate quantity of yarn to the handloom sector."[19]

The Sathyam Committee recommends the scrapping of the Reservation Act (of 11 items) and the hank yarn obligation which, despite their ineffective implementation, have provided the only means of support to handlooms. The report presumed that there would be no handloom industry after 2005 and that all handlooms would be converted to powerlooms by then.[20] Thus, NTP (2000) has become the "noose for weavers and their families for whom the loom is not only a means of livelihood but a way of life."[21]

Table 18: Total cloth production by handloom and powerloom

(in million Sq. mtr)

Year	*Production by Handloom*	*% share in total production*	*Production by Powerloom*	*% share in total prod.*
2000-01	7506	19	23,803 (mn. Sq. mtr.)	59.15
2001-02	7585	19	25,192 (mn. Sq. mtr.)	59.9
2002-03	-	18.4	25,954 (mn. Sq. mtr.)	-
2003-04	5536*	14.22	27,258 (mn. Sq. mtr.)	63
2004-05	4,238*	13.12	28,803 (mn. Sq. mtr.)*	62
2005-06	6,108	13	29,627 (mn. Sq. mtr.)	63
2006-07	6,536	13	32,879 (mn. Sq. mtr.)	62
2007-08	6947**	13	34,725 (mn. Sq. mtr.)	62
2008-09	6,677	-	33,648 (mn. Sq. mtr.)	61

Source: Annual Report, Ministry of Textile, GOI.
* Provisional or expected production, excluding cloths made of wool, silk, and hand spun.
** *Annual Report, Ministry of Textile, GOI, 2008-09.*

The main problem with the Sathyam Committee Report, which the government is to implement in phases, is its way of looking at the handloom industry, says Dr. K Srinivasulu. "Deviating from the well-accepted method of categorising weavers on the basis of the organisation of production into cooperatives, master weavers and independent weavers, the report seeks to divide them into three groups on the basis of the 'quality of cloth' they produce. In the first tier are weavers who produce "unique, exclusive, high- value-added items" (highly skilled weavers). In the second are producers of 'medium-priced fabrics from not-so-fine counts of yarn' (semi-skilled). And in the third tier are those who produce 'plain and low-cost textile items (unskilled)."[22] Seemathini Niranjana argued that "the assumption here is that producers of high value cloth will also receive high remunerations, unlike producers of lower-value cloth. Based on this assumption, policy recommendations suggest either a shift in the direction of producing finer cloth, or a shift away from handloom weaving altogether. The rationale for such an assumption is questionable, since field visits reveal that producers of 'luxury' fabrics are not necessarily well-paid, that is, the 'high value' of the cloth is rarely translated into wage terms."[23]

Uttar Pradesh Textile Policy

As mentioned earlier in the first chapter about the factors influencing the late initiation of economic reform, however, UP formulated textile policy with an aim to generate more jobs and attract investments in textile and apparel manufacturing industries. State proposes schemes, strategies and programmes for power supply, infrastructure, textile parks, human resource development and provisions to attract big players with substantial investment in the state in this sector. To put forward the State as key player in the segment, government had make efforts to make the textile policy more lucrative and on the theme of States like Tamil Nadu and Gujarat.

Within Tenth Plan (2002-07) UP through State Industrial Policy 2004 promised to invest to restructure the Village and Small Sector and make it viable. However, if we look at the Plan outlays and its usage it can be said that handloom sector in particular has been grossly neglected. Under Tenth Plan Rs. 130 crore for the handloom sector was allocated but only Rs. 46.31 crores released in first three years of the Plan. Rs. 83.70 crores had to be released and spent by the department. Given the attitudinal problems of department it was doubtful that such a huge amount would have been spent by it in such a short span of time. Even if the allocation was made the usage quality of fund would be a matter of concern. On part of physical targets, it appears that the handloom sector had the target of producing 510 million meters of cloths each year and generation of 25,000 employments every year. Against these targets, achievement was to the tune of 97.6 per cent in 2002-03 and 91.0 per cent in 2003-04 with regards to the production of handloom cloths. As for the achievement of employment generation target, it was reported to be 32.7 per cent in 2002-02 and 77.3 per cent in the year 2003-04. During the year 2004-05, both the production of cloths and the generation of employment were reported to be 100 per cent of the annual target.

However, the achievement with regard to the largest component of handloom sector i.e. Deen Dayal Hathkargha Protsahan Yojna, was less than 30 per cent in the first three years of Tenth Five Year Plan. As the installation of computers in the Directorate, restructuring of cooperative societies, strengthening of Directorate, assistance to Handloom Corporation and Uttar Pradesh Industrial Cooperative Association (UPICA) etc. are concerned, though outlay had been made, yet neither any annual allocation nor utilisation of funds was reported in the last three years. In some cases, like establishment of Textile Centre, Development of Knitwear/Garment Centre, Preservation of arts and crafts though annual allocations for the first two years had been indicated, hardly any utilisation was reported against the annual allocations. "All these indicate that the planned development of Handloom sector is yet to be established in the real sense."[24]

Textile policy of Uttar Pradesh, 2008-2013 was meant to restructure different sectors of textiles – organized mills sector, handloom, power loom, knitting, and garments. Taking in view the changing scenario of textile trade in India over last couple of months, it was suggested to have a second round of discussions with veteran industrialists and technical experts to take their opinion for incorporating in the policy. The other features of the policy were: In line of the removal of Value Added Tax (VAT) on yarn, readymade garments should also be exempted from VAT; adequate supply of good quality of electricity power is to be ensured; subsidized power for power loom sectors to be continued; for organized sector, instead of providing subsidized charges (electricity charges per unit), low cost electricity charges should be proposed which may be less than the present charges by a certain percentage; amendment of age old lopsided labour laws – urgently required; In view of high cotton prices and high yield in recent years, techno-economics of cotton cultivation in UP can be assessed so as to eliminate dependence on cotton procurement from far off places; infrastructure like road and transportation should be improved in Noida as the place houses huge number of garment export units; As Noida is a garment hub, fabric is mostly procured from other states. Some kind of freight subsidy should be given; the policy must address labour law anomalies and labour overtime issues; textile and garment exporting units should be allowed to adopt hire and fire policy to compensate the seasonal nature of these businesses; the facilities in ITI's, polytechnic, textile institute (Government Central Textile Institute) and research institute (North India Textile Research Association) in UP should be updated to facilitate the manpower training and development for textile and garment industry; Uttaranchal model should be followed for revival of closed and loss making state owned spinning mills i.e. allowing private participation with long term lease; technical textiles have great future hence should be addressed separately in the policy.

In 2012 Government of UP introduced Infrastructure and Industrial Investment Policy whose objective is integrated development of whole State. It aims for 11.2 per cent industrial growth rate along with 10 per cent State Gross Domestic Product (SGDP). It has priorities development of infrastructure. It promises to provide suitable condition for the participation of private agency in to the development of infrastructure. To have suitable condition for industrial growth, State has promised to give 100 er cent exemption from stamp duty to the units that are coming up in Eastern, Central and Bundelkhand region. These exemption are extended to the food processing unit, food park, agro-industry, BPO, IT, Bio-Tec, solar etc. But, government has shown no energy to rejuvenate handloom industry. In a passing reference, policy draft has mentioned the better implementation of the on-going schemes. Although, twice the policy draft mentioned about the presence of traditional industries but there has been no analysis of the problem that handloom industry of UP is facing today. This approach lacks seriousness.

Effect of Textile Policies during Liberalization on Handloom

Post-ATC handloom industry has further dwindled in terms of production and employability. Presenting the status of handloom industry of India Working Group Report on Handloom for the 12th Five Year Plan mentioned that "Competition from the machines, changing consumer preferences and the pursuit of less demanding means of livelihood have threatened the vibrancy of the handloom industry. Traditional hand woven products are in danger of becoming obsolete and weaving skills face dilution and decline."[25]

Table 19: Gender-wise Employment in the Handloom Sector.

		Female Workers			*Male Workers*			
Source	*Year*	*Full Time*	*Part Time*	*Total*	*Full Time*	*Part Time*	*Total*	*Grand Total*
Handloom Census	1987-88	779038	1859459	2638497	1410117	145153	1555270	4193767
Handloom Census	1995-96	603247	1500640	2103887	998286	223915	1222201	3326088
NSSO 55th Round Household Survey – Weekly status	1999-00	N.A	N.A	992938	N.A	N.A	2043100	3036038
NSSO 55th Round Household Survey – Usual Status	1999-00	N.A	N.A.	1132123	N.A	N.A	2135104	3267227
NSSO 55th round Enterprise Survey	1999-00	554714	254941	809655	1394747	91117	1485864	2295519
NSSO 56th round Enterprise Survey	2000-01	959658	265718	1225376	1717868	65118	1782986	3008362

Source: Examining Employment Figures in the Handloom Sector, NCAER, All India Artisans and Craftworkers Welfare Association (AIACA), 2006.

Report of the Steering Committee on Handlooms and Handicrafts for 12th FYP explain the economic status of weavers that "Despite the welfare-oriented policies implemented by the Government, almost half of the handloom weavers belong to the most backward and poorer sections of the population. Nearly 47% of all handloom weavers possess Below Poverty Line cards and 10% have Antodaya Anna Yojana Cards. About 29.4% of all handloom workers have never attended school and 12.7% are educated only up to primary school level. The high incidence of poverty and illiteracy among weaver families is accompanied by poor access to basic necessities including health, water, sanitation, housing and livelihood facilities. The role of women in the handloom industry is largely unacknowledged"[26]. The percentage share of handloom in total cloth production has reduced to 19.11 per cent from 22.89 per cent in 1995-96. Below, the two tables show the shrinking productivity of handloom.

Table 20: Production of Cloth in Mills, Handlooms, Powerlooms and Hosiery Sector

(In Million Sq. Meters)

Year	*Mill*	*Handloom (HL)*	*Powerloom (PL)*	*Hosiery (H)*	*All Sectors*	*Percentage shares*			
						Mill	*HL*	*PL*	*H*
1995-96	2019	7202	17201	5038	31460	6.42	22.89	54.67	16.01
1996-97	1957	7456	19352	5533	34298	5.70	21.74	56.42	16.13
1997-98	1948	7603	20951	6394	36896	5.28	20.61	56.78	17.33
1998-99	1785	6792	20689	6277	35543	5.02	19.11	58.21	17.66

Source: Report of the Steering Committee on Handlooms and Handicrafts, 12th FYP.

Table 21: Total cloth production by Handloom (1999-2008)

Year	*Total Cloth Production by Handloom (in million square metres)*	*% share in total cloth production*
1999-00	7352	19
2000-01	7506	19
2001-02	7585	19
2002-03	-	18.4
2003-04	5536*	14.22
2004-05	4,238*	13.12
2005-06	6,108	13
2006-07	6,536	13
2007-08	6947**	13
2008-09	6,677	-

Source: Report of the Steering Committee on Handlooms and Handicrafts, 12th FYP.

Due to the erroneous policy of government handloom was made to lose to the powerloom. "National trade policy has been a major factor in the crisis in Banaras. Over roughly a decade from 2002 to 2010 duty levied on imported silk yarn (from China) remained at 30% while duty on imported silk fabric was reduced from 30% to 10% (Ministry of Textiles, Sericulture Division). Thus Chinese silk yarn, a key input to the industry, became expensive over time; the most dramatic increase being from Rs. 1,750 per kg in August 2010 to Rs. 3,300 per kg in December 2010. Emphasizing the need for imported yarn, Badruddin Ansari, the Chairman of the UP Handloom Co-op Federation, claimed that domestic silk yarn production is 16000 metric tons while the demand is 28000 metric tons. Even as yarn became expensive, simultaneously Chinese silk fabric imports soared despite an anti-dumping duty having been in force during this period. Chinese imports increased four-fold between 2005 and 2010 (from about 400,000 meters to 1.6 million meters of silk fabric per day)."[27]

The policies have affected the life of 12.5 million weavers around the country somewhat uniformly.[28] Going by the Shivaraman Committee's estimate, the addition of 2.90 lakh powerlooms should have displaced 17.4 lakh handlooms (at the displacement rate of 6 handlooms per every new powerloom), which in turn means a loss of 41.76 lakh jobs per annum in the handloom sector (at the rate of 2.4 persons employed on each handloom). But the 1987-88 handloom census show a decline of handlooms to the tune of 2.39 lakh and another 2.46 lakh recorded as being rendered dormant. According to K. Srinivasulu, "This is a gross underestimation that makes the handloom figures suspect unless one wishes to assume that handlooms coexisted very happily with the phenomenally growing powerloom sector, withstanding the intense competition from the latter."[29] The effect of handloom dislocation can be seen at the ground level in handloom dominated areas such as Andhra Pradesh and Banaras. This chapter will make a comparative study of the handloom industry of Banaras with Andhra Pradesh and Mau to explore the impact of economic reform and globalisation.

Liberalization and Banaras Handloom Industry

It can be understood from the data as well from the fame of *Banarasi* silk sari that Banaras handloom mostly uses silk as yarn to weave. The fate might be similar to handloom in and around the country, but the procedure of effect of globalisation in places such as Banaras and Andhra Pradesh could be different from powerloom of Mau which uses cotton and silk both. As has been noted earlier, Banaras handloom industry mainly used silk yarn and produced sari and any disturbance in supply and demand chain could affect the weavers badly. This is exactly what happened with the Banaras handloom industry. Today, this industry has been continuously facing slump in demand of sari, that too of higher input. To understand this, let's have a look at the demand of silk items at the international level and government silk policy.

Table 22: Changing pattern of World Fiber Demand

(Million tonnes)

Fiber Variety	*1981*	*1990*	*1997*	*Percentage Changes*		*Percentage Shares*		
				90 over 81	*97 over 90*	*1981*	*1990*	*1997*
(A) Man-Made Fibers								
1. Cellulosic	3.20	2.76	2.31	-15.94	-19.48	10.32	7.21	5.14
2. Synthetic	10.83	14.89	21.68	37.94	75.00	34.92	38.90	48.22
3. Total	**14.03**	**17.89**	**23.99**	**25.80**	**35.92**	**45.24**	**46.11**	**53.36**
(B) Natural Fibers								
1. Raw Cotton	15.30	18.59	19.45	21.50	4.63	49.34	48.56	43.26
2. Raw Wool	1.62	1.97	1.43	21.60	-37.76	5.22	5.15	3.18
3. Raw Silk	0.06	0.07	0.09	16.67	28.57	0.19	0.18	0.20
4. Total	**16.98**	**20.63**	**20.97**	**21.49**	**1.65**	**54.76**	**53.89**	**46.64**
(C) Total Fiber Demand	***31.01***	***38.28***	***44.96***	***23.44***	***17.45***			

Source: Compendium of Textile Statistics, 1997, GOI, P. 222-223, and 1999, p. 303.

The total fiber demand has gone up from 31.01 million in 1981 to 38.28 and 44.96 million ton in 1990 and 1997 respectively. The remarkable up-side down turn can be seen in the per cent shares of natural and man-made fibers. In 1980 natural and man-made fibers shares 54.76 and 45.24 per cent, whereas, in 1997, it turned to 46.64 per cent and 53.36 per cent respectively. Within natural fibers, raw cotton and raw wool demand has gone down, with the exception of marginal gain by raw silk. Thus, at the international level silk has been in demand, which can also be seen from India's – the second largest silk producer in the world – export of silk items. "Silk exports amounts to 238 million US $ accounting for only 2.25 % of the textile export from the country and 0.75 % of its total export."[30]

Table 23: Silk Export Earning (1953-99)

Value: In Rupees; Unit: In Lakhs

Year	*Finished Silk Goods*	*Silk Waste*	*Total Export*
1953	17.07	30.51	47.58
1956	25.80	26.08	51.88
1960	103.06	34.02	137.08

(Contd...)

1965	244.97	37.41	282.38
1970	1349.92	73.25	1423.17
1975	1501.59	73.92	1575.51
1980	5160.26	34.96	5195.22
1985-86	15921.14	60.67	15981.81
1990-91	43593.75	459.32	44053.07
1995-96	84516.45	91.16	84607.61
1998-99	105398.42	3235.15	108633.57

Source: Datta and Nanavati, Global Silk Industry: A Complete Source Book, 2007, pp. 65.

However, if we disaggregate the export of silk variety-wise, on the one hand, data reveals the continuous slowdown of Mulberry silk sari, on the other hand spurt in demand of mixed/blend sari mainly produced by powerloom. Government policy on silk too affected the silk market in domestic as well as international market. Raw silk production in India is inadequate to meet the domestic demand. It is estimated that against the demand of around 28,000 ton per annum the domestic production is around 19000 to 19,500 tons. The gap is of nearly 8000 to 8500 tons. To meet the demand of exporters, the government has allowed the import of raw silk under OGL as per WTO compatibility (Table 24). This import policy is erroneous. Instead of strengthening domestic production of raw silk government readily agrees to import. Although it brings down the rising price of silk but badly effected sericulture farmers. Secondly, this mechanism to stop inflation of raw silk does not work for the weavers. The traders always gave raw materials to weavers on high prices.

Table 24[31]: Import of Silk in India

Year	*Quantity(in ton)*	*Value(‘ In Crores)*
1999-00	5018	412.74
2000-01	4713	475.15
2001-02	6808	624.73
2002-03	9054	647.15
2003-04	9258	628.41
2004-05	7948	607.21
2005-06	8383	779.71
2006-07	5565	673.37
2007-08	7922	734.44
2008-09	8392	903.06
2009-10	7338	933.70

Source: DGCIS, Kolkatta.

Thirdly, government kept high custom duty on raw silk and low on silk fabrics. It may be noted from table 25 that 2002-03 onwards the basic custom duty on raw silk has been kept at 30 per cent level. In case of silk fabric the basic custom duty has been reduced gradually from the level of 30 per cent (2002-03) to 10 per cent (2009-10). It means raw silk becomes costlier than the silk fabric. Traders focused on marketing of silk fabrics, which gives competition to weavers in India. They have to compete with the foreign ready-made silk products.

Table 25: Government impose duty on import of silk

Years	*Basic Custom Duty*	
	Mulberry Raw Silk (5002 00)	*Silk Fabric (5007 00)*
2000-01	35%	35%
2001-02	35%	35%
2002-03	30%	30%
2003-04	30%	25%
2004-05	30%	20%
2005-06	30%	15%
2006-07	30%	12.5%
2007-08	30%	10%
2008-09	30%	10%
2009-10	30%	10%

Source: DGCIS, Kolkatta.

Table 26: Variety-wise Certified Export of Silk Sari (Mulberry and Blended/Mixed)

(Unit: lakhs; Qty: sq. mtrs. Value: Rs.)

Year	*Sari (Mulberry)*		*Sari (Mixed/blend)*	
	Qty.	*Value*	*Qty.*	*Value*
1980-81	25.09	1038.81	0.01	1.34
1981-82	25.10	1241.75	0.03	2.34
1982-83	29.48	1648.13	0.28	9.74
1983-84	28.40	1570.18	1.17	62.15
1984-85	31.88	1597.06	1.44	99.91
1985-86	37.17	1986.33	2.24	179.52
1986-87	42.50	2319.49	3.67	307.62
1987-88	59.25	3174.60	4.99	389.83
1988-89	47.48	3299.64	4.98	444.31
1989-90	36.71	3254.12	4.58	552.75

(Contd...)

1990-91	28.53	3094.54	4.08	612.36
1991-92	40.14	5044.18	3.55	623.94
1993-94	55.56	7002.54	4.28	894.42
1994-95	52.49	7375.25	5.17	1016.06
1995-96	43.13	6677.15	4.87	1083.19
1996-97	34.67	6619.60	5.00	1019.38
1997-98	29.13	6358.23	6.86.	1508.47

Source: Datta and Nanavati, Global Silk Industry: A Complete Source Book, 2007.

Table 27 exposes the fact that in export the powerloom produced silk-goods have actually dominated the silk-goods produced by handloom.

Table 27[32]: Handloom and Powerloom Silk-goods certified for Exports

(Unit: Lakh; Qty.: Sq. mtrs.; Value: Rs.)

Year	*Handloom*		*Powerloom*	
	Qty.	*Value*	*Qty*	*Value*
1990-91	191.17	24086.67	133.37	19507.08
1991-92	214.87	34350.03	172.01	32738.45
1993-94	241.16	37717.93	225.16	49904.32
1994-95	258.66	40575.16	351.67	52121.01
1995-96	188.23	36960.21	304.33	47556.24
1996-97	161.47	34630.82	319.36	53015.71
1997-98	139.32	36810.13	262.91	53632.31

Source: Datta and Nanavati (2007:137)

The international and national trend and its impact could be seen in Banaras. In 1999-00 the total production of silk sari was 14.2 tonnes worth Rs. 4261 crores ($ 9.83 million), whereas, in 2000-01 the total production had gone down to 9.24 tonnes worth Rs. 2720 crores ($ 5.95 million) at all India level. This has direct bearing on the production of state and local level, in this case Banaras. Table 28 shows the production figure of silk sari in Banaras.

Table 28: Exports of Natural Silk Goods from Certification Centre CSB, Banaras

(Value in rupees lakh)

Year	*Dress Material*	*Saris*	*Scarves/ Stoles*	*Readymade*	*Carpets*	*Others*	*Total Turnover*
1993-94	131.25	**763.03**	45.04	28.33	116.90	51.99	2346.52
1994-95	1513.92	**870.68**	39.33	36.89	67.95	128.47	2657.25

(Contd...)

1995-96	1220.61	**550.60**	26.90	38.27	114.31	96.24	2046.94
1996-97	1083.39	**798.37**	86.56	7.14	75.65	85.33	2136.44
1997-98	1123.20	**902.25**	50.65	16.49	81.72	141.81	2316.12
1998-99	1792.28	**1026.20**	116.83	10.84	47.26	208.42	3201.83
1999-00*	1098.72	**355.40**	53.44	6.17	55.79	289.99	1859.50
2001-02	1842.00	**385.28**	420.34	6.63	14.79	266.70	2915.73
2002-03	1629.14	**137.00**	458.19	6.34	29.29	119.33	2379.28
2003-04	2972.00	**22.37**	848.97	2.07	2.10	255.38	4103.28
2004-05	1845.84	**5.24**	821.93	171.83	6.77	118.30	2803.50
2005-06	2332.79	**34.20**	617.87	0.00	0.00	334.30	3305.65

Notes: * Data for April to October only; Data for the year 2000-01 is not available.
Source: Certification Centre, Banaras.

Considering 1998-99 as base year, the above data underlines the ailing silk sari business of Banaras. In 1998-99 Banaras had produced sari worth Rs. 1026.20 lakhs, which almost wiped out of business as it produced sari worth Rs. 34.20 lakhs in 2005-06. But, the data still does not reveal the percentage share of powerloom and handloom in total production of sari in Banaras. As per the government records, *Banarasi* silk weaving industry has shrunk more than 50 per cent in a decade. "As per the records of 1998-99, there was a consumption of 11,000 metric tons of silk yarn in *Banarasi* silk weaving industry. But, now this consumption has declined to 5,000 metric tons," revealed Principal Secretary (silk) Sushil Kumar. According to another official estimate the sari segment of Banaras which typically consists of Satin-based work (largely Karnataka yarn) and Organza type work (largely Chinese yarn) recorded the decline of 50 per cent and 30 respectively.[33]

The decline has been due to the lack of demand of sari of high-end for which Banaras is famous. The weave-rich varieties of *Banarasi* sari are: *Kimkhab, Jangla, Tanchoi, Vaskat*, Cutwork, *Tishu* and *Butidar*, which range from Rs.8,000-10,000 and takes 15 days to a month or even two. The input is too high as compared to Mau and Andhra Pradesh sari, which has been low-end product. The other reason is copyright violation of the handloom design by powerloom owner leaked by *gadiddars* and *grihastha*. The powerloom produces copy design sari at faster rate and flush it in market before handloom produced reach there. Even the hallmark designed specifically for handloom is used by powerloom owner. It is difficult for an average customer to distinguish handloom product from a powerloom product. There are simple, practical ways of educating and empowering the customer but the trade channels do not perceive any benefit from such education and have not invested in it. Further, under the quota regime, handloom was not within the purview of quota. It had been permitted to exploit its full potential. However, after the disintegration of MFA and coming of ATC the advantage is also wiped out.

It is not very surprising that *Banarasi* sari did not even get mentioned in Oxford Asian Textile Group Newsletter.[34] It contained a complete chapter on the 'Indian Sari'. It described about *Paithani* sari of Aurangabad (Maharashtra); *Chanderi* Sari (Madhya Pradesh); *Maheshwari* Sari; *Patola* sari (Patan, Gujarat); *Bailuchari* sari (Bengal); *Jamdhani* sari (Dhaka); *Gadwal* sari (Gadwal, Andhra Pradesh); *Kanjeevaram* sari (Tamil Nadu), but forgets about the famous Banaras sari. The missing space is epitome of decline market share of Banarasi sari. The downturn has primarily affected those regions of Banaras handloom industry which produces high-end product (sari) and uses handloom. Thus, Bajardiha, the extension of Madanpura is worst hit by the combined effect of powerloom unwind by economic reform.

Table 29: Area-wise use of yarn in Banaras

Madanpura and other Area:	***Silk and silk-cotton kora silk, mainly Chinese yarn. Low-end work***
Lohata	Silk-Nylon, Polyster-nylon, Polyster-viscose. Lower-end and middle-end work. Largely crepe and work on it
Badibazar and Pililothi	Middle-end Traditional Work. Satin-based Work. Mainly Karnataka Yarn
Rampur	Higher end work
Chandeli	Higher end work

Source: Oxford Asian Textile Group, Newsletter No. 26, October 2003.

Madanpura escaped the wrath of economic reform as they shifted to powerloom. However, recent shift and installation of Computer Embroidery Machine (CEM) has challenged the existence of the powerloom in Banaras. Today, Banaras has some 300 such machines, which cost approximately Rs 14-15 lakh.[35] But, it is minuscule and remaining weavers used cheap pit-loom to produces silk items like sari.

Table 30[36]: Technical details along with the cost of component of Banaras handloom

Part	*No. of Unit*	*Material used*	*Cost*
Cloth beam Holders (Kunta)	2	Wood: Sakua	1000
Warp beam Holders (Kunta)	2	Wood: Sakua	1000
Sley Stand	2	Wood: Sakua	3000
Jala Frame	4	Stone : Local	400
Sley unit	1	Wooden sley (swing beat-up) throw shuttle type: Wood: Sakua	1200
Reed with Heald shafts	1 set	Steel reed along with Heald shafts. Staves made up of sakua wood and consists maximum of 2200 nylon wires in each shaft.	1550
Shuttles	2	Buffalo horn	0100
Pirns	1 gross	Plastic pirns of 4”	0050
Cloth Roller	1	Sakua wood – 1 No. with MS rod of5/8 “dia and 18” length	2600
Warp Roller	2	Sakua wood – 1 No. with MS rod of 5/8 “dia and 18” length	4000
Lease Rod	2	aluminum lease rods	0100
Weaver’s Seat	1	Sakua wood 35” X 5.5” X 1”	1400
Peddles for heald shaft with stand and grate.	2	Bamboo	0400
Temple		Sakua wood	0100
Heald shaft dead weight (stones of 2 kgs each) –	4 Nos	Stones	0200

Source: CSRTI, CSB, Varanasi, 2011.

In terms of technology, Banaras has induced several changes in neighbouring areas known for handloom products. Chanderi is one such case. About 20-25 years ago, the jacquard mechanism for the border of Chanderi saris was introduced in Chanderi by the artisans from Banaras who also introduced the rolling log at the same time.

Table 31: Components of Jacquard

240 hooks Jacquard (wooden frames) – 1 No	3000
Harness threads – Nylon - 1 kg,	200
Cotton – 1/2 kg	50
Clips– 400 no.s	200
Bamboo peddle and wooden (Sakua) Jacquard lifting lever	200

(Contd...)

Bamboo for tying Pagiya – 2 Nos.	100
Deadweight for jacquard (Metal) – 2 Nos.	150
Cards (250 nos.)	500
Subtotal	**4400**

Source: Sarguamani, Jayanta Ghosh and Dinesh Tomar (2011).

It is clear from the table that cost of the loom is low compared to other looms (power and Shuttleless). The uniqueness of these looms is the production of specific design (imaginary, own creations/thoughts etc.) using different colour weft threads and lifting of warp with *jala* (Nylon/ Cotton threads). The designs produced are simple or complicated that are perfect in appearance with less/no distortion which catches the heart of the viewer. But handlooms, especially of Varanasi, are the best to produce design that are incomparable with any other type of loom for which special skill is needed and cost of the loom is low compared to latest looms. However, before weavers start weaving they engage themselves in pre-production works which are as follows:

(a) Degumming: It involves cleansing of gum from raw material which is known as '*Khara*'. The raw silk with gum is called as '*Kora*'.

(b) Dyeing: Adding colour of own choice according to the demand in market.

(c) Throwing or Unwinding: The coloured and dyed silk material filled on reel is called as '*Nali bharna*'. It is mainly done by female and child member of weavers' family.

(d) Sizing and Beaming: Before weaving starts, '*Tana*' is set up to decide the length of the product. The tana's threads check-up very minutely in open field by group of weavers.

(e) Reeding and Warping: After rewinding *tana*, it is kept on Handloom, then filled '*Nali*' kept on sides to build '*Bana*'.

One thing can be concluded that the powerloom has really threatened the existence of handloom and converted major handloom centres into the powerloom hub. The comparative case study of Mau vis-à-vis Banaras, the focus of this study, explains this phenomenon clearly. Mau, a major sari production centre of Eastern Uttar Pradesh has been seen as glaring example of success of economic reform. Once it was figured as a handloom centre completely transformed itself into the powerloom hub in and around 1980.

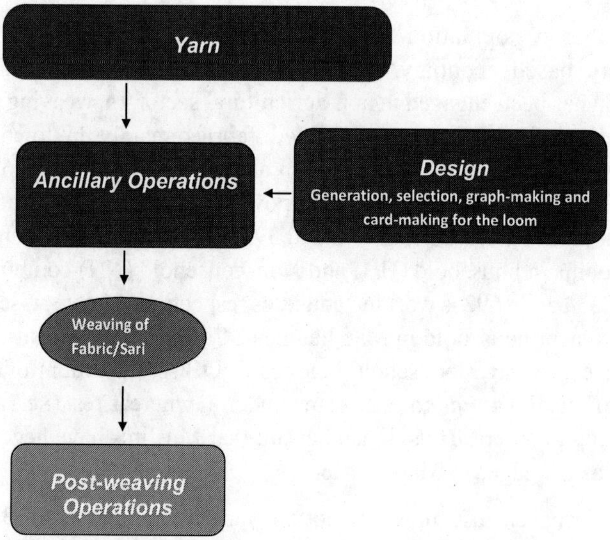

Figure 2: Production stage of sari at handloom in Banaras

Table 32: The shift from handloom to powerloom in Mau[37]

Year	*Total No. of Respondents*	*Per cent*
1980-85	180	60
1986-90	90	30
1991 - Onward	30	10
Total	300	100

Source: Fieldwork.

The process of shift from handloom to powerloom well began in early 1980 and completed at the initial phase of economic reform. By 1990, of the total, 90 per cent of respondents had changed to powerloom. The reason could be well recorded during the field work. An overwhelming percentage of population argued that by the 1980 handloom was not a viable source of livelihood. The income was less and work was labour intensive.[38] Thus, shift to powerloom was seen as the freedom from meagre resource and maximisation of the profit. The lack of brand tag associated with Mau product unlike *Banarasi* sari of Banaras helped the weavers to switch over swiftly without any fear to the brand product. But there have been many low income level weavers who were unable to transform technologically and stuck to handloom whose fate will be discussed in next chapter.

Mau has a population of approximately 18.49 lakh[39] primarily agriculture based economy.[40] However, a substantial percentage of population has been engaged in non-agricultural sector i.e. weaving cotton bedspreads, sari, dress material, mixed fabrics mainly in town area. According to Joint Census of handloom and powerloom (1995-96) Mau had 14,273 household units engaged in powerloom activity.[41] Of the total, 13, 874 households were with loom and 399 without it.[42] Mau has total of 19, 026 looms in household (HH) and Non-household (NH) combined, in which 17,334 and 1692 is working and idles respectively. Caste-wise 21.75 per cent weaver household in Mau belongs SCs and 1.59 per cent to STs. 74.38 per cent weaver household belongs to OBCs, maximum of which belongs to Muslim as *julaha* caste came under it, whereas rest (i.e.2.28 per cent) belong to others. Thus, it can be said that Muslims have hegemonic presence as a weaver in Mau district.

These weavers use more of cotton yarn as compared to Banaras weavers who used silk yarn for the production of saris. According to the Census (1995-96) 103,833 kg/month of cotton yarn used by Mau weavers as compared to 57,896 kg/month by Banaras loom. But, Banaras used 231,356 kg/month of silk as compared to 58,547 kg/month by Mau. In both the places almost 2/3rd percentage of loom engaged in producing sari. 72.77 per cent in Mau and 78.90 per cent of loom in Banaras were producing sari. But, interestingly, despite large percentage of loom were engaged in producing sari in Mau, it was producing much less sari than Banaras loom. 3,483,090 (linear meters) of sari as compared to 1,182,660 (linear meters) produced by Banaras. Thus, it can be concluded that silk sari production at that time was dominated by Banaras district. On the other hand, Mau was much ahead to Banaras in producing cotton items such as *Dhoti, Lungi, Gamchas/Angawastra* and towel/napkin. Unlike Banaras' market structure Mau has two layers ultimately control by the *Grihastha* or *seth*.

However, with the production of mixed silk sari, which is easier to produce on powerloom, from Surat and Kolkatta began to take over the Banaras handloom silk saris market. The powerloom began to copy the Banaras silk sari and produce it on affordable price. The powerloom sari cheap in price, better in quality than Banaras product and produced at higher speed acts as a bane to Banaras handloom. As the powerloom had engaged in producing mixed silk sari, the grown demand of silk forced India to import it from China and other places. The imported silk from China cost lesser than Indian grown silk and also better in quality, intensified the demand. According to a report Chinese silk cost $ 1-1.25/metre, whereas Indian silk cost $ 2.5 – 4/metre.[43]

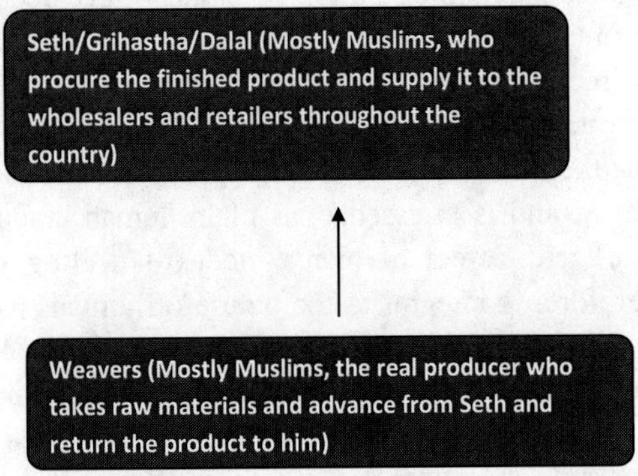

Figure 3: Structure of Market in Mau, Uttar Pradesh

Thus, Chinese silk fabric exports to India grew by a whopping 6500 per cent in 5 years (2001 – 2005) 1.5 million meters in 2000-01 to 91 million meters in 2004-05. This had badly affected the Bangalore silk production market, which made Deve Gowda ban Chinese silk import from 1995 to 1998. Probably because of its superior quality, smuggling of Chinese yarn into the region began. Soon realising that their need for Chinese yarn would only grow, the weavers demanded an OGL to import Chinese silk. Government policy aimed at more productivity and competitiveness in international market lifted the ban. "The big blow to weavers came during 1999-2000, when the Indian Government allowed duty-free imports of Chinese plain crepe fabric."[44] In 2001, India also abolished its quantitative restrictions on silk imports on demand from the WTO. Since then annual growth rates of silk imports have soared exponentially. This gives free ride to powerloom of Mau.

However, once the field for competition was set, the Mau powerloom too faced its heat from the domestically organised powerloom of Surat and Maharashtra. According to Jalis Ahmad, "a Communist Party of India (CPI) activist and shopkeeper in Mau who buys and sell saris, said that in 2002-03 Mau was facing competition from Surat, because Surat had processing plants that could smoothen the rough texture of synthetic fibre, bringing it closer to the texture of silk."[45]

Conclusion

The impact of advancing technology on weavers across the nation is deleterious. Long before, speaking on the impact of technology at the General Council meeting of the International Working Men's Association, Marx noted: '...what strikes us most is that all the consequences which were expected as the inevitable result of machinery have been reversed... The influence of machinery upon those with whose labour it enters into competition is directly hostile. Many handloom weavers were positively killed by the introduction of the powerloom, both here and in India'.[46] Marx argued that the technology is an extension of the productive organs of the human body, and is in essence, as plain human labour was at an earlier stage, part and parcel of man's mode of dealing with nature. Technology, therefore, is integral to the nature of humans as part of the specific nature of their existence as a species, and the specific form that the evolution of this particular species has taken subsequently. But it would be interesting to know the processes what turn technology, which is a product of human labour, into an external, alien force that comes to rule over labour itself?

The first stage in the process, which turns technology into alien force for labour, was in the manufacture, where 'the revolution in the mode of production begins with labour power.' In manufacture, masses of workers are gathered together under one roof, and the task of each one is broken down into some basic element of the series of actions that go into the making of a particular artefact. At the same time, manufacturing also brings under one roof all the elements of producing goods that were produced by different classes of craftsmen and artisans in separate locations. Manufacture is an age of ever-increasing and brutal exploitation. But, as the physical limits of such exploitation are reached, even as capitalism demands ever-increasing production and as working class resistance to this grows, the stage is set for the next phase of the development of the forces of production, namely by the introduction of machinery. Thus, Marx notes the origins of the technological drive of capitalism which ever increases with the liberalization process in the third world economies.

According to a research "liberalised regime has also affected the level of technology acquisition in the manufacturing sector by encouraging technology imports. Three main sources of technological advancement in manufacturing sector include import of embodied technology (e.g., capital goods), import of dis-embodied technology (through royalty payments, technical fees and lump-sum payments) and in-house research and development (R and D). In the post reforms period, the import of capital goods has been on an average 2.4 per cent of the total imports and this has not increased much overtime as seen in Table 33. One for the reasons of this could be domestic machinery replacing imported machinery in the process of import substitution. The in-house R and D efforts by industrial firms have also been relatively low in India though they have shown a tendency to improve consistently overtime. R and D intensity increased to 3.3 percent in 1996-97 from 0.5 per cent in 1990-91. The top one-tenth industrial companies spent on an average about 8 per cent of their sales on R and D during 1996-99."[47]

Table 33: Trends in Technology Acquisition in Indian Manufacturing: (1990-91 to 1997-98)

Year	*Import of Capital Goods as a Percentage of Total Imports*	*RandD Expenditures as a Percentage of Total Sales*	*Import of Technology as a Percentage of Total Sales*
1990-91	2.4	0.5	0.7
1991-92	2.1	0.9	0.9
1992-93	2.0	1.6	1.5
1993-94	2.6	1.6	2.5
1994-95	2.6	1.9	3.1
1995-96	2.8	2.5	4.4
1996-97	2.5	3.3	4.8

Source: The Handbook of Statistics on Indian Economy, DGCIandS and Author's estimation from Prowess (C.M.I.E.). Note: Import of technology includes import of embodied as well as dis-embodied technology.

"But a considerable volume of technology has entered Indian industry through the route of technology imports i.e., purchase of technology. Imports of technology increased from 0.7 per cent of total sales in 1990-91 to around 5.0 per cent in 1996-97 (Table 33). In absolute terms, the payment for royalty and technical fees increased from USD 25.1 million in 1985 to USD 200.8 million in 1998. However, it is still much lower than those found in other developing countries (e.g., a comparative figure for Malaysia is USD 2392 million, USD 1002 million for Indonesia, USD 420 million for China and USD 804 for Thailand)."[48] Hence, more emphasis of technology without taking care of labour in handloom sector, which is labour intensive industry, displacing weavers and creating an army reserved labour for mechanised weaving in the same or for other sector in the country. Arjun Sengupta committee report, 2007, on condition of worker in unorganized sector pointed out that "This (Handloom) occupation is the lowest in the hierarchy of technologies of textile of textile manufacturing…The intermediate technology of power looms, organized in small factories and workshops, has been on the expansion taking advantage of both low cost of production as well as electro-mechanical technology…The problem for handloom workers is that there is no demand for these workers in the powerlooms sector since no traditional skills are required. While it would be desirable to have a technological shift to enhance productivity and income, the losers are not necessarily the gainers. This poses a huge dilemma and calls for policies for rehabilitation and provision of sustainable livelihood mechanisms."[49]

Weavers have been recognizing the worsening effects of technology on handloom. Mohammad Jallaluddin, who works on the loom, owned by Suleiman, said, 'The power looms are the biggest culprits. Every design, which bunkars (weavers) innovate and prepare and weave on the handloom, is copied on the power loom and that leads to decline in the price of the new design. "The production technology has more or less remained ancient-pit type handloom where the weaver sits with his legs in the pit," said Hazi Jamaluddin. "During the medieval period skilled Muslim weavers from the West Asian countries came to India along with Moghuls. These weavers found Varanasi complementing to their art of intricate pattern of weaving and settled there under the patronage of the then Muslim rulers,"[50] adds the elderly Hazi. The continued use of the ancient production technology however proved to be a stumbling block in increasing the production. An improvement was made by incorporating a device in the handloom, which lifted the warp threads according to the design punched on paper cards so that the weft thread shuttle could weave through the design without any manual intervention. This device called Jacquard, made it possible to reproduce any given design.

References

1. K. Srinivasulu, '1985 Textile Policy and Handloom Industry: Policy, Promises and Performance', *Economic and Political Weekly*, Vol. 31, No. 49, 1996.
2. L.C.Jain, '1985 Textile Policy: End of Handloom Industry', *Mainstream*, July 20, 1985.
3. Ruddar Datt, '1985 Textile Policy: End of Handloom Industry', *Mainstream*, July 20, 1985.
4. India's artisans: A Status Report, SRUTI, 1995, p. 43.
5. K. Srinivasulu, op. cit. pp. 3198-3206.
6. Vasanthi Raman, *The Warp and the Weft: Community and Gender Identity among Banaras Weavers*, Routledge Publication, New Delhi, 2010, p. 237.

7. K.D.Saksena, *Dynamics of India's Textile Economy: Towards a Pragmatic Textile Policy*, Shipra Publication, New Delhi, 2002, p. 468.
8. *Ibid.*, p. 468.
9. Bandyopadhyay and T. Sengupta, 'Cotton Textile Industry in India: Implications for MFA Phase Out', in D. Sengupta, Chakraborty and Banerjee (ed.), *Beyond the Transition Phase of WTO: An Indian Perspective on Emerging Issues*, Academic Foundation, New Delhi, 2006, p. 146.
10. D. Sengupta, Chakraborty and Banerjee (ed.), *Beyond the Transition Phase of WTO: An Indian Perspective on Emerging Issues*, Academic Foundation, New Delhi, 2006.
11. S. Niranjana and S. Vinayan, "Growth and Prospects of the Handloom Industry", Planning Commission, 2001, New Delhi.
12. Nambiar, 1993, p. 36.
13. L.C. Jain, Handlooms face Liquidation: Powerlooms mock at Yojna Bhawan, *Economic and Political Weekly*, Vol. 18, No. 35, 1983, pp. 1517-26.
14. *Ibid.*
15. Asiya Chaudhary, Changing Structure of Indian Textile Industry after MFA (Multi Fiber Agreement) Phase out: A Global Perspective, *Far East Jounral of Psychology and Business*, Vol. 2, No. 2, February 2011.
16. Indian Express, September 2, 2004.
17. Financial Express, Bombay, 23rd May, 2005.
18. Sunit Arora, Indian Express, Jan. 05, 2006.
19. India: Economic News, 'Highlight of the National Textile Policy, 2000', Vol. XI, No. 10-11, Washington, 2000.
20. Vasanthi Raman, op. cit., p. 170.
21. Asha Krishnakumar, 'Perilous Policies', *Frontline*, Vol. 18, No. 8, April 14-27, 2001.
22. *Ibid.*
23. Seemanthini Niranjana, '*Growth and Prospects of Handloom Industry*', Planning Commission, Dastkar Andhra, 2001.
24. A.N. Pandey, Industrial Development in Uttar Pradesh, Chapter four, in Diwakar and Nayak (ed), *Development Challenges: Afflicting Uttar Pradesh*, Manak Publication, New Delhi, 2007.
25. Ministry of Textile, 'Report of Working Group on Handloom for the 12th Five Year Plan', GoI, p.22.
26. Steering Committee Report, '*Handlooms and Handicrafts*', 12th Five Year Plan, VSE Division, Planning Commission, GoI, p. 27.
27. Amit Basole, 'Knowledge, Gender and Production Relations in India's informal Economy', Ph.D., 2011, p. 137.
28. Narshimha Reddy, Weaving Woes on the Handlooms, *India Together*, February, 2006. There is no consensus about the total strength of weavers in the country. According to 1995-96 'Joint Census of Handloom and Powerloom' the numbers

of weavers was 65 lakh, whereas, Working Group of Textile Industry for 10th Plan 120 lakh person involved in handloom weaving and allied activities.

29. K. Srinivasulu, '1985 Textile Policy and handloom Industry: Policy, Promises and Performance', *Economic and Political Weekly*, Vol. 31, No. 49, December 7, 1996, p.3202.
30. Datta and Nanavati, *Global Silk Industry: A Complete Source Book*, APH Publishing House, New Delhi, 2007.
31. Source: DGCIS, Kolkatta.
32. Datta and Nanavati, *Global Silk Industry: A Complete Source Book*, APH Publishing Corporation, New Delhi, 2007, p. 137.
33. Diagnostic Study of Handloom Silk Cluster Varanasi, Uttar Pradesh, p. 14.
34. Oxford Asian Textile Group, Newsletter No. 26, October 2003.
35. Vasanthi Raman, op. cit. p. 245.
36. Sarguamani, Jayanta Ghosh and Dinesh Tomar, *Cost Estimation and Technology of Banaras Hand loom [Pit loom]*, Textile testing Laboratories, CSRTI, CSB, Varanasi, UP, India, 2011.
37. Data collected from Fieldwork in Mau in June 2010.
38. Fieldwork in Mau.
39. Census 2001.
40. According to 1991 Census, of the total population percentage of worker was 33.2. Of the total work force 68.3 per cent were directly involved in agriculture.
41. By mid of 1980 there was large scale conversion to powerloom from handloom in Mau.
42. Compiled from Joint Census of Handlooms and Powerloom, 1995-96.
43. Rahul Kodkani, *Varanasi Weaver in Crisis*, UCSD Chapter, 2007 p. 18.
44. Sujata Madhok, "As the Looms go silent in Benaras", *The Hindu*, 2009.
45. Vasanthi Raman, op. cit. pp. 257. According to Imtiaz Ahmed (one of the informants of V. Raman) at least 15 persons died due to starvation in Mau between late 2002 and early 2003. Author further mentioned the newspaper reports which bring forth the plight of weavers in the area of Mau and Mubarakpur. It records that some 150 families from Mau and Azamgarh pawned off their wives' jewellery and parted with all their savings on the assurance from tricksters and conmen that they would get jobs in the Gulf.
46. Prabhat Patnaik (et. al), '*Marx's Capital: An Introductory Reader*', Leftword publication, New Delhi, 2011.
47. Rashmi Banga, 'Impact of Liberalization on wages and Employment in Indian Manufacturing Industries', Working Paper No. 153, 2005, New Delhi p. 9.
48. *Ibid.*, p. 10.
49. Arjun Sengupta, '*Report on Conditions of work and promotion of livelihoods in the unorganized sector*', National Commission for Enterprises in the Unorganised Sector, New Delhi, 2007.
50. T. K. Bose, "Globalisation: Pushes Varanasi Weavers to Hunder & Death", Chaturdisha, ActionAid. Access from https://www.scribd.com/document/8947031/Report-on-Weaver-of-Varanasi-India.

Chapter - 3

Handloom Weavers of Banaras – The Unfolding of Economic Reform

Effect of Liberalization on the Banaras Weavers

The previous chapter focused on the policy initiatives to introduce economic reform in the textile industry, and their impact on the handloom of the country in general and Banaras in particular. Economic reform has affected the trade and export potential of a country, in which the textile sector has a major share. "It contributes around 5 per cent of GDP and accounts for over a third i.e. 37 per cent of country's total export. However, India's share in the global textile trade is a meagre 2.5 per cent, compared to 11.5 per cent of China and 7.5 per cent of Hong Kong. On the other hand, silk exports account for only 2.25 per cent of the textile export from the country and 0.75 per cent of its total export."[1] The users of cotton and pure-silk yarn in handloom are among the worst affected groups across the country, as the Indian textile industry is predominantly cotton-based with 70 per cent of the raw material consumed being cotton. The item-wise growth in the production of handloom cloth is shown below in table 34.

Table 34: Item-wise growth production of cloth on handloom

Year	*Cloth in Handloom Sector*				*Percentage Share*		
	Cotton	*Blended*	*100% Non-Cotton*	*Total*	*Cotton*	*Blended*	*100% Non-Cotton*
1988-89	3911	26	56	3998	97.95	0.65	1.40
1989-90	3837	14	73	3924	97.78	0.36	1.86
1990-91	4237	11	47	4295	98.65	0.26	1.09
1995-96	6239	18	945	7202	86.63	0.25	13.12
1996-97	6441	52	963	7456	86.39	0.70	12.91
1997-98	6699	69	835	7603	88.11	0.91	10.98
1998-99	5861	111	820	6792*	86.29	1.63	12.07

Source: Textile Statistics, 1999, GOI, p. 67.

* Share in total cloth production is 22 per cent.

In the four year period between 1994-95 and 1998-99, the total cloth production from handloom reduced considerably (table 35). According to the annual report published by the Ministry of Textile, the share of handloom in total cloth production reduced to 13 per cent in the year 2007-08. The share of cotton cloth in the total output of the handloom sector has also gone down from 97.95 in 1988-89 to 86.29 in 1998-99.[2] In the export sector as well, cotton fabrics produced by handloom have lost to the power-loom, while cotton itself has given way to other sectors of the textile industry.

Table 35[3]: Sector-wise Export of Cotton Cloths

Year	*Cotton*				*Total Cotton*	*% Change over previous year*
	Mills	*Power*	*Knitted*	*Handloom*		
1992-93	414	622	92	85	1,213	-
1993-94	413	725	105	79	1,322	8.98
1994-95	458	949	130	78	1,615	22.16
1995-96	466	998	115	60	1,639	1.49
1996-97	486	1,271	131	48	1,936	18.12
1997-98	476	1,315	110	43	1,944	0.41
Percentage Change						
1997-98 over 1992-93	14.97	111.47	19.56	-97.67	60.26	-

Source: Compendium of Textile Statistics, 1997 (pp.144-145) and 1999 (194-195).

The downturn in business had a direct bearing on patterns of employment and job-switches in Uttar Pradesh and Banaras. The people who lost their jobs shifted to the status of marginal worker and even non-worker.

Table 36: Category-wise total number of workers in Uttar Pradesh

State (Uttar Pradesh)	*Industrial category*	*Census year*	*Rural*			*Urban*			*Total*		
			P	*M*	*F*	*P*	*M*	*F*	*P*	*M*	*F*
	Main Worker	**1981**	29.71	50.98	5.90	26.99	47.30	2.99	29.22	50.31	5.39
		1991	30.52	50.10	8.36	26.56	46.19	3.75	29.73	49.31	7.45
	Marginal Worker	**1981**	1.75	0.51	3.14	0.31	0.17	0.47	1.49	0.45	2.67
		1991	2.94	0.41	5.18	0.57	0.18	1.03	2.47	0.36	4.87
	Non-worker	**1981**	68.54	48.51	90.96	72.70	52.53	96.54	69.29	49.24	91.94
		1991	66.54	49.49	85.84	72.86	53.63	95.22	67.86	50.32	87.68

Source: Census 1991, Uttar Pradesh. P=Person; M=Male; F=Female.

As the Banaras silk handloom is mainly concentrated in the urban centre of Banaras[4], it can be presumed that the increase in unemployment occurred there as well. Table 37 elaborates this point below. Table shows the increase in unemployment of males in rural as well as urban areas. The lack of employment opportunities had pushed workers either into marginal jobs or into unemployment.

Table 37: Category-wise total number of workers in Banaras

District (Banaras)	*Industrial category*	*Census year*	*Rural*			*Urban*			*Total*		
			P	*M*	*F*	*P*	*M*	*F*	*P*	*M*	*F*
	Main Worker	1981	28.33	48.32	6.75	26.38	49.19	2.95	**27.80**	47.73	5.77
		1991	29.71	46.43	11.33	26.44	45.12	4.75	**28.82**	46.06	9.58
	Marginal Worker	1981	1.39	0.34	2.53	0.11	0.08	0.14	**1.05**	0.27	1.91
		1991	3.65	0.48	7.13	0.49	0.12	0.91	**2.79**	0.38	5.48
	Non-worker	1981	70.28	51.34	90.72	73.51	53.73	96.91	**71.15**	52.00	92.32
		1991	66.64	53.10	81.53	73.07	54.76	94.34	**68.39**	53.56	84.94

Source: 1991 Census, Varanasi, Uttar Pradesh. P=Person; M=Male; F=Female.

The table below shows that 43 out of 56 i.e. 76.78 per cent of respondents in rural areas of Banaras, shifted from weaving to other jobs or to working as manual labours under the National Rural Employment Guarantee Act (NREGA). As NREGA is not meant for the urban poor, the weavers of the city are engaged in rickshaw pulling, selling vegetables, working in power-looms, polishing, dyeing and others jobs.

Table 38: Detail of respondents regarding the shift in their job in Banaras[5]

Sr. No.	*Name*	*Age*	*Village*	*Whether earlier a weaver*	*Shifted to which Job*
1.	Sewaram	80	Sarnath	No	
2.	Natwai	70	,,	Yes	Other job
3.	Chhawinath	67	Tadiya	Yes	,,
4.	Rajkumar	40	Daghariya	Yes	NREGA
5.	Balwanta	48	,,	No	
6.	Rambharose	48	,,	No	
7.	Sohanlal Gupta	40	Sajoi	No	
8.	Sitla Prasad	28	Badhaini	Yes	Other job
9.	Kanhaiya lal	30	,,	Yes	,,
10.	Shiv Kumar	35	,,	Yes	,,
11.	Vishnu	35	,,	Yes	NREGA
12.	Ramasare	35	,,	Yes	Other job

(Contd...)

13.	Shivlal	37	Sajoi	Yes	NREGA
14.	Bechan	45	,,	No	
15.	Ramchandra	30	Sahwaazpur	Yes	NREGA
16.	Ramlakhan	36	,,	Yes	,,
17.	Tejbahadur	33	,,	Yes	,,
18.	Umashankar	35	,,	Yes	,,
19.	Rajnath	32	,,	Yes	,,
20.	Amarjit	32	,,	Yes	Other job
21.	Mangla	32	,,	Yes	,,
22.	Prabhunarayan	25	,,	Yes	,,
23.	Satyakant	35	,,	Yes	,,
24.	Sakeel Ahmad	48	Sajoi	No	
25.	Ramkishun	33	Sahwaazpur	Yes	NREGA
26.	Shivshankar Patel	25	Badhaini	,,	Other job
27.	Ram Narayan	41	Sahwaazpur	,,	,,
28.	PremShànkar	35	Badhaini	,,	,,
29.	Ravishankar	22	Sahwaazpur	,,	,,
30.	Lalman	29	,,	,,	,,
31.	Chhotelal	28	Badhaini	,,	,,
32.	Kharpachhu	30	Kanthipur	,,	,,
33.	Gangaram	55	Badhaini	,,	,,
34.	Mulendu	30	,,	,,	,,
35.	Ramdular	30	,,	,,	NREGA
36.	Bhupendra	38	,,	,,	,,
37.	Amarnath	50	,,	Yes	Other job
38.	Santkumar	40	Tadiya	,,	NREGA
39.	Kishori	55	,,	,,	Other job
40.	Rajesh	28	Lohta	,,	,,
41.	Hira	55	Koraut	,,	,,
42.	Kailash	35	Tadiya	,,	,,
43.	Bholai	50	,,	,,	,,
44.	Udaya	31	,,	,,	NREGA
45.	Matin	42	Chhitanpura	,,	,,
46.	Madanlal	42	Sarwanpur	,,	,,
47.	Omprakash	23	,,	Yes	Other Job
48.	Lalmani varma	55	Parmandapur	No	
49.	Mobin ahmad	60	Koilabazar	Yes	Other Job
50.	Ramgopal	58	Mataldei	No	
51.	Radheshyam	46	Tadiya	Yes	NREGA
52.	Rajkumari devi	27	Chhitauni	No	
53.	Kewaladevi	40	,,	,,	
54.	Champadevi	40	,,	,,	
55.	Dauladevi	40	,,	,,	
56.	Anita devi	35	,,	,,	

Source: Fieldwork in Banaras in September 2009-Janurary 2010.

Thus, the closure of handlooms has forced weavers to migrate from Banaras to cities such as Bangalore, Surat, Mumbai and other places, and take up various jobs in the cities. While analysing the Andhra weavers' migration pattern, a study argued that "Handloom is much more sustainable than common views and standard government policies recognize. Instead of a linear migration out of weaving into other forms of livelihood, weaving communities show a more strategic mobility – flexibly departing from and again returning to weaving, depending on circumstances."[6] It is considered to be 'flexible mobility'. However, this kind of flexible mobility has not been observed in case of the migrant Banaras weavers, who became completely detached from their traditional jobs.

According to the Census of 2001, UP topped the chart with 2,672,620 (-2.6 million) out-migrants from the State. The negative impact is certainly visible on the day-to-day lives of Banaras' weavers. Iqbal Ahmed said that the "declining fortunes of the handloom sector compelled him to send his sons, Vakil Ahmed and Aftab Ahmed, to Surat and Ahmedabad respectively."[7]

Table 39: Variation in migration profile of 1991 – 2001 for Uttar Pradesh based on migrants by last residence (duration 0-9 years).

Uttar Pradesh	*2001 Census*	*1991 Census*	*Variations (%) 1991-2001*
	Persons	*Persons*	*Persons*
In-migrants (from other States	1,431,551	728,329	96.6
In-migrants (from abroad)	61,248	58,960	3.9
Total in-migrants	1,492,799	787,289	89.6
Out-migrants	4,165,419	2,457,996	69.5
Net migrants (+/-)	**(2,672,620)**	**(1,670,707)**	**60.0**

Source: Census 2001, Data Highlights – Table D1, D2 and D3, pp. 6.

"Earlier, we used to get Rs.1,200 for weaving one *Banarasi* silk sari; today the traders are not willing to pay more than Rs. 800," he said.[8] Their wages have been dwindling along with a sharp increase in working hours. Table 40 shows the income of weavers divided into two categories i.e. owner weavers and labourer weavers. 45.2 per cent of owner weavers earned 9000 or above, whereas more than fifty per cent of labour weavers earned between Rs. 1500-3000 in a month. But the most surprising finding is that 31.1 per cent of labour weaver earned less than Rs.1500, which could be even less than the official minimum wages of the state.

According to a project report sponsored by the Ministry of Commerce and Industry, UNCTAD-India and Department for International Development (DFID) argued that "There has been an absolute decline in earnings @ at least 30% to 40% over the last 10 years. A weaver who was getting Rs. 100 per day in the mid-nineties gets Rs.60 per day now. If we factor in inflation, the decline is sharper."[9]

Table 40: Monthly Income of Weavers in Banaras

Monthly Income Group (Rs)	*Owner Weaver (%)*	*Labour Weaver (%)*
Below 1500	None	31.1
1500-3000	10.9	**51.1**
3001-6000	25.4	17.8
6001-9000	18.2	None
9001-above	**45.2**	None

Source: B.Gupta, *Varanasi Zile mein Silk Udyog ka ek Addhyan*, 2001, Ph.D Thesis, BHU.

The report further pointed out that "The earning reported includes, besides wage payment for weaving work, the following, a) Reeling/bobbin filling work put in by the women in the family; b) The economic or notional rental for loom-area provided by the weaver (the convenience of working from home is stressed to the exclusion of fact that the weaver provides space for production facility; his family bears the loom noise. The discussion typically emphasizes weaver advantage and blanks out rent saving benefit to CGG; c) National interest on investment in looms and depreciation thereon (in some cases CGG invests in looms). If we factor in return on the above-cited three components, it seems that the return on weaving labour on average, is in Rs. 40 to 45 ranges. A weaver, typically, works on a few designs (single digit) in a year. He is required to spend four to five days for readjusting the loom and related tasks for changing over from one design to another. This is not paid for."[10]

Generally speaking, the weaver handling silk or very fine cotton cloth had incomes between three and five times that of a weaver making cloths variously called 'coarse' or 'ordinary', basically generic men's and women's wear. Between these easily identifiable extremes, there were a great many types of weavers who combined rural and urban, local and long-distance trade, high and low skill, more capital or little capital. They strove to join the elite, but were often pushed by circumstances to regress to labouring or other occupations. These basic hierarchies influenced how groups of weavers responded to long reversal in fortunes. The rural labouring castes engaged in coarse weaving on the side, tended to leave the industry for general labour and semi-skilled services. The urban communities and silk weavers responded differently. When the silk weavers had to leave weaving, they tended to shift to skilled professions and trade rather than labour. In general, in the 1921 or 1931 Censuses, the percentages engaged in weaving among silk or fine cotton weaver castes were usually higher than that with the services castes. They diversified and innovated within weaving. They migrated from depressed regions and resettled as weavers at points of flourishing handloom trade. This study has found further steep declines in the wages, and increases in working hour durations in a day. Table 41 shows the wages of weavers who are not differentiated as owner weaver and labour weaver.

Table 41: Monthly Income of Weavers in Banaras

Monthly Income Group (Rs.)	*% of total respondent*	*Total person*
Below 1500	42.85	129
1501-2000	40.47	121
2001-2500	11.90	36
2501-3000	4.76	14
Total	**100**	**300**

Source: Fieldwork in Banaras in 2009.

Data in table 41 shows that 83.32 per cent of weavers earn not more than Rs. 2000 a month, which is Rs. 66.66 average daily income of a weaver. A family of 2-3 working males could fetch around Rs.133.32 - 199.98. That is one explanation for the continuance of large and joint families in Banaras. However, if all the males are married, the average individual income reduces, as dependency increases. In addition, the cited income never accounts for the labour of women, children and other family members that is integral to the production of handloom weaves such as *Banarasi* saris. In the silk industry, children are the worst sufferers. Pushed to penurious conditions, weavers have to make their children sit at the looms and add to the earning of the family. Children help in creating design patterns (*Buti*) and also operate the shuttle (*Dharki phekna*), which speeds up the production process. If the weavers have looms more than what family members can operate, they even hire adults and children.

Children can be hired either on a little amount or in lieu of the loan disbursed to their parents. Bonded labour, however, can move from one owner to another provided the new loom's owner pays off the outstanding debt to the first loom owner.[11] The role of women in the Banarasi sari weaving process is quite critical, but they are neither given recognition nor good remuneration. Work done by women is most strenuous, repetitive and quite un-stimulating. The work of sari *katran* is done by women by continuously sitting for 6 to 7 hours. Women, who do the cutting, earn a pittance of Rs. 5 to Rs. 15 a day by putting up a hard toil. Usually, they carry out the cutting work at their homes. However, women working in the sari industry are few, particularly those doing *Anta* and *Nari* filling work. Moreover, they work either to augment family incomes or to run the household, in the absence of their spouses.

Given the low wages in *nari bharai* and the financial constraints in the setting-up of handlooms, women are forced to move out of their homes and work as labourers, despite social constraints. The *gaddidar* engages women for the katran work, *Anta, Nari* filling and even for cutting work. Though in the weaving of saris, women are not involved, this has become the norm. They are involved in the menial tasks, such as '*nari bharna', 'taana kheechna', 'anta bharna',* making holes in cardboards for jacquards, cutting of threads and finishing of the woven sari. However, they have been kept away from the entire sari weaving process. They are not allowed to sit on the handlooms, as they are seen to be weak and incapable of sitting at the looms. There is no attempt to adapt the looms in accordance with the needs of women. In addition, there is a feeling that if the women were to come on the looms, men will lose their jobs, and the cost of the sari will drop drastically.

In the *Banarasi* sari sector, the various players transfer costs to women, who bear the brunt of subsidising the production. In fact, if the women did not do the menial jobs without getting any remuneration, the cost of the finished product would be much higher than what it is at present.[12] By not providing adequate healthcare and welfare infrastructure for the women workers, the government is also responsible for transferring this cost on to women, who often suffer silently or live considerably reduced life spans. The absence of crèche or day care facilities for the children of women putting up long hours, affects the children adversely. Denied congenial growth, education and good parenting, the children suffer the consequences when they are adults. Many children are drawn towards drugs, criminal or other nefarious activities. The *gaddidars* and master weavers in tandem with the male weavers or members of a family transfer significant amount of production costs, such as *Nari bharai* on the women members of the household. However, this cost goes un-accounted while deciding the market price of the finished product. Measuring the financial implications on the transfer of the above costs on to women of the sector, needs further attention.

Hafiz Mohammad Umar, a resident of Bajardiha, says "At times it is difficult to earn Rs.30 to 40 a day, and even if one is able to make Rs.100 per day on the loom, the amount does not suffice to feed the large families which an average weaver invariably possesses."[13] Interestingly, the Planning Commission's estimates of poverty do not place these weavers below the poverty line. According to the latest estimates of the Planning Commission, anyone with a daily consumption expenditure of Rs. 28.35 and Rs. 22.42 in urban and rural areas respectively, is above the poverty line. The new poverty estimates for 2011-12 will only add to the furore triggered by the Commission's affidavit in the Supreme Court in October, in which the BPL cap was pegged at an expenditure of Rs. 32 and Rs. 26 by an individual in the urban and rural areas respectively, at the going rate of inflation in 2010-11.

There are some economists who feel that the estimate and methodology followed by Planning Commission is accurate. S.S.A. Aiyar, research fellow, CATO institute, argued that "Rapid GDP growth is the best antidote for poverty. That is the big message that comes blaring out of the poverty data for 2009-10. Record GDP growth of 8.5% per year between 2004-05 and 2009-10 has reduced poverty at a record rate of 1.5 percentage points per year, double the 0.7 percentage points per year in the preceding 11 years. There can be no better refutation of the leftist myth that fast growth has benefited only a small rich coterie while bypassing the poor. Unfortunately, the good news has been drowned out by quasi-illiterate screams from politicians and sections of the media that the data has been fudged. The allegation is false. The data has not been fudged, and should be cause for celebration."[14] However, Left parties termed it as 'fraudulent'. In spite of the national outrage when the Planning Commission had given its earlier estimates to the Supreme Court, it has retained the same poverty measure suggested by the Tendulkar Committee. This has meant an absurdly low national poverty line of Rs. 22.40 per day for an adult in rural areas and Rs. 28.65 per day for an adult in urban areas, in 2009-10. Anyone spending more than this is being categorized as non-poor. "On the basis of these flawed figures, the Planning Commission claims that the proportion of BPL persons has gone down by 7 per cent between 2004-05 to 2009-10."[15]

"This shows the huge gap between the members of the Planning Commission and the reality lived by crores of people in this country who have been burdened by relentless price rise amidst meagre incomes. It hardly needs to be stated that these are destitution lines and it is a shame that an institution chaired by the Prime Minister should produce such absurd figures. What is shocking is that even with these gross under-estimates, large sections of our population are shown to continue living in destitution. The proportion ranges from 37-39% in states like Uttar Pradesh, Jharkhand, Madhya Pradesh and Odisha to around 50% in Bihar and Chhattisgarh. Shockingly, the North Eastern states of Assam, Manipur and Nagaland are showing an increase in destitution levels. This calls the bluff of 'inclusive growth' under the UPA government."[16] Subsequently, weavers started experiencing extension of working hours to equalise the low payment. Table 42 presents the increase of work hours input of a weavers in the production process.

Table 42: Working Hour of weavers in Banaras

Working Hour	*% of total respondent*	*Total person*
8-10	12	35
10-12	26	79
12-above	**62**	**186**
Total	100	300

Source: Fieldwork in Banaras in 2010.

186 persons i.e. 62 per cent of the total respondents work for 12 hours and more in a day, which leaves them with little time for amusement and leisure. Earlier, they would go for '*shair*' (picnic) at the local spot with their families, but today the game of survival has eliminated the personal space of a labourer. Weavers, whom this researcher met in course of visits to Bajardiha, Lallahpura and Bhaghwa Nala, work on the looms for more than 12 hours a day. During the marriage season when the demand for Banarasi saris increases, the weavers have to work for long hours. Even prior to Eid festivals when weavers need money, most of the weavers toil for almost 16 hours a day. Weavers toil hard, starting their work at 8.00 a.m. till 6.00 p.m. at a stretch spanning 10 to 12 days but earn a miniscule Rs. 350 on a sari. The increasing pressure on weavers has pushed them towards malnutrition death and the extreme step of suicide. Table 43 gives the details of death of weavers who died of hunger and committed suicide due to economic hardship.

Table 43: List of dead weavers in Banaras (January 2003 to March 2007)

Sr. No.	*Name*	*Age*	*Place*	*Date*	*Reason*
1.	Shivsatti	-	Chhahi,	03-01-2003	Suicide
2.	Jaychand Mauyra	20	,,	03-08-03	,,
3.	Sabnam	6	,,	,,	,,
4.	Malti		,,	,,	,,
5.	Nuruddin	-	Saraiya	23-06-03	Hunger
6.	Daddan	-	Gorai Gaon	16-08-03	,,
7.	Dharmaraj	-	Mirzapur	27-09-03	,,
8.	Rekha	-	,,	,,	,,
9.	Bachchi	-	,,	,,	,,
10.	Kaushar Jahan	-	Bajardiha	27-03-04	Suicide
11.	Jamil	20	Jaitpura	31-03-04	Hunger
12.	R. Patel	22	Rohaniya	21-06-04	,,
13.	T. Ahmad	-	Koniya	01-08-04	,,
14.	Shira	12	Sevapuri	Aug. 04	,,
15.	Razia	20	Bajardiha	09-08-04	,,
16.	Badruddin	-	Kauvapur	15-08-04	Suicide
17.	Raju	13	Phoolpur	26-09-04	Hunger
18.	Moni	7	,,	,,	,,
19.	B. Hasmi	55	Harhua	01-10-04	,,
20.	Parvati	-	Tophapur	11-10-05	Suicide
21.	Parvati's daughter	6	,,	,,	,,
22.	Parvati's Son	7 month	,,	,,	Hunger
23.	Chhendi	-	Sevapuri	28-03-06	Hunger
24.	Fulchand	50	Belwa	18-06-06	,,
25.	Durgawati	-	Sevapuri	12-02-05	,,
26.	Teras Nath	28	Sobrana	12-08-06	Debt
27.	Jiutram	-	Changwar	02-02-06	Debt
28	Md. Iqbal	45	Bakrabad	Aug. 04	Malnutition
29.	Nuruddin	-	Jaitpura	18-10-04	Unpaid wage
30.	Kaju	16	Changwar	27-10-06	,,
31.	Ibrahim	-	Saraiya	13-08-04	Hunger
32.	Gulijar	30	Bajardiha	20-05-04	Financial Problem (FP)
33.	Md. Ikram	45	Lohta	Aug. 04	Hunger
34.	Rukhsana	24	Bajardiha	20-05-04	FP
35.	Jiwata	28	Adampura	July 04	FP
36.	Tara	-	Sarnath	June 04	FP
37	Ramesh Maurya	42	Lohta	26-02-05	FP
38.	R. Prajapati	30	Chandpur	16-03-05	FP
39.	Usha Devi	30	Pindra	21-04-05	FP
40.	R. J. Ansari	40	Jagjiwanpura	24-04-05	FP

(*Contd...*)

41.	Rita	26	J. Belauri	15-05-05	FP
42.	Surekha	-	J. Naraicha	14-05-05	FP
43.	G. Rajbhar	-	Sarnath	07-06-05	FP
44.	U. Devi	26	Barani	13-05-06	FP
45.	Surekha W/o Babalu	22	Naraicha	14-05-06	FP
46.	Farid	35	Lallapura	09-06-06	FP
47.	Neeraj	-		12-06-07	Suicide
48.	Md. Islam	38	Lohta	03-11-06	FB
49.	Lalman		Bhatauli	7-08-04	Hunger
50.	Bansu	-	Sarnath	June 2007	Hunger

Source: Lenin Raghuvanshi, *Suicide and Malnutrition amongst Weavers in Varanasi*, PVCHR, 2009, p. 14. List provided by CPM Secretary of Varanasi.

On May 9, 2013 two children in Bajardiha died of hunger and continuous malnutrition. Though the medical report describes it as death due to tuberculosis, the health officials admit that the tuberculosis directly related to poverty. "Tuberculosis and poverty are two sides of the same coin," chief medical officer MP Chaurasia said. "The abject poverty of the people and pathetic living condition in the locality really moved us," the CMO added. Medically, the children died of tuberculosis but the family's financial condition could not be overlooked. Attempts to suicide have been recorded in 2012. Wasim Ahmad, 20, resident of Lallapur (Sigra) tried to kill himself due to economic hardship.[17] He was living a life of distress after separation from his family. Earlier he was weaving on his own handloom but problems pushed him to be a wage earner in the powerloom sector.

However, it is not easy to rely on the statistics of suicide death. Even Durkheim was not fond of the quantitative method employed to record suicides. He found that "recording of motives is done by untrained enumerators in offices of vital statistics, as well as that the motives ascribed by suicides to their acts are unreliable."[18] But a more trenchant view of suicide statistics is presented by psychoanalysts like Gregory Zilboorg. "Statistical data on suicide as they are compiled today deserve little if any credence; it has been repeatedly pointed out by the scientific students of the problem that suicide cannot be subject to statistical evaluation, since all too many suicides are not reported as such. Those who kill themselves through automobile accidents are almost never recorded as suicides; a great many genuine suicides are concealed by families; and suicidal attempts, no matter how serious, never find their way into the tables of vital statistics. It is obvious that under these circumstances the statistical data available cover the smallest and probably the least representative number of suicides; one is justified, therefore, in discarding them as nearly useless in a scientific evaluation of the problem."[19] The factoring in of religions such as Islam, which do not permit suicides, complicates the scenario. Islam argues that "Do not take life, which Allah made sacred, other than in the course of justice" Quran (17:33). Further, Quran speaks that Allah decides how long each of us will live. "When their time comes they cannot delay it for a single hour nor can they bring it forward by a single hour" (Quran -16:61) and "Do not destroy yourselves. Surely Allah is ever merciful to you" Quran (4:29). But against the ideal of Islam, Muslims weavers in real life have been victim to socio-economic conditions, quite similar to the farmers of Vidharbha. The tendency of Muslims and other social groups from around the world to commit suicide in violation of religious doctrine has been termed as "symptom of secularisation" by Dominique Avon.[20]

Those who are surviving in these adverse conditions are prone to many diseases such as tuberculosis (TB) resulting in slow death. In a case recorded on May 9 2013, an entire family of six were afflicted by TB, and while the father died ten months earlier, the mother and her five children suffered from severe malnutrition and tuberculosis. Eventually, the family lost two of its younger members - a son and a daughter, leading to the pertinent question, 'Is India fit for its Children?.'[21] The prevalence of TB cases in weaver-dominated areas is very high. For instance, in Lohta 35-50 suspected TB patients go to the centre every day for the sputum test and out of them 10-15 are found positive for TB.[22] Most of the TB patients come from poor handloom weavers' families, who find it difficult to maintain daily food. Besides, non-hygienic living condition and insufficient healthcare facilities increase the possibility of spreading the infection. According to the reports of the chief medical officer (CMO) (dated July 21, 2009) sent to the DG, Health Services, as many as 101 TB patients were put under Directly Observed Treatment Short-Course (DOTS) from January to June in the Lohta area while the number of new patients during this period was 66. According to the report of PVCHR and Asian Human Rights Commission (AHRC) prepared in 2008 "weavers are suffering from high level of tuberculosis, particularly Multi Drug Resistance Tuberculosis (MDTRB), which can be induced from exposure to silk and cotton fibres."

Table 44: AHRC/PVCHR Weaver Tuberculosis Study and Consultation (2008)[23]

Month	*Patients Diagnosed*	*With TB*	*Female*	*Male*
March	20	20	7	13
April	20	10	7	3
June	14	14	4	10
July	16	16	6	9
August	16	16	7	10
Total	**86**	**67**	**31**	**36**

Source: Source: Dr. Lenin Raghuvanshi, *Suicide and Malnutrition amongst Weavers in Varanasi*, PVCHR, 2009, p. 7.

The plight of the life of the weavers' families underlines government neglect, exploitation and starvation. The deteriorating health of weavers has not only affected them, but has made the industry sick as well. It would be an illusion to think of weavers spending on basic healthcare services when their livelihood is threatened and they are striving hard to arrange for the days' meal. The lack of food and infections with diseases are threatening their livelihood while the State-sponsored public health services are not reaching them. "Fifty percent of children in weaver families, even in Lallahpura are malnutritioned. In blatant violation of Supreme Court orders, a number of children can be seen to survive on a mere bowl or two of plain rice and some bread. Sometimes they get nothing at all,"[24] said Gufran. Ahmed Mohammad Aslam added, "Under such circumstances, education is a distant dream. What do you expect a weaver to do with such a meagre earning of Rs 35-40 per day? Buy medicines, food or send his children to school," asked Gufran.

The weavers in the study area are prone to several chronic diseases which are consequent upon malnutrition and lack of money to access healthcare services. The failure of government policies related to public health services is taking their lives away. The weavers' family is facing extreme poverty and suffering from disease since their income is not enough to fetch daily food and proper treatment. Moreover, they do not receive any benefits from the government and are the victims of widespread corruption rampant in the system. The relatively heavy work for handloom weaving requires the weavers to spend hours in a weaving pit with the weaving machine. Given the physical condition of a starving weaver and the presence of the infectious elements in the surroundings, poor health services create the most congenial environment for the illness to spread vigorously in the community. They have no choice but to approach the primary health centers due to their poverty, where they do not get proper treatment due to the neglect of the doctors and staff, insufficient medical supplies, facilities and corruption.[25]

Cases of malnutrition and starvation clearly indicate the complete failure of public food distribution system and relevant government agencies. Since the government adopted the exclusionary approach through Targeted Public Distribution System (TPDS) in 1997, most of the weavers are out of the social safety network. Earlier, it was not the case with functioning of PDS around the country. Abraham Koshy argued that "The public distribution system (PDS) in India, with a network of more than 3.3 lakh fair price shops, covers over 90 per cent of the country's population. In addition to essential commodities such as sugar, edible oil and kerosene, nearly 18 million tonnes of foodgrains, which constitutes nearly 15 per cent of the net food production in the country, are made available to the beneficiary population at subsidized prices through the fair price shops. The quantum of subsidy involved is also large; in 1986-87, the food subsidy was estimated to be in the region of Rs 2,060 crore. However, since the PDS has been set up to act as a buffer against price increase, shortages and non-availability of essential commodities, its benefits are expected to accrue more to the vulnerable sections of the society."[26]

However, the current debate regarding replacement of TPDS with cash-transfers is very problematic. In India the idea was first argued in the Government's Economic Survey (ES) for 2010-11, and the Finance Minister made an explicit announcement in his budget speech for replacing some subsidies on goods with cash transfers. Many scholars like Arvind Subramanian joined Devesh Kapur and Partha Mukhopadhyay (KMS) to argue that since current annual allocations for Centrally Sponsored Schemes with food, fertilizer and fuel subsidies, add up to a figure of nearly Rs. 2,00,000 crore, why not transfer Rs. 1 crore to each village. The proposal sounds reasonable, but its actual implementation could be dangerous for the masses. It is important to take a critical view of this proposal. Some of the problems of direct cash transfers are given below:

(a) Cash transfers cannot and should not replace the public provision of essential goods and services, but rather supplement them. For instance, providing small amounts of cash to allow people to visit local private quacks will hardly compensate for the absence of a reasonably well-funded public health system that provides access to preventive and curative services.

(b) In the period of such a price steep rise in essential commodity cash transfers are less effective.

(c) Further, government shows complete failure in understanding the rural complex lifestyle where most of the time villagers are under debt provided by local moneylenders on high interest rate. Lenders in the nexus with bank manager will try to grab the money meant for the family.

(d) This society is a patriarchal in nature. Men control the economy. So if men are addicts or less responsible towards his family, he can waste money and members depending on him go hungry.

These general problems also afflict the weavers' community of Banaras. Apart from these, weavers face corruption in day to day delivery of items. Right from the distribution of yellow, red and white cards and the distribution of food items, the system is totally corrupt.[27] Bribes are so common in practice that it makes the life of the pity weavers miserable. Weavers are out of reach of PDS shops and at the mercy of contract holders. It can be said that poor weavers are sandwiched between utter poverty, corruption and malpractices of system.

About 60 per cent weavers have abandoned their traditional occupation. Either they have migrated to cities in search of livelihoods as unskilled labourers or have become rickshaw pullers or brick-kiln workers in and around the city. A few shocking instances of hunger deaths, selling blood and even selling their off-springs in highly distressed circumstances have also been reported by the media in recent times. "The driver of our vehicle for the field visit introduced himself to us: 'My condition is as bad as this car', said the driver referring to the vehicle hired to travel to few villages and talk to weavers to hear the story from the horses' mouth. He surprised us when he added, 'I was a weaver myself about seven years ago. There were three handlooms running in our house then and we were doing well. It was about 10-12 years ago when the bad luck hit us. Our *Banarasi* handloom saris stock would remain piled up in traders' store for a long time. We were told that people did no longer want to buy the *Banarasi* handloom saris as they are very expensive'. It was shocking to know when Rajan, 37, the driver lamented in emotionally choked voice, 'My village had more than 600 weavers 10 years ago. Today, there are just about 10 or 12 of them existing somehow. The handlooms are lying idle and abandoned only to be heaped and crumbled one day under the load of dust and rust.'[28]

"Another instance is Akhtar (40), a resident of the weaver-dominated Lohta locality of Varanasi. He was once the proud owner of eight handlooms, weaving Banarasi saris. Now a rickshaw-puller, Akhtar hopes of bringing back smiles to his family. Akhtar was among the twenty-one weavers of Lohta-Kotwa area who were given new cycle-rickshaws by a Guwahati-based NGO, Centre for Rural Development (CRD), under the Rickshaw Bank Project funded by the Punjab National Bank (PNB)."[29] "Fifteen years ago, I owned eight handlooms and even employed workers. However, the slump in *Banarasi* sari market has forced me to a pull a rickshaw to feed my family," he said. "Through the project, I will be the owner of a rickshaw after just 450 days. Till now, I have been hiring a rickshaw for Rs 25 daily," he added.[30] According to Mohammad Taha, a teacher and resident of Rewari Talab, slump in handloom silk industry has pushed many weavers to powerloom sector as labourers, and also into the criminal activities. In fact, a number of respondents believe that there has been increase in some anti-social activities in the past few years. 52 per cent respondents nodded affirmatively when asked about the rise in criminal activities around the neighborhood. They also argued that it was a recent phenomenon as the environment was not as such earlier and that there was many a drop-out from school due to slump in the income of weavers.

Table 45: Criminal Activities in Banaras

Nature of criminal activities	*Number of Respondents feel the rise in criminal activities*
Snatching	15
Burglary	109
Others (selling blood, prostitution, drugs etc.)	31
No criminal activities	145
Total	**300**

Source: Field work in Banaras in 2010.

Before the analysis of education among weavers of Banaras, a succinct discussion is needed regarding the background of weavers' education levels, both at the national and state levels. Amit Basole has focused on education of weavers at the all-India level. He found out that "The vast majority (97.6 per cent) of weavers report having no formal technical education or vocational training (Government of India, 2006)." Here, one important consideration is that access to formal technical institutions is conditioned on completion of high school, a fact clearly underlined by the NSS data which shows that only those who have completed some form of college education report also having received formal vocational training. One might think that this lack of formal training is not surprising given that handloom weaving is still a profession dominated by hereditary apprenticeship methods. However it is significant that this fact includes powerloom weavers too. And though we are not able to separate powerloom from handloom weavers, since the survey did not collect this information, we know that they constitute a significant proportion of the weaving population. If formal training was important in the powerloom sector it would show up in the aggregate data. The fact that over 97 per cent weavers are not formally trained suggests that non-formal methods of training are predominant in both sectors.

As noted above, vocational training has been defined very broadly here to include traditional apprenticeship methods and on-the-job training. It is surprising then that only 27.2 per cent report having received hereditary or other non-formal training, while 72 per cent report having no form of vocational training at all, despite the broad definition of what constitutes such training. Uttar Pradesh still lags behind the national average with respect to education (64.8 per cent). Literacy rates differ widely between rural and urban areas and between males and females. "Thus, literacy rate in rural areas in 2001 was only 53.6 per cent as compared to the literacy rate of 70.8 per cent in urban areas. The male literacy in UP is 68.8 per cent and female literacy 42.2 per cent. The corresponding figures at the national level are 75.3 per cent and 53.7 per cent respectively."[31] Before interventions by the State could reach the least advantaged population, economic reform was implemented by the government. Privatisation of everything including education became inevitable after the State's retreat from social sectors. Banaras could not remain untouched by such development. The education system, which till now was socially stratified, also became highly privatised.

Table 46: Range of Monthly fees in Varanasi's Elementary Schools

Fee Range	*Govt. Schools*	*Low-fee Private School*	*Medium-fee Private School*	*Elite Private School*
Fee Range (INR)	0	50-150	150-1300	1300-2460
Fee Range CAD)	0	1.07-3.21	3.21-27.84	27.84-52.68

Source: Emily Christine Antze's 'They should stand on their own feet', 2011, p. 54.

Antze noted that "discovering that wealthy, middle-class and poor children all received such dramatically different kinds of education, I wondered to what extent meaningful social mobility was possible through education, given that the kind of education available to children in Varanasi seemed to promote social stratification rather than equality. I also wondered to what extent the low-income parents sending their children to school in this inequitable system were aware of this tension and whether it influenced them in the process of choosing a school and planning for education for their children."[32] In these circumstances, weavers started community funded madarasas in the neighbourhood in order to impart education to their wards. Banaras has two types of madrasas: exclusively for girls and another for boys. Madrasas uphold the Islamic principle of separating the two sexes in public life. Nevertheless, they have played a role, especially in girls' education.

With time, weavers realised the importance of modern education. Initially, only few madrasas accepted the new method and syllabus, and their numbers increased substantially with the realisation of importance of modern education. Today, most of the madrasas teach English, Maths, Science, Social Sciences and vocational training courses along with imparting religious education. There have also been efforts from non-governmental organisations in the field of education. PVCHR and Human Welfare Association (HWA) are such an organizations working around Varanasi focusing on out of school child laborers, particularly from the hard to reach communities facing exclusion in primary schools. HWA initiated a Project Promoting Elementary Schooling (PES) in Eastern Uttar Pradesh from July 2005 with the support of Dachser, Germany, Terra des Homes, Germany. The project is aimed at the children from the *julaha* Muslim (minority) communities.

Lohta had five registered madrasas. These madrasas attract more than 2500 children. One amongst them, 'Madarasa Faizul-Uloom' alone attracts more than 1500 children up to middle school. These madrasas have almost 60 per cent of children from the Muslim *julaha* or weaving community. The Muslim community is also reluctant to send its daughters to schools far away and prefer those located within the village. The Human Welfare Association recognized this and initiated Education Centres, upgrading the facilities and offering vocational training and scholarships. It sought to inspire parents and draw the girls out of their homes in order to expose them to modern education, albeit within the four walls of the Madrasas. 'The idea is not to disrupt the comfort level of the parents. They feel a strong sense of security for their daughters with limited mobility in the precincts of the immediate neighbourhood' comments Dr Rajnikant.

The HWA together with UNICEF and Panchayati Raj Department of the State of UP provided a package of services to draw the Muslim girls to the madarasas and to synchronise the school syllabus with the one followed by the government run and assisted schools. The madrasas were earlier teaching only Urdu and Arabic. They introduced basic education curriculum of the State which includes subjects like Maths, Science, English and Social sciences. Teachers and management of the madrasas were trained by subject- matter specialists to focus on teaching techniques, quality and on management of educational institutions. The management of the madrasas were encouraged to register as 'educational institutions' so that they could become entitled to receive aid from the State.

Other programmes included the 'School Hygiene and Sanitation Programme' providing toilet and urinal facilities in the madarasas along with training of the teachers and management committee. Construction of toilet facilities has resulted in an increase of 20 per cent in school attendance by girls of the Muslim community. They also promoted a child rights forum to promote school sanitation and hygiene education. The organization also started vocational training in hand embroidery, tailoring, cutting, stitching, painting, *Zari/Zardozi, mehndi* courses, craft making and beautician training for adolescent girls in the madrasas. This was done to attract girls in the age group of 14-18 years to the school, and also to leverage the interest of the girls in the age group of 6-14 years, who would eventually benefit from these courses. Parents were also interested in these vocational programmes being offered in the madrasas as the dwindling income from the traditional work of Benarasi saris was not enough to provide some measure of food security to the family.

So far, 300 girls have been provided with scholarships of 500 INR or $ 11 per month for attending 6-10th grades. This has been achieved with the support of the Rajiv Gandhi Foundation, in partnership with the Sri Sivasubramniya Nadar Educational and Charitable Trust founded by Shiv Nadar, Chairman, Hindustan Computers Limited (HCL) Technologies as his private initiative. These are called 'Vidya Gyan Scholarships' for Muslim and Dalit girls in three districts of Uttar Pradesh. HWA is responsible for the implementation of the Scholarship Programme in Lohata area of Varanasi district. All these girls are being helped separately with additional tutoring to improve upon their English, Maths and Science skills so that they can improve their achievement levels. They have additionally provided resources for 110 girls to receive computer education for a period of one year. They have also started a community library to facilitate and improve the reading skills of the girls in the Madrasas."[33]

However, the financial crisis in the handloom industry of Banaras causes early drop-out of students. While interviewing the male head of the family, this research found that due to the economic reasons, most of the parents have stopped sending their children to school, or even to the madarsa. Table 47 below illustrates that 59.37 per cent respondents have cited economy as the reason for dropping out of students. However, the finding that surprises is that 14.84 per cent feel education to be of little use for their children, as they would eventually have to join the weaving profession.

Table 47: Reasons for Drop-out in Banaras

Reasons for de-schooling of children	*Number of Respondents*
Economic	178
No Use of education	45
Marriage	77
Total	**300**

Source: Field work in Banaras in 2010.

Though the enrolment of children of weaver families in elementary education is comparable to the enrolment for Muslims across the country, their dropout rate from primary to upper primary is very high. Mahfooz Alam, a weavers' leader, concurs that the financial condition of weaver families has worsened and they also started keeping their children away from schools. Testifying to the problem of dropping out due to the financial crisis, weaver Salim argued that "affording the fee of even Rs 5-10 for the local madarsas was difficult for the weavers. Locals estimated that youth who had received education up to junior high school would be less than one per cent in the population of about one lakh."[34] Apart from the economic issues, these madarasas are afflicted by intra-community sectarian politics, which really lessens the ambit of educational coverage, as a Muslim student of one sect does not attend madrasas of another sect. The list of schools belonging to various sects in one particular area is given below:

Table 48: List of Schools/Madrasa in Banaras

Sr. No.	*Name of School*	*Sect*	*Places*
1.	Jamia Hamidia Rizvia	Barelwi	Hatiya Madanpura
2.	Jamia Hamidia Rizvia (Niswan)	,,	Pandey Hata
3.	Hamidia Rizvia Higher S. School	,,	Hatiya Madanpura
4.	Hamidia Rizvia Girls inter college	,,	Pandey Haveli
5.	Madarasa Jamia Faruquia	,,	Rewari Talab

(Contd...)

6.	Faruqi Girls Highschool	,,	Pandey Haveli
7.	Jamia Zinatul Islam	,,	Rewari Talab
8.	Zinatul Islam Girls High School	,,	Rewari Talab
9.	Al-Falah Convent School	Sunni	Rewari Talab
10.	Madrasa Mohammadiya Ahl-e-Sunnat	Ashrafi	Madanpura
11.	Madrasa Hifazatul Iman	Shia	Rewari Talab
12.	Jamia Islamia	Deobandi	Madanpura
13.	Jamia Islamia (Niswan) Madarasatulbanat	Deobandi	Madanpura
14.	Jamia Islamia (Arabiya)	Deobandi	Rewari Talab
15.	Jamia Islamia	Deobandi	Ansar Nagar
16.	Jamia Islamia	Deobandi	Asfaq Nagar
17.	Qudratullah Gulzar-e-Taleem (Nursury and Girl) ,,	Deobandi	Rewari Talab
18.	Jamia Salfiah (Markazi Darululum)	Ahl-e-Hadith	Rewari Talab
19.	Ummahtul Momineen Girls inter college	Ahl-e-Hadith	Pandey Haveli
20.	Ummahtul Momineen Nursery School	Ahl-e-Hadith	Pandey Haveli

Source: Fieldwork in Banaras in 2009.

While speaking at a public hearing organised in 2008 in Banaras city, weavers from four districts including Varanasi, Mirzapur, Bhadohi and Chandauli discussed the causes and possible remedies of the current crisis of silk handloom weavers of Varanasi. This public hearing was organised by HWA. Amresh Kushwaha said that rise in the price of silk yarn as well as fluctuations in its price have proved harmful for weavers. As a remedial step, a scheme to step up yarn banks has been started. A scheme to providing handloom mark has also been started.

"Razizaan Ali, who spoke next also supported these two steps, said that in addition there should be greater opportunities for weavers to sell their products directly. There should be more emporiums where their product is sold and the government should step up the efforts to promote handlooms."[35] Aminuddin of Nakhighat challenged this view of the traditional working system by saying that the real weaver, the real artisan is exploited in this system. If something is given by one hand, it is snatched by another hand. Rates given to weavers are very low and they can't survive on this. The reality is that most government funds also reach only those who are already rich and prosperous. He said committees and delegations do not even bother to meet the poor weavers who are the real sufferers of the crisis. "Please meet them and know their problems", he implored.

Vibhuti Shankar, development activist from Mirzapur district, said that at the time of a crisis situation for weavers Central Silk Board is running away from its responsibilities. It is beyond comprehension why the market has been opened so blatantly for Chinese imports while Indian weavers' livelihoods are destroyed. Hazi Nasir Ahmed said that earlier weaving was an important pillar of Banaras economy but now it is in a bad state.[36] The work of carpets in neighbouring areas has also deteriorated. Problems relating to electricity availability and bills as well as silk yarn should be solved on priority basis. Nurul Hassan Ansari asked why UP Handloom is not promoting the products of weavers now. He said weavers have suffered due to unjust policies and neglect.[37]

Jagriti, a Gandhian activist emphasised the importance of self-reliance and Mahatma Gandhi's thinking on khadi and handloom for the survival of handloom weaving. Unity of the community and Hindu-Muslim unity is also very important, she said. She said children from weavers' families who come to an educational centre run by them said that they eat only one meal in a day, at other times when they are hungry they just drink some water. Mohammad Sharif Ansari said that 47 suicides of weavers have been reported here, but the real weaver is still being ignored while the rich persons who dominate their work and its export are cornering all the benefits. He said that some so-called experts and visiting senior officials do not even understand who the real weaver is. They meet traders and exporters in the name of meeting weavers and only listen to the views and opinions articulated by traders and exporters. He said that just as in agriculture there are traders; landlords and actual farmers (cultivators), similarly in weaving there are *gaddidars, grihastas* (master-weavers) and actual weavers. He said that existing co-operatives should be dissolved as now most of these are not serving the intended purpose of extending benefits and facilities to real weavers. New co-operatives should be opened to take the benefits to real weavers while avoiding serious mistakes made earlier.

Yanim Mobaddin Ansari of Bunkar Kalyan Parishad said that British rule had inflicted the worst injustice on weavers, and subsequently weavers made a very important contribution to the freedom movement. He also said that existing co-operatives should be dissolved. The government should also provide direct relief by waiving loans taken by weavers. Riyazul Hasan Ansari said that remedial steps which benefit the entire sector should be emphasised. Better quality and stable colours should be available. Training to prepare products more in demand should be provided. Relief from fluctuations of yarn price should be provided by giving agencies for silk yarn to members of weavers' community. A minimum support price for products should be ensured by the government. Razia Begum, BDC member from Lohta village said women make an important contribution to weaving work.[38] She said that till some years ago, weavers could do their work in a satisfactory way.

But now the situation has deteriorated to such an extent that after he completes a new sari the weaver cannot be sure whether he'll be able to get some minimum price to support his family and to start work on the next sari. This is why weavers are leaving this work and women too are taking up other work like that of beads. She emphasised the need for girls' education to open up more opportunities for them. Iqbal Bhai of Kotuwaan emphasised the need of loan waivers for handloom weavers. "Ainul Haq used to be a handloom weaver who became seriously ill. He came with his small children to the public hearing to tell the story of how in the absence of social security weavers and their families have to suffer greatly when illness disrupts their life. For instance, when grants were approved by the government for his treatment following media reports of his serious illness, formalities like doctor preparing estimates of the approximate expenditure of his treatment could not be completed."[39]

The women like Zarina, the widow of a weaver in Bajardihan in Varanasi, have been worried about the survival of her children. "If we wake up at 6 am and work the whole day we earn only Rs 10. With the Rs 10 I earn I get half a kilo atta and I make chutney and make them sleep," says Zarina. "When they cry out of hunger, I keep them quiet by telling them that I too will leave you like your father."[40] After his father died last year, 12 year old Wakil in Katuadihan near Lohta started working as a helper for Rs 10 a day. His mother Nasirun also earns Rs 10 a day from her work on finishing woven saris. Her seven children survive on food they beg from their neighbours. "Every evening I beg for food and feed these children. Tell me what should I do? How should I manage? If I manage, I cook once a day and in the evening we beg food from others,"[41] says Nasirun, the widow of another weaver.

"Uma Shankar (S/o. Shri Kharpattu harijan), a resident of Rasipatti village, used to work as weaver, he had two handlooms, but before two years his handlooms closed due to collapse of sari industry in the era of imperialistic globalization. After this he switched over to rickshaw pulling, but due to lack of food his health has deteriorated thus making the condition more miserable by keeping him away from his daily source of income. This has led to a situation where there is no food for himself and his family."[42] Similar fate met with Raziya and her husband who were once the pride of their village. They owned five looms. Razia and her husband made enough to keep all nine members of his family content. Now, Nurool is suffering from acute anaemia according to doctors. "But we have no money for the treatment," sighs Raziya. They have been out of business for the last 27 months as there are very few takers for the Varanasi silks they wove for a living. Raziya Biwi argued that "My three-year-old son is dying of starvation. My husband lies unconscious beside him. My remaining six children are now beggars. The youngest feeds only on sugar and water as I'm incapable of feeding him." "Over the past two years, she and her husband Nurool Haq have done everything from selling her jewellery and a small plot that they owned; the money is gone now and they are starving."[43] 'Who knows who will die and who will live?' she ponders miserably. In Kotwan village, Ghulam Rasool and Raziya Biwi sold Subhan Ali, their two-month-old son, for Rs. 2,000. "At least I knew the buyer-a distant relative who has the means to look after Subhan. The thought that he could feed him was of some consolation,"[44] she admits. Today with their son back at home, the couple earns from a vegetable shop in the village. "No matter what happens, I'm not going back to becoming a weaver," says Ghulam.[45]

The anecdotes of hardship have been noted by many researchers on the topic. "Weavers living in Bajardiha and other *bastis*, who were at the centre stage of the Banaras silk industry, now face hunger and desperation. Gone are the days when the uniqueness of the creation was appreciated and patronised at a great cost. The weaver was a producer as well as creator of designs. Now the industry in this changed scenario has shifted to producing at large volumes with low quality design at a low cost. With the change in time the buyer's preferences changed. The demand for high valued intricately patterned heavy silk sari, for which Varanasi was famous, declined. Today's fashion is marked by fast change in design, low cost of production and low inventory."[46]

The conditions in Mau in terms of wages, working hours and education are better than in Banaras. In Banaras 95.22 per cent of total respondents fall below the average income of Rs. 2,500 per month i.e. Rs. 83.33 per day. The number of working hours also differs in the two districts. In Banaras 60.90 per cent respondents work for over 12 hours in a day, whereas in Mau weavers spend average of 7-8 hours in a day though this depends on the supply of electricity. The decent income also acts as push factor for the spending on education by the weavers of Mau. In Banaras, total Muslim literacy is 54.4 per cent with 44.9 per cent literacy among the women.[47] In contrast, the quality education infrastructure in Mau city is a result of private initiatives.

Those weavers that continued within the handloom segment due to the lack of capital have been hard hit by diminishing government subsidies and closure of mills in the aftermath of liberlisation. This resulted in the total control of businessmen over the required raw materials, as they began to charge high prices. This increased the input cost of a product and lessened the income of weavers.

Table 49: Wages of Mau's Weavers

Income Group	*Total No. of Respondents*	*Percentage*
< 2,500	0	0
2,501 – 5,000	60	20
5,001 – 7,500	120	40
7,501 – 10,000	105	35
Above 10,000	15	5
Total	**300**	**100**

Source: Fieldwork in Mau in 2010.

This has forced Mau handloom weavers as well to commit suicide. In January, 2010, Mahmud Alam, 25, committed suicide. In the coming months 6 more handloom weavers killed themselves. The problem has affected not only the handloom segment of the weaving community, but also the powerloom workers. These days the sari trade of Mau is passing through economic slump and hard competition. The saris of Surat have started giving tough competition to Mau saris. As compared to the latter, the former is of better quality and available at cheaper rate. As a result the saris of Surat have started replacing the saris of Mau in the markets of Mau and the adjoining areas where Mau saris earlier had monopoly. Further, "Mau's powerloom industry is now facing the challenges of Chinese Machines that are entering into this trade. This machine is used for embroidery which was earlier done manually and the cost of a Chinese machine is around 15 lakh. Due to this machine, the number of employable workers has drastically reduced. At the same time, it has presented a crisis of existence before small traders. Although the number of these machines is very small at the moment, they may lead to a great crisis in the future. Presently there are about 25 such machines in Mau."[48]

Apart from this common problem across the country, Mau and Banaras have similarity in one sense: both are clouded by a communal atmosphere, perhaps as a result of Muslim domination in these places. While economic hardship compounded by maladministration has provided the conditions for nurturing communalism in Mau, the media and warring factions of right wing political parties have been vying for dominance.[49]

Table 50: Distribution of Looms according to using Cotton, Silk, and Wool (in thousands)[50]

State	*Cotton*	*Silk*	*Wool*	*Total*
UP	145.1 (4.92 %)	66.5 (13.80 %)	11.1 (2.56 %)	222.7 (5.77 %)
AP	166.4 (5.65 %)	282.7 (5.87 %)	145.5 (33.62 %)	594.5 (15.40 %)
Tamilnadu	288.4 (9.79 %)	59.9 (12.43 %)	0.5 (0.11 %)	348.8 (9.03 %)
Karnataka	46.1 (1.56 %)	13.1 (2.72 %)	126.7 (29.26%)	185.9 (4.18%)

Source: Sabrang, 2005.

* Figure in bracket referred to the percentage share of loom in total yarn-wise loom in India.

However, unlike in Mau, suicide due to distress is not a new phenomenon in the handloom sector in Andhra Pradesh. As early as 1991, Andhra Pradesh recorded the suicide of weavers and their family members. According to Asha Krishnakumkar's analysis of powerloom and handloom sectors of various places in Andhra Pradesh 'In Dubakka – a handloom centre in Andhra Pradesh – the slide began in 1985 when powerlooms began to be encouraged by the government. The situation worsened in 1991 after the Centre began to push the liberalization policies vigorously and launched a frenzied export drive, which covered cotton and yarn. The weavers' condition reached its nadir in 1996 when the Andhra Pradesh State Handloom Cooperative Society (APCO) stopped the Janata cloth scheme. The last straw was the virtual collapse of APCO in 1998.'

Traditional powerloom weavers in some places like Sircilla, Karimnagar district of Andhra Pradesh too have been affected badly. Asha Krishnakumar notes that "there are about 60,000 traditional powerlooms in the state. Over 60 per cent of the 40,000 powerlooms in the major centres of Chittoor, karimnagar and Nalgonda districts have been lying idle since 1999. In Sircilla, of the 10,000 powerlooms (the unofficial figure is 12, 000), 2,000 have been abandoned and another 2,000 sold at the scrap value. Only some 6,000 are working and that too at less than 20 per cent of their capacity.[51] This is due to introduction of high productivity Jet looms in powerloom centres like Surat and Bhiwandi. So the fate of weavers depends on the fast changing technology in the textile industry. Powerloom that overtook handloom is now getting destroyed by high productive CEM or Jet looms in the organised sector.

Thus, the worst affected among all are the handloom weavers. Wages for weaving a sari declined from Rs.120 to Rs.80. A weaver who used to earn Rs. 1,800 a month until 1997, hardly earns Rs.640 now, the lowest in 30 years. For instance, "Aleti Anjaneyalu (32) of Dubakka worked for a cooperative society and sometimes for master weavers producing tie-and-dye saris since the age of 15. In 1986-87, he earned Rs.1,000 to Rs.1,200 a month, a good income by his standards. His monthly income in 1997 fell to less than Rs.800. At this time he was paying an interest of Rs.450 on the loans he had taken and a house rent of Rs.200."[52] As the debts and the pressure to repay them mount, weavers go into depression. Some of them resort to suicide. The table 51 present the list of suicide death in the of Guntur and Prakasham districts.

Table 51: Starvation Death list from two districts in Andhra Pradesh

Name/ Guntur District	*Sex*	*Age*	*Village*	*Date*	*Cause*
U. Radhkrishnamurthy	M	45	Gullapalli	Sept. 4	Starvation
V. Raghavamma	F	55	,,	,,	,,
A. Nagamalleswari	F	55	Bhattiprolu	Aug. 30	,,
P. Balakrishna	M	45	,,	Sept. 12	,,
C. Markandeyulu	M	55	Kotharaddypalem	Sept.14	,,
B. Lakshmikantham	F	40	Bhattiprolu	Sept. 19	,,
R. Harichandrudu	M	56	,,	Sept. 23	,,
P.V. Venkamma	F	58	Mangalagiri	Sept. 26	,,
R. Suryanarayana	M	60	,,	Sept. 27	,,
Kota Narayana	M	59	Tenali	Sept. 28	,,
P. Varalakshmi	F	58	Gullapalli	Sept. 17	,,
C. Ramaiah	M	60	Manglagiri	Sept. 28	,,
A.K. Rao	M	60	Illavaram	Sept. 30	,,
R.Setharavumma	F	42	Manglagiri	,,	,,
J. Ramaswami	M	55	,,	Oct. 1	,,
C. Venkateswarlu	M	60	,,	Oct. 6	,,
S. Narayanamma	F	50	,,	Oct. 10	,,
Munagala V.S. Rao	M	46	Bhattiprolu	Oct. 17	,,
K.S.Rao	M	51	Rajole	,,	,,

(*Contd...*)

M. Uppari	M	25	Bhattiprolu	Oct. 18	,,
V. Gurnadham	M	40	Nidubrole	Oct. 20	Suicide
V. Kotaiah	M	55	Manglagiri	Oct. 23	Starvation
Suseela	F	35	,,	,,	,,
A. N. Rao	M	34	Repalle	Oct. 28	,,
P. Ramakottaiah	M	69	Ilavaram	Oct. 27	,,
T. Nagaraju	M	26	Manglagiri	Oct. 30	,,
K.M Rao	M	42	Ilavaram	Oct. 31	,,
Gundega Arlaiah	M	58	Phiranglipuram	Nov. 1	,,
J. Lakshmamma	F	62	Ilavaram	Nov. 2	,,
G. Venkataratham	M	57	Kanagala	Nov. 3	,,
T. Veeranjaneyulu	M	55	Manglagiri	Nov. 7	,,
Prakasam District					
P. Venkateshwarlu	M	50	Ramakrishnapuram	Sept. 5	,,
J. Suryanarayana	M	50	Chirala	Sept. 7	,,
G. Basavaiah	M	50	,,	,,	,,
R. Pothuraju	M	47	Perala	Sept. 16	,,
K. Vishwanatham	M	60	Chirala	Sept. 17	,,
N. Ramanjaneyulu	M	65	Chimakurthy	Sept. 27	,,
B. V. S. Rao	M	45	Chirala	Sept. 22	,,
T. Radha	F	25	Epurupalem	Sept. 24	
G. Venkateshwarlu	M	32	Chirala	Sept. 30	,,
Goli Venkateshwarlu	M	47	Epurupalem	Oct. 1	,,
J. Papaiah	M	55	Valaparla	Oct. 12	,,
V. Bhadramma	F	58	Amadagiripatnam	Oct. 18	,,
K. Ramulu	M	60	Chirala	Oct. 22	,,
K. Lakshminarayana	M	32	Epurupalem	Oct. 24	Suicide
K. Balaiah	M	55	Thotavaripalem	Oct. 23	Starvation
G. V. Rao	M	60	Chirala	Oct. 27	,,
J. Venkateswarlu	M	49	Thotavaripalem	,,	,,
R. Bhadraiah	M	52	Chirala	,,	
S. Pidayya	M	58	Vetapalem	Oct. 31	,,
D. Lakshmirajyam	F	32	Epurupalem	Nov. 5	,,
C. Jayalakshmi	F	55	Epurupalem	Nov. 4	,,
D. Sathibabu	M	20	Devangapuri	Nov. 8	,,
M. Uppari	M	25	Bhattiprolu	Oct. 18	,,
V. Gurnadham	M	40	Nidubrole	Oct. 20	Suicide

Source: Frontline, December 6, 1991, pp. 52.

Many handlooms under household (HH) unit get closed down in Andhra Pradesh.

Table 52: Total number of working and idle looms in Andhra Pradesh

District	*Beginning*				*Present*			
	Active	*Idle*	*Total*	*% Idle*	*Active*	*Idle*	*Total*	*% Idle*
Narayanavanam WCS, Chittoor	1,000	0	1,000	**0**	35	137	172	**79.65**
Kamalapur WCS, Karimnagar	600	600	1,200	**50**	420	190	610	**31.15**
Maripallegudem WCS, Karimnagar	300	0	300	**0**	30	110	140	**78.57**
Choutuppal WCS, Nalgonda	200	0	200	**0**	250	396	646	**61.30**
Kuntlagudem WCS, Nalgonda	60	0	60	**0**	156	78	234	**33.33**
Koyyalagudem WCS, Nalgonda	50	0	50	**0**	400	233	633	**36.81**
Sivaji WCS, Prakasham	210	0	210	**0**	80	976	1,056	**92.42**
Sri Venkateswara WCS, Prakasham	28	0	28	**0**	120	289	409	**70.66**
Abhyudaya WCS, Prakasham	120	35	155	**22.58**	25	140	165	**84.85**
Chirala WCS, Prakasham	NA	NA	NA	**NA**	160	690	850	**81.18**
Sri Uma Maheswara WCS, Vijayanagaram	500	69	569	**12.13**	188	164	352	**46.59**
Payakaraopeta WCS, Visakhapatnam	18	45	63	**71.43**	75	162	237	**68.35**
Sri Sambamoorthi WCS, Visakhapatnam	60	0	60	**0**	150	29	179	**16.20**
Polavaram WCS, Krishna	45	0	45	**0**	208	31	239	**12.97**
Rayvaram WCS, Krishna	NA	NA	NA	**NA**	95	32	127	**25.20**
Sri Ramalingeswara WCS, Krishna	NA	NA	NA	**NA**	20	94	114	**82.46**
Saraswathi WCS, Guntur	340	60	400	**15**	47	92	139	**66.19**
Harijana WCS, Guntur	120	0	120	**0**	80	76	156	**48.72**
Jogipet WCS, Medak	1,000	0	1,000	**0**	150	1,125	1,275	**88.24**
Upparpalli WCS, Kadapa	170	30	200	**15**	70	10	80	**12.50**
Madhavaram WCS, Kadapa	170	0	170	**0**	30	24	54	**44.44**

Source: Economics of Handloom Weaving, EPW, May 24, 2008.

Note: WCS= Weavers' Cooperative Society, NA = Not Available.

There has been migration on large scale as a part of the strategies to avoid the agony of hunger, debt and disrespect. Simanthinee Niranjana has looked at the reasons for the migration while studying four villages around Chirala region.

Table 53: Migrational Status of Weavers in Andhra Pradesh

Native place	*Number*	*Reasons for migration*
Hastinapuram, Chirala	24	-
Peddapuram, East Godavari	01	Closure of co-operative there in late 1970s
Molapalem, near Bapatla	01	Cyclone
Mangalagiri	01	Domestic problems
Narasipatnam, Vizag	01	Stocks destroyed in riot, started afresh
Salem, then, Ongole	01	Low income as peon, domestic troubles
Annavaram, Rajamundhry	01	Cyclone
West Godavari	01	Politics in co-operative – not getting work
Proddatur, Ongole, Tadpatri	01	Low wages there
Nalgonda	01	-not indicated
Palapura, Pandilapalli	01	- ,,
Vetapalem	01	- ,,
Total	**35**	

Source: Niranjana Simathinee, Report on Growth and Prospect of the Handloom Industry, Study Commissioned by Planning Commission, Dastkar Andhra, 2001

Further, there has been a systematic deterioration of living conditions: the weavers of Dubakka, Medak district subsist on painfully low levels of nutrition, and with almost no access to healthcare facilities. Poor nutrition seems to have made them susceptible to various infections. Desperate to provide food and medical attention to the family, the weavers end up taking loans. While reporting about the condition of handloom weavers in Chirala district, M. M. Rao, founder President of Rashtra Chetna Jana Smakhya mention the complexity in the life of weavers there. "It has turned the wage-work equation against the weavers like never before. Says elderly Saraswati Amma of Devangapuri village in Chirala: In our times we were poor, but not as badly crushed as now. We used to make simpler saris but the wages were commensurate. Now my son and daughter-in-law have to strain their eyes for hours weaving these ornate designs to earn just Rs 330 for one sari. The weaving process of each of these heavy-work saris alone takes up two long days, she says, along with spool and weft work of at least two more days.

Malikamma of the same village, whose son Venkat Subbarao committed suicide three years ago, agrees. “When I was young, my husband used to work at the loom while I did the spool-winding and weft work. We could earn enough to bring up four children. But today you can’t earn a living unless the entire family is roped in the work. At least four workers are needed per loom, while earlier two were sufficient.” One of the reasons that led to Subbarao’s suicide, she explains, is that his wife did not know loom work and the family weas unable to sustain itself on his work alone. The extraordinarily long hours of work are taking their toll on weavers’ health. Sulochana suffers from constant headache, eye-strain and body ache. Sivasarada’s father Ranga Rao developed tuberculosis while in his 40s, and the family had to take a loan of Rs 40,000 for treatment. The doctor says I should not work for more than four hours a day, he says. The cases of tuberculosis, asthma, nerve weakness, eye-strain and body ache have risen steeply among the present generation of weavers, and are also manifesting themselves at an early age, Says Sajja Srinivasa Rao, district president of RCJS. “Many women have had to undergo hysterectomy at the age of 35-40. The reason is that we are forced to work for 12 to 14 hours a day.”[53]

Conclusion

Fieldwork and interviews of weavers in Banaras suggests that globalisation is responsible for the marginal difference of income between the loom-less and loom-owning Banaras weaver. However, an important question that arises is this: if the demand for silk saris and other materials were on the decline due to the growing preference for man-made and mixed fabrics, how are economic reform and policies of the WTO responsible for the plight of the Banaras silk industry? First of all, as reported earlier, the reform itself reflected a shift in the ideological position of government from employment to productivity and earning foreign exchange through export. Indian government advocated and very readily agreed on the ATC under WTO. The inborn effect of the agreement was the influx of Indian market with silk yarn at cheaper rates from countries like China. This available material has been used by the powerloom sector to produce cheaper material as compared to handloom products.

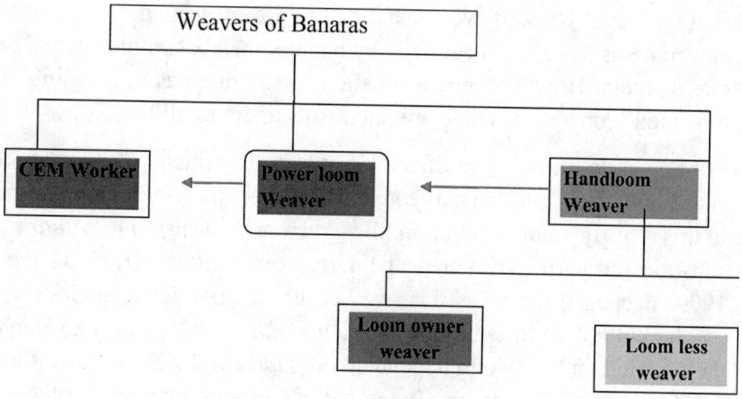

Figure 4: Types of Weavers in Banaras

The product also being good in quality has been preferable to customers. According to one estimate, Chinese silk fabric exports to India grew by a whopping 6500 per cent in 5 years (2001 – 2005) 1.5 million meters in 2000-01 to 91 million meters in 2004-05.[54] A.K.Shukla, Deputy Director, Weaver Service Centre, argued that the Banaras silk handloom was destroyed by the cheaper powerloom product from Surat, Ahmedabad, Bangalore and other places. In addition to that, with the onset of globalisation in India, the government introduced different duty taxes on the finished product and raw materials, which also doomed the market for handloom. For instance, the duty on finished products is only 10 per cent against 25-30 per cent duty on the raw materials, which automatically increases the input cost for producing handloom goods.

"The craft is now dying primarily because of the sale of fake Banarasi saris made in power looms and also because of the sale of cheap imports' as per Dr Rajni Kant working with the community. 'There wages and net income have declined. In absolute terms, it is now half of what it was five years ago. Payments to weavers are often not made immediately and given through a postdated check. Most of the weavers are now wageworkers, working for a master weaver or a trader and are totally cut-off from the market. The design function has also gone from their hands to the master weavers or local designers employed by the traders. The import of silk fabric has increased during the last decade, which has adversely impacted the industry'.[55] Today, in Banaras, most of the powerloom sector uses this cheaper material imported from China, Taiwan and other countries. The powerloom and Computer Embroidery Machine (CEM) copy the exact design of a Banarasi handloom sari and sell it under the tag of original

Banarasi sari. Now, if we looked at the government policy, it restricts eleven items to be produced only by handloom, silk sari of Banaras being one of them. However, open violation of the rule has been going on as informed 'corrupt' officials are silent spectators to all these.

Secondly, the closure of the Kanpur mills, which was the source of yarn for Banaras' weavers, affected the prospect for handloom in this area. In this already volatile situation, the government decision to withdraw the subsidies on yarn by 2 per cent for five consecutive periods in the late 1990s deepened the crisis further. Weavers did not get subsidies on yarn and had to buy at inflated rates from *gadiddars* or traders. This depleted their capital and left them dependent on *gaddidars*, who supplied the raw materials at arbitrary prices. Today, a *gaddidar* or trader decides the prices of both the raw materials and finished product. The weavers have no bargaining power. Once a proud skilled labour, today they work as bondage labourers. Finally, due to the unavailability of the raw materials, weavers themselves turned to synthetic raw materials like nylon for weaving silk saris. However, such tactics used for survival in the weaving business turned against them. The originality that the *Banarasi* sari was once famous for seems to have died along with the innocence of weavers. Thus, opening of the market, which inundated the markets with cheap finished products, along with the insensitive decision of the government to withdraw subsidies from raw materials, on which handloom was dependant, created a condition extremely unfavourable to the Banaras silk handloom and left a deep mark on the *julaha* community.

References

1. Datta and M. Nanavaty, *Global Silk Industry: A Complete Source Book*, APH Publishing Corporation, New Delhi, 2007.
2. Record shows the overall decline in the production of cotton cloth in all the sectors of textile industry. Powerloom share of cotton cloth production declined from 51.96 per cent in 1988-89 to 28.30 per cent 1998-99. Similarly, Mill – organised sector – too experiences the decline in cotton cloth production from 72.36 in 1988-89 to 62.24 per cent in 1998-99. This is due to the increasing demand and production of mixed and 100 per cent non-cotton cloth.
3. Table 10 of Chapter 1 dealing with Silk-goods produced on handloom lost to powerloom.
4. 70 per cent of handloom located in City and 90 per cent of total weavers in the city are Muslims.
5. The list has been prepared after the interview during the fieldwork. I got help from the *Bunkar Dastkar Morcha*, an organisation working for the welfare of the weavers and peasants in Banaras and its adjoining areas.

6. A. Mamidipudi, Syamasundari B., W. Bijker, 'Mobilising Discourses: Handloom as a Sustainable Socio-Technology', *Economic and Political Weekly*, Vol. xlvii, No. 25, 2012, p. 1.
7. Atiq Khan, 'Handloom Fall Silent here, Weavers leave Varanasi', *The Hindu*, September 12, 2006.
8. *Ibid.*
9. P. Nayak, Rout, S. Shaikh and Rajnikant, 'Dream of Weaving: Study and Documentation of Banaras Sarees and Brocades', Textile Committee, Ministry of Commerce, GOI, 2007, p. 54.
10. *Ibid,* p. 55.
11. During field visit research had not encounter with the case of bonded labour. Children mostly work on loom of own family as an assistant.
12. The inference was drawn after interaction with male respondents in Banaras.
13. During fieldwork in Banaras
14. S.S.A.Aiyar, Rapid GDP Growth – Best Anti-dote for Poverty, *Economic Times*, 28th March, 2012.
15. PTI, "Poverty Line at 28.65: Planning Commission faces Criticism for Figures", *Economic Times*, 20 March 2012.
16. http://www.cpim.org/content/fraudulent-poverty-estimates.
17. Dainik Jagran, Varanasi, 27 April, 2012, p. 3.
18. Emile Durkhiem, *Suicide: A Sociological Study*, Routledge, New York, 1950, p. 18.
19. *Ibid,* p. 18.
20. Suicide, Islam and Politics: Reflections on the events in Tunisia, www.Ideas.net, 2010.
21. India had launched ICDS program way back in 1974 to deal with the supplementary nutrition (SN) to the young children and the lactating mothers. There is another scheme called SABLA which dealt with nutrition of adolescent girl of age group 11-18 years. In 201-13 union budget has allocated Rs. 77235.95 crore for children welfare. Now, the question arises that whether this amount allocation is enough to ensure equity. Is it inclusive enough? The incident answers the question. It is not only with health of minorities' children are being compromised. Protection, participation, development and education all are compromised in Banaras. In Banaras alone, no minority student has benefited from educational loan scheme after 2009-2010. According to district minority welfare officer Vijay Pratap Yadav, close to 700 minority students were the beneficiaries of this scheme till 2010, however, due to lack of funds at UPMFDC, no further loans were provided.
22. *Times of India*, Varanasi, November 26, 2009.
23. Dr. Lenin Raghuvansi, op. cit. pp. 7. Details provided by Dr. Ajay Kumar Gautam of Sarojini Naidu Hospital which uses x-ray and montex testing.
24. *Ibid,* T.K. Bose, p.28
25. Issue came up during interview in Banaras.

26. Abraham Koshy, 'Malfunctioning of Public Distribution System: An Empirical Analysis', *Vikalpa*, Vol. 16, No. 1, 1991, p. 43.
27. Respondents views on the PDS.
28. Kumar Gautam, 'Dying Skill and Starving Weavers: The Crisis of Banarasi Handloom', CENTAD, September 2008.
29. Editor, 'Weavers to own cycle-rickshaw soon in State', *Indian Express*, February 04, 2008.
30. *Ibid.*
31. Source: http://planning.up.nic.in/apd/hdr-2006/chapter-3.pdf.
32. Emily Christine Antze, op. cit., p. 5.
33. Sudhanshu Joshi, *India: Madarasas Modernise to Meet the aspirations of Muslim Weaver Community Girls*,
34. Editor, 'Unemployed and Uneducated due to down turn in the silk industry of Banaras', *Times of India*, Varanasi, March 14, 2009.
35. *Ibid.*
36. Fieldwork interview in Banaras.
37. *Ibid.*
38. Craftrevival.org
39. *Ibid.*
40. Voices From Folk School of Dalit Bahujan and Marginalised, PVCHR, Varanasi, 2008.
41. *Ibid.*
42. *Ibid.*
43. PVCHR, 2005.
44. Sutapa Mujherjee, 'Looms of Doom', *Outlook*, September 24, 2004.
45. *Ibid.*
46. Tarun K. Bose, *Globalisation Pushes Varanasi Weavers to hunger and Death*, Actionaid, Varanasi, 2007.
47. Sachar Committee Report, 2006, p. 277. The percentage of Muslim literacy is much lower than the district total literacy rate i.e. 66.75 per cent and 48.07 total female literacy rate of Banaras (Census 2001).
48. Mau Violence – An Exclusive Citizens Report, *Sabrang*, 2005, p. 3.
49. The tussle was between the BJP and Hindu Yuva Vahini for the political control over the "Hindu" votes.
50. *Ibid.*, p. 27.
51. Asha Krishnakumar, 'Weavers in Distress', *Frontline*, Vol. 18, No. 8, April 14-27, 2001.
52. *Ibid.*
53. Aparna Pallavi, 'Fake not Fair', *Down to Earth*, April 14th, 2008.
54. Rahul Kodkani and UCSD Chapter, 'Varanasi Weavers in Crisis', Varanasi, 2006.
55. Nesar Ahmad, '*Handloom Cluster: Globalisation and indigenous Artisan Economy – A case Study of Varanasi Silk Sari Industry*', PVCHR, 2007.

Chapter - 4

Government Policies and Weavers' Response to the Crisis

Government Policies for Handloom

The government could not afford to neglect a sector that played a vital role in generating employment and GDP. It has from time to time formulated policies, which may have been meagre in scope and limited in reach, but did try to address the problems faced by the handloom industry after economic reform. In collaboration with the various State governments, the Centre has launched several schemes to bring some respite to the ailing industries. Some of the previously introduced schemes include project package with fund sharing of 50 per cent by each body, quality control project, handloom prize project, thrift fund, collective insurance, health package and Bunkar Bahboodi fund. However, the textile industry in general, and handloom in particular, has been experiencing two pronged problems i.e. non-implementation of policy and wrongly designed policy. For instance, the safety to handloom through reservation act was well intended.[1] But its non-implementation fetched no result, as handloom was clubbed together with household powerlooms, which gave leverage to the latter. Studies point out that "by 1974, almost 90% of the powerloom units fell into the category of 'small' with less than 5 looms, and the reservation actually benefited these powerloom units rather than handlooms."[2]

The government's realisation of policy failure is reflected in the critiques contained in various reports. According to the Report of the Working Group on Village Industries, "A large number of …artisans are facing difficulties due to flight of raw materials from the rural areas… The KVIC is yet to evolve a strategy for supply of raw materials…the artisans are willing to work…but for want of raw materials, they remain without work for long spell."[3] Further, "schemes up to the end of the Seventh Plan have not been able to provide assistance to large sections of craftsmen in so far as production-related inputs are concerned and the marketing of their products is still left largely to…private trade. Consequently, they have not made any discernible impact on their earnings and standard of living."[4] To sum up the whole argument, the author had argued that "there is of dearth of schemes both for working and fixed capital, as far as the individual craftsman is concerned. There is no data on actual utilisation of these schemes by the craftsmen, but the general feedback has been indicative of a very low order. Most of the problems faced are implementation rather than policy related."[5] During the 10th Five Year Plan period, 12 schemes were run by the government to help the weavers. At the time of mid-term review for the 11th Five Year Plan, the report noted down the current status of the handloom industry. It says that "The traditional handloom weaving in India has been kept alive by those professionally skilled weavers household, which inextricably is linked with the age-old tradition of weaving. However, the sector is beset with various problems, such as obsolete technology[6], unorganised production system, low productivity, inadequate working capital, conventional product range, weak marketing links, overall stagnation of production and sales and above all, competition from powerlooms and mill sector."[7]

The government's budgetary allocations to deal with problems faced by the handloom sector are as follows. 1. During the XI Plan period, 12 schemes of the 10th Five Year Plan were merged into five schemes (i) Integrated Handloom Development Scheme, (ii) Handloom Weaver's Comprehensive Welfare Scheme, (iii) Marketing and Export Promotion Scheme, (iv) Diversified Handloom Developments Scheme, and (v) Mill Gate Price Scheme.

Table 54: Allocation of funds during 2009-11

Sl. No.	*Name of the Scheme*	*Amount Allocated during 2009-10 (Rs. In Crore)*	*Amount Allocated during 20010-11 (Rs. In Crore)*
1.	Integrated Handloom Development Scheme	115.57	168.00
2.	Handloom Weavers Comprehensive Welfare Scheme	119.80	116.14
3.	Marketing and Export Promotion Scheme	49.60	58.59
4.	Diversified Handloom Development Scheme	13.72	17.78
5.	Mill Gate Price Scheme	30.60	65.00

Source: Ministry of Textile, Lok Sabha, Unstarred Question no. 1133 answer on 28-11-2011.

Government's Policy intervention in Banaras

The government has from time to time provided assistance to the powerloom weavers. In the year 2008-09 the State government had waived off the electricity bill worth Rs. 50 crore.[8] However, the experience of Banaras has been different from that of the other Andhra Pradesh and Mau, where the handlooms and powerloom weavers benefitted from the cumulative effect of varied factors. As has been said earlier, the condition of weavers did not improve despite some significant aid from the government. The situation in Banaras has prompted a study by Craft Revival Trust sponsored by Planning Commission to recommend a wide range of policy initiatives to uplift the status of weavers.[9]

The Study has made some specific recommendation vis-à-vis Banaras. "Common Facility Centre: In Cholapur cluster, a 2 year old project for a CFC was funded at Rs 30, 00,000. The consolidated facility was to have a dye house, yarn depot, computer centre, design lab, and show room. However, there was no government land available for building the CFC. Therefore the money could not be acquitted and was returned to the government. Therefore it is important to find a space to create a common work area along with other facilities to facilitate production. Sourcing: There should be availability of yarns through yarn banks set up by the government. Yarns should be available at fixed rates. The fluctuation in the price of raw material causes heavy loss to the weavers as they have to buy the yarn at high cost and when they are selling the finished product the yarn prices slash. Weavers have to suffer huge losses due to price fluctuation. Also the yarns must be available at subsidized rates. Introduction of a silk bank so there is no unavailability of silk yarns. Review of the Mill Gate Scheme: There are currently a number of problems identified in the scheme, these include the following: time taken for freight to arrive; the subsidy covers only a small part of the actual transportation cost. - Much of the silk arrives from Bangalore and cost of transportation is very high and takes 20-25 days. National Handloom Development Corporation (NHDC) has only some yarn in stock; the silk available is only Grey Yarn. Market Outreach: National Marketing Platform – Extensive advertising and marketing is required to establish the USP of Banaras and distinguish the Banaras tradition from other saris."[10]

"Key terms: quality, design and motif, quality and durability. Increase exposure visits for weavers to improve the outcomes of the workshop. National Level Branding – Create an identity for the Banarasi sari through development of a branding campaign aimed at increasing awareness about products from the region. Develop Annual Business Plan and Market Strategy with Key Performance Indicators (KPI's) to move towards a service delivery and business model. Government officers and WSC have to develop business plans, with a set of objectives and key performance indicators, in consultation with the expert committee. Reporting against this criterion monitored and evaluated: Non-compliance or failure to meet established KPI's will result in funding loss, including funding for responsible staff positions. Need of government funded advertisement through a forum like 'Jaago Grahak Jaago' to educate the buyers about the difference in handloom and power loom products. Training and Skills Development: Develop a comprehensive training program to improve weaver meta-skills to develop capacity in design, production, and entrepreneurship in partnership with private and public sector, and institutions. Design exchange/training to build professionalism in weavers."[11]

"Research and development: Institute of Handloom Technology holds a three year diploma in weaving. Entrants to the college and graduates do not generally have links to the Banaras handloom sector. The curriculum must include field visits and projects to work with the craftsperson at grass root level. To introduce more professional courses that creates a platform for interaction with weavers. Product Development Strategy: Develop market research, forecasting and convert this into practical terms, for example, training modules so that design and marketing inputs flow to designers. Provide opportunities, such as workshops, for urban designers to build capacity, and interface with local designers. Introduce product labeling and handling. Introduce quality benchmarks: WSC focuses on-field training as well as on-campus training of weavers and dyers; product development; design development and identity cards. They produce designs and sell these to traders; their designers hold workshops. WSC should produce, and disseminate a check list for each step of the production process, including marketing, and product materials, and information. Introduction of labels on care instructions, quality and the content of the raw material in product should be done. Introduction of the quality standards according the international rules training the weavers to weave according these standards and put a price tag and other labels to the finished product."[12]

"Weave the Handloom Mark into the Banaras sari, using a technique that cannot be copied by power loom. Advertise this as the key authentication mark. Local, domestic and international advertising about the mark should be promoted. To protect handloom products from imitation power loom in the market, introduce mechanisms for monitoring, and imposing penalties on traders, and, importers selling imitation products. Less paper work as the weavers do not copyright their designs due to too much paper work and lengthy procedures they have to follow. Improve governance and accountability: There is a WSC in Banaras. There is also an IIHT, Silk Board Office, and an NHDC office. All these are located on the same campus, adjacent to the major weaving colonies of Banaras city. In certain rural clusters, officials visit frequently, whilst in other areas, the weavers reportedly had no contact with government officials. Therefore it is necessary to; provide regular consultation of officials with weavers, and host meetings. Develop structures and create positions for weavers to improve accountability. For instance: hold meetings every three months in each cluster by the WSC, in which all the weavers and people associated with Banaras weaving are invited: advertise both formally (newspaper, posters) and informally (word of mouth). This could be an interactive sessions where WSC officials explain the current schemes and their benefits. Concerns and actionable items can be taken up by staff. At the end of each financial year, the concerned WSC official would submit a report in which the outcomes of the 4 meetings would be tabled."[13]

The picture of weavers' lives as painted in the previous chapter is only worsening today, and nothing has much changed except the form, factors and intensity of exploitation. Below is a critical analysis of the government's schemes in Banaras.

(1) Integrated Handlooms Development Scheme: "The scheme aims to focus on formation of weavers group as a visible entity, develop the Handloom Weavers Groups to become self-sustainable, inclusive approach to cover weavers both within and outside the cooperative fold, skill up-gradation of handlooms weavers/workers to produce diversified products with improved quality to meet the market requirements, provide suitable workplace to weavers to enable them to produce quality products with improved productivity etc. Under the scheme, clusters, covering about 300-500 looms under each, are taken up for development in a timeframe of 3 years at an upper cost of Rs. 60.00 lakh per cluster."[14]

Table 55: Budget Allocations: Union Ministry of Textiles (in Rs. Crores)

Sr. no.	Year	*Handloom Budget*			*Total Budget*			*Handloom % of total*
		Plan	*Non-Plan*	*Total*	*Plan*	*Non-Plan*	*Total*	
1.	1997-98	107.00	96.50	203.50	260.00	479.00	739.04	27.5
2.	1998-99	89.80	61.80	151.60	260.00	726.58	986.58	15.3
3.	1999-00	81.80	56.50	138.30	266.00	740.10	1006.10	13.7
4.	2000-01	112.00	53.29	165.29	457.00	754.30	1211.30	13.6
5.	2001-02	116.00	40.50	156.50	650.00	660.00	1310.30	11.9
6.	2002-03	117.00	35.83	152.83	715.00	870.50	1585.50	9.63
7.	2003-04	129.77	125.91	255.68	760.00	947.84	1707.84	14.9
8.	2004-05	119.36	132.37	251.73	878.00	902.31	1780.31	14.1
9.	2005-06	131.00	63.89	194.89	1150.00	858.25	2008.25	9.7
10.	2006-07	150.00	91.29	241.29	1349.50	1696.25	3045.75	7.9
11.	2007-08	252.00	68.75	320.75	2243.00	893.68	3136.68	10.22
12.	2008-09	255.00	70.32	325.32	500.00	823.51	3323.51	9.7
13.	2009-10	255.00	73.07	328.07	2500.00	889.00	3389.00	9.68

Source: Compilation by Centre for Handloom Information and Policy (CHIP), 2006; Ministry of Textile, GOI.

Handloom weavers, who are not covered by the clusters, are supported through a 'Group Approach', which will be implemented in a project mode. A set of 10 weavers or more is provided financial assistance for (i) Basic inputs; (ii) Training in weaving, dyeing, designing and managerial disciplines; and (iii) Construction of Work-sheds. During the year 2007-08, an amount of Rs. 110.50 crore was released under the scheme to various implementing agencies such as State Government/UTs, WSC etc., mainly towards Cluster Development Programmes and Marketing Incentive. A sum of Rs. 35.78 crore was released for the development of 251 clusters against a target of 250 clusters for the year. During the year 2008-09, against the Revised Estimate of Rs. 108.98 crore, a sum of Rs. 108.98 crore has been released. Against a target of 100 clusters for the year 2008-09, 131 clusters have been sanctioned and a sum of Rs. 19.70 crore has been released so far. Under Group Approach Project, 548 projects have been sanctioned to various State Government/UTs and a sum of Rs. 26.08 crore has been released. Financial assistance provided to the Uttar Pradesh state for overall development and welfare of handloom weavers during the last three years and in the current year are as below:

Table 56: Financial Assistance to Uttar Pradesh

Sl. No	*Financial year*	*Financial assistance provided to the state of Uttar Pradesh.(Rs. in lakh)*
1.	2006-07	974.00
2.	2007-08	371.00
3.	2008-09	1367.00
4.	2009-10 (up 30.06.2009)	Nil

Source: Ministry of Textile, Lok Sabha Unstarred Question no. 770 answered on 09-07-2009

Under the first phase of the Integrated Handloom Development Schemes, the government of India sanctioned four handloom clusters in Uttar Pradesh. Barabanki, Mubarakpur, Varanasi and Bijnor were the four handloom clusters with the fund of Rs. 2 crore each. In the second phase, out of 10 sanctioned clusters in Uttar Pradesh, 4 were from the Varanasi sub-region. Table 57 gives the details of clusters sanctioned in the Banaras sub-region.

Table 57: Clusters Sanctioned, Cost and total expenditure in Banaras sub-region

Name of the Cluster and District	*Name of the implementing Agency*	*No. of weavers*	*Total Project Cost (in Lakh)*	*Total amount released*	*Total Expenditure*	*% of Expenditure*
Bajardiha, Varanasi	AD. HandT, Varanasi	500	38.250	8.2966	8.2966	100
Saraiyan, Varanasi	AD. HandT, Varanasi	500	38.750	9.7966	9.7966	100
Dulhipur, Chandauli	AD. HandT, Varanasi	500	38.250	8.2966	8.2966	100
Adalhaat, Mirzapur	AD. HandT, Varanasi	500	60.000	11.0466	11.0466	100

Source: Handloom and textile Industry Director, Kanpur, Uttar Pradesh, 07-10-2009.

During the third phase period of 2007-08, 2 out of 14 sanctioned clusters in UP were under the Varanasi sub-region. The details of the clusters are given below in table 58. In the fourth phase of implementing cluster formation during 2008-09 in UP, 7 out of 11 clusters were in Varanasi, which received Rs. 69.051 lakh in first instalment. Table 59 given below notes down the details of clusters.

Table 58: Clusters Sanctioned, Cost and total expenditure in Banaras in Phase 2

Name of the Cluster and District	*Name of the implementing Agency*	*No. of weavers*	*Total Project Cost (in Lakh)*	*Total amount released*	*Total Expenditure*	*% of Expenditure*
Majhwaan, Mirzapur	AD. HandT, Varanasi	500	40.35	12.687	12.6174	99
Cholapur, Varanasi	AD. HandT, Varanasi	. 300	57.85	19.06	7.13116	37

Source: Handloom and textile Industry Director, Kanpur, Uttar Pradesh, 07-10-2009.

Table 59: Clusters sanctioned, its cost and total expenditure in Banaras in Phase 3

Name of the Cluster and District	*Name of the implementing Agency*	*No. of weavers*	*Total Project Cost (in Lakh)*	*Total amount released (in Lakh)*	*Total Expenditure*	*% of Expenditure*
Badagaon, Varanasi	AD. HandT, Varanasi	320	39.5	11.988	9.801	81.76
Dulhipur, Chandauli	AD. HandT, Varanasi	312	35.47	10.29	6.861	66.76
Jalilpura, Varanasi	AD. HandT, Varanasi	315	25.7	7.692	5.393	70.11
Sikandarpur, Chandauli	AD. HandT, Varanasi	350	35	9.305	6.711	72.12
Sarai Mohna, Varanasi	AD. HandT, Varanasi	320	34.85	9.576	6.886	72.00
Harsos, Varanasi	AD. HandT, Varanasi	345	56.13	13.5	12.0	88.88
Lallapur, Varanasi	AD. HandT, Varanasi	320	30.34	6.7	4.171	62.26

Source: Handloom and textile Industry Director, Kanpur, Uttar Pradesh, 07-10-2009.

Under the Group Approach scheme, a total of 64 proposals were sent to the Varanasi sub-region Weavers' Service Centre. Table 60 shows the mode of monetary help provided to the weavers under this scheme.

Table 60: Mode of monetary help provided to the Weavers in Uttar Pradesh

Sr. No.	*Expenditure On*	*Amount (each Weaver)*	*Per cent Share of Amount*		*Weavers' percentage*
			GOI	*State Gov.*	
1.	Margin Money	6000	70	20	10
2.	Handloom Supply	8000	70	20	10
3.	Jacquard Supply	6000	70	20	10
4.	Equipment Supply	2000	70	20	10

Source: Textile and Silk Industry, UP, 03-10-2009.

Apart from these schemes, the weavers under BPL having 20 sq/mtrs of land could avail Rs. 25,000 from the government to establish workshops.

(2) Handloom Weavers Comprehensive Welfare Scheme: Under this scheme, two programs are run by the government i.e. 'Health Insurance scheme' (HIS) and 'Mahatma Gandhi Bunkar Bima Yojana' (MGBBY) for the weavers of the country. Health Insurance scheme is implemented through the ICICI Lombard General Insurance Company Ltd.[15] The scheme envisages covering (a) not only the weaver but also his wife and two children (b) all pre-existing diseases as well as new diseases and (c) substantial provision for OPD. The ancillary handlooms workers like those engaged in warping, winding, dyeing, printing, finishing, sizing, *Jhala* making, jacquard cutting etc. are also eligible to be covered. The annual limit per family is Rs. 15,000 out of which OPD cover will be Rs. 7,500. Till now more than 43 lakh weavers are enrolled under the scheme and ICICI Lombard has settled over 53 lakh insurance claims.[16]

Table 61: Weavers covered under the scheme during the last three years in Uttar Pradesh

Year	*Weavers covered under Health Insurance Scheme*	*Weavers covered under Mahatma Gandhi Bunkar Bima Yojana*
2006-07	88,372	17,163
2007-08	431,921	14,350
2008-09	371,617	21,560

Source: Ministry of Textile, Lok Sabha Unstarred Question no. 770 answered on 09-07-2009.

Table 62: Detail of Receipt and Settlement of Medical claim under HIS in Varanasi

Year	*Kind of claims*	*Claims Received*		*Claims Settled*		*Claims Outstanding*		*Claims Disallowed + Rejected*	
		Number	*Amount*	*Number*	*Amount*	*Number*	*Amount*	*Number*	*Amount*
2007-08	OPD	5717	32911679	4370	22848618	1268	7710270	79	2352791
	IPD	4910	27363286	4307	20779463	497	2199699	106	4384124
	Total	10627	60274965	8677	43628081	1765	9909969	185	6736915
2008-09*	OPD	1634	11930603	553	3780176	1061	7613216	20	537211
	IPD	201	1515422	29	213177	169	1208869	3	93376
	Total	1835	13446025	582	3993353	1230	8822085	23	630587

Source: ADI, Banaras.

The MGBBY is being implemented through the life insurance Corporation of India. The funding pattern of the annual premium of Rs. 330/ - per member under the scheme is as below:

Table 63: Share in Contribution for MGBBY

GOI Contribution	Rs. 150/-
Weavers' Contribution	Rs. 80/-
LIC's Contribution	Rs. 100/-
Total Premium	Rs. 330/-

Source: Handloom and textile Industry Director, Kanpur, Uttar Pradesh, 07-10-2009. * Data till June of Year.

During the 11th Plan, the benefits available under the MGBBY have been substantially increased as compared to what was available during the 10th plan. The details of comparative benefits are as given below in table 64.

Table 64: Benefits given to weavers under different circumstances

Sr. No.		Benefits during the 10th Plan	Benefits 1.10.07 onward
1.	Natural Death	Rs. 50,000	Rs. 60,000
2.	Accidental Death	Rs. 80,000	Rs. 1,50,000
3.	Total Disability	Rs. 50,000	Rs. 1,50,000
4.	Partial Disability	Rs. 25,000	Rs. 75,000

Source: Handloom and textile Industry Director, Kanpur, Uttar Pradesh, 07-10-2009.

According to the official record, a total of 155 insurance claims were made till June 2009 in the Varanasi sub-region. Of these, 133 claims worth Rs. 6,780,000.00 have been paid by LIC. In the first quarter of the year 2009-10, 10 out of 13 claims worth Rs. 550,000 have been paid. In addition to the above, under the MGBBY, a scholarship of Rs. 300/- per quarter per child is paid to students studying in standard IX to XII for a minimum period of four years, or till they complete XII standard, whichever event occurs earlier. The benefit is restricted to two children of the member covered. Under this scheme, as per official data, 3375 students in the Varanasi sub-region have received scholarship as on 30th September 2009.

(2) Marketing and Export Promotion Scheme: The Marketing and Export Promotion Scheme is the amalgamation of the Marketing Promotion

Programme and Handloom Export Scheme. With some modifications and additions, it is being implemented during the 11th Plan as a Centrally Sponsored Scheme (CSS) with the following two components: Marketing Promotion and Handloom Export Promotion. Under this scheme, Varanasi has organised four handloom expos in the year 2009-10. Table 65 given below presents the details of the expos in the district of Varanasi.

Table 65: Detail of the Expos in Banaras

Name of the Exhibition	*Time Period*	*Proposed budget (in lakh)*	*Number of Participant*	*Number of Beneficiary*	*Discount to the beneficiary*
Ganga Mahotsva Mela, Varanasi	Nov. 2009	2	25	525	Free Stall/Electricity/ aid
Diwali Mela, Sarnath, Varanasi	Oct./Nov. 2009	2	25	525	Free Stall/Electricity/ aid
Shivratri Mela, Varanasi	Feb./March 2010	2	25	525	Free Stall/Electricity/ aid
Holi Mela, Obra, Sinbhadra	Feb./March 2010	2	25	525	Free Stall/Electricity/ aid

Source: Weaver Service Centre, Banaras.

(4) Diversified Handloom Development Scheme (DHDS): Design Development and Training Programme (DDTP) of the 10th Five Year Plan is being implemented as a central sector scheme in a modified form during the 11th plan and as "Diversified Handloom Development Scheme (DHDS)." The Scheme aims at upgrading the skills of the handloom weavers through organisation of workshops and exhibitions, design development, documentation of traditional designs and providing linkage and meeting the market requirements. This scheme includes components such as strengthening of Weavers Service Centres/Indian Institutes of Handloom technology, setting up of New WSCs/IIHTs, National Centre for Textile Design (NCTD), Research and Development (R and D) and Conducting Third census and issue of Identity cards to handloom weavers.

(5) Mill Gate Price Scheme (MGPS): This scheme was introduced during 1992-93 with the objectives of providing all types of yarn to the handloom weavers' organisations at the price which it is available at the Mill Gate. Under the Scheme, the Government of India reimburses the

transportation expenses involved in the supply of the yarn. National Handloom Development Corporation (NHDC) is the nodal agency for implementation of the scheme.

(6) Banarasi brocade covered under Geographical Indication (GI): Banarasi silk products have been registered under Geographical Indication (GI) rights with the name 'Banaras Brocades and Saris'. This is the first ever GI status that any product in Eastern UP has received. The GI is aims to curb others from processing or marketing any product under the same name and is like intellectual property rights. As GI status is the measure to restrict the misuse of Banarasi sari brand, it would benefit around 12 lakh people who are directly or indirectly associated with handloom silk industry of the region, said an official. According to the certificate issued by the registrar of GI, Banaras Brocades and Saris come under four classes (13-26) that include silk brocades, textile goods, silk sari, dress material and silk embroidery. This registration is for 10 years, which can be renewed further. Nine organizations had applied for the GI registration of world famous Banarasi sari and brocade, to the Chennai-based Geographical Indication Registry in July 2007 and they received the GI status on September 4, 2009. The nine organizations were, Banaras Bunkar Samiti, Human Welfare Association (HWA), joint director industries (eastern zone), director of handlooms and textiles Uttar Pradesh Handloom Fabrics Marketing Cooperative Federation, Eastern UP Exporters Association (EUPEA), *Banarasi Vastra Udyog Sangh, Banaras Hath Kargha Vikas Samiti* and *Adarsh* Silk *Bunkar Sahkari Samiti*. However, the question that how GI status would be able to stop powerloom products labelled as authentic[17] handloom product from the same (Banaras) region, would instigate a critical inquiry.

Nevertheless, the applicants and weaver community apprehend that like the policy of Handloom Mark, this GI shall be futile exercise and not serve its purpose. In his field interview, Amit Basole found the overwhelming perception about the GI rule. "The government is trying to use patent law to protect this industry. This shows the government's intellectual bankruptcy. It is like trying to keep a tree alive by watering its leaves instead of its roots. It won't have any effect. When a product comes to the sales counter if a buyer likes it she will buy it, if she doesn't she won't. You are trying to save the product by patenting it; first let us look at the execution. It's impossible. Take for example Bhadohi's rug-mark that is supposed to tell you if child-labor has been used in making a carpet. It costs Rs. 20 to put this stamp. If it is there on a carpet it is free of child labor, if it is not there, then the carpet has been made from child-labor. The same thing will happen here. And then, the people who will implement it, the officials, do they have the wherewithal to tell if a fabric is from Surat or Banaras? We are from this trade, we also get fooled, what barometer do they have to tell fabrics apart?"[18]

HWA's president Rajnikant points out that the Handloom Mark, which is two years older than the GI, has failed to take off in Banaras. There are no more than 400 weavers registered in Banaras with handloom mark. Not even 10 societies are registered . . . [recently] there was a circular that only those weaver cooperative societies who have been registered under the mark can participate in government sponsored exhibitions. No mention of whether the products they sell should also have those tags. 90 per cent handloom weaver cooperative societies sell powerloom cloth. One can anticipate that this will be problem with the GI also, since those producers who are best positioned to apply for and take advantage of the GI are often the same who have enough capital to own powerlooms. The powerloom prepared products with look of handloom product, question the authenticity of Banarasi sari and artisanship. This further added marginalisation to the urban Muslim artisans, which was the initiated during colonial India during the search of 'traditional Indian craft'. Mira Mohsini argued that "The notion of 'traditional Indian craft' – born from colonial experiences and shaped by actors within the 'craft world', including government officials, politicians and development workers – has been historically produced by a romantic search for an authentic India. However, this dominant narrative excludes urban craft production in favour of locating 'tradition' and authenticity in village cottage industries, as most visibly evidenced by the promulgation of home-spun cloth (khadi) as an enduring symbol of the nation-state. It is these discursive formations and normative categories, which seek to define the meaning of authenticity that have profound and detrimental impacts on a large proportion of Muslims residing in urban areas who are involved in artisanal occupations."[19]

(7) Others: In the 2011 budget, the government has announced debt waivers of Rs. 3,000 crores to the weavers through co-operatives. It has targeted 15,000 handloom co-operatives and around 300,000 weavers across the country. The government has proposed reduction in import duty on raw silk (not thrown) from 30 to 5 per cent as well. For systematic analysis of the policy and its performance, this research will undertake a comparative study of Banaras vis-à-vis Andhra Pradesh and Mau. The deteriorating condition of weavers in Andhra Pradesh described in the last

chapter showed that policies were either ineffective or problematic. For instance, many societies in Andhra Pradesh became dysfunctional due to the lack of yarn as prices were on the rise. The government decided to merge such sick entities with the productive co-operatives. "In this process 668 co-operatives, or roughly one-third of the total, were liquidated. 622 societies were merged with 323 societies, and only 502 (less than one-fourth) were considered independently viable, and retained. In all, thus, there were 825 societies in the State. The highest percentage of co-operatives closed down was in Prakasam district (83 per cent), followed by Nellore district (75.6 per cent), Karimnagar (73 per cent) and Guntur (69 per cent). Clearly, in the rediscovered zeal for co-operatives, too many had been formed without any consideration for their viability."[20]

The Andhra Pradesh government's relentless effort to rejuvenate co-operative societies went in vain as these "co-operatives as an institution of implementation did not resolve the weavers' crucial dependence on the 'master-weaver', an entrepreneurial marketer who would negotiate orders and then contract them out to weavers. Master-weavers perform a vital function, interfacing between consumer demand and production. But as a consequence they also hold inordinate power. Cooperatives can become 'captured' by these elite, distorting contracts and revenue distribution."[21] But, there are some rays of hope in the policy initiative to form a cluster in Andhra Pradesh.

Table 66: Important Statical Information of the Cluster in Andhra Pradesh

1.	No. of Weaver Population	209737
2.	Total No. of weavers	60000
3.	Total No. of working handlooms	18000
4.	No. of weavers co-op societies	13
5.	No. of societies working	12
6.	Total No. of handlooms in Co-operative societies	4630
7.	Total No. of handlooms working in Co-operative societies	865
8.	Total No. of handlooms working in Non Co-operative fold	17135
9.	No. of photo Identity cards issued under co-operative fold	4330
10.	No. of photo Identity cards issued under non co-operative fold	6708
11.	Total No. of photo Identity cards issued	11038
12.	No. of weavers benefited under Project Package Scheme	1875
13.	No. of weaver families benefited under I H V D S	100
14.	No. of weavers benefited under Health Package Scheme	7256
15.	No. of weavers benefited under Handloom Development Centre	850
16.	No. of weavers benefited under Bunakar Bheema Yojana	2650

(Contd...)

17.	No. of Quality Dyeing units	1
18.	No. of House-cum-worksheds sanctioned	2021
19.	No. of beneficiary under Thrift Fund-cum-savings and Security Scheme	150
20.	No. of beneficiary under Deenadayal Hath Kargh Prostaha Yojana	300
21.	No. of Artisan Credit Card Scheme - Target	1655
22.	No. of Artisan Credit Card Scheme - Issued	211
23.	No. of weavers benefited under IHTP	40
24.	No. of weaver death cases	24
25.	No. of weaver cases sanctioned	20
26.	Netha Bazar (completed)	1
27.	Textile (Handloom) Park	1

Source: Diagnostic Study Report on Chirala Handloom Cluster, Andhra Pradesh, 2008.

This has helped in providing continuous employment to the weavers, which enhances their wage earning. Though the wages are not increasing in proportion to the increase in essential commodities cost, "the average earnings of the weaver will be from Rs.18000 to 24000 per annum."[22] The programme of cluster has become successful in Andhra Pradesh as it has the culture of group-working in co-operatives and corporations. Secondly, weavers in Chirala have been responding and adapting the production to changes in market demand - a trend that is not seen in many other places like Banaras. For instance, '*Telia Rumal*' (used as head-cloth by the labouring classes) was the most famous product of this region for long time. But once the Chinese entered into its production, and the powerloom began to imitate the product, its demand reduced to the minimum. The weavers of Andhra Pradesh immediately changed the items of production and shifted to the weaving of jacquard saris, trying various blends such as polycot, sico, etc. Currently, the production of dress materials and *dupattas* has taken over. This ability to keep pace with changing market trends could be a major strength of the handloom industry in this region. Some of the products being woven are described in Table 67 below.

Table 67: Diverse Handloom Products in Andhra Pradesh

Product	***Type (counts)***
Real madras Handkerchiefs (RMKH)	40s – jacquard
Saris, dress materials	80s count
Polycot zari	80s
Cotton dress materials	80s × 60s
Plain yardage, dupattas	60s
Shirting	60s × 40s
Saris	60s

Source: Simanthinee Niranjana, Report on Growth and Prospects of the Handloom Industry, Commissioned by the Planning Commission, 2001

Another success story of government intervention was recorded in Pochamalli in Andhra Pradesh, which has been famous for its hand woven tie and dye design. The results of the intervention are summarised below in table 68.

Table 68: Policy's Achievement in Pochampalli, Andhra Pradesh

S. No.	*Parameter*	*Before*	*After*
1.	No. of Weavers brought into Coop.folds	Nil	1000
2.	No. of weavers enrolled under insurance (Bunkar Bima Yozna)	150	725
3.	Members share capital	Nil	Rs. 1.00 Lakh
4.	Number of MAC Societies	Nil	9
5.	Production	Nil	220 Lakh
6.	Sales	Nil	240.4 Lakh
7.	Average wage	Rs. 1900	Rs. 2300

Source: Sameer Sharma, Entrepreneurship Development in Networks of Weaver Cluster of Pochampalli, *Journal of Rural Development,* Vol. 23 (3), 2004, pp. 350-351.

The collective working of experienced of weavers in UP has been poor. The co-operatives never succeeded beyond the small numbers, and therefore the industry remained un-organised for a majority of weavers.

Table 69: Weaver in Co-operative and Non-co-operative folds in Banaras and Mau

		BANARAS		
Sr. No.	*Institutions*	*Male*	*Female*	*Total*
1.	Co-operative	32366	2815	35181
2.	Non-co-operative	92270	20254	112524
		MAU		
3.	Co-operative	31,500	3500	35000
4.	Non-co-operative	60885	6800	67685

Source: Dream of Weaving-Study and Documentation of Banaras Sarees and Brocades, Human Welfare Association and Textile Committee, GOI, 2007, p. 71.

"The coverage of co-operatives in UP is negligible: only 5,575 or 2 per cent of the full-time weavers are members of co-operatives."[23] Today, as per official claim, UP has the largest number of co-operative apex institutes in India with membership of 2434 primary societies and 64,866 weaver members covering 77,034 looms.[24] But during the fieldwork in

Banaras none of the respondents claimed to be members of co-operatives. Rather their attitude was very negative towards the co-operatives, and most of them demanded the immediate closure of co-operatives.

Anju Grover, member of Global Information Network, has captured the weavers' perception of co-operatives in Banaras, really well. "Cooperative societies just hold meetings and do nothing concrete for the welfare of weavers. Nothing comes out of the meetings. Our condition is no better than that of individual weavers and we too suffer from improper facilities, said Gaavesh Sarvar, a local weaver and cooperative member. Long hours at the loom have damaged Sarvar's health. He complains of swelling legs during the cold winters and worries that he has no insurance cover. 'We often fall sick for days, and these are times when we cannot earn any money, but have to borrow to pay the costs of medical treatment.' Another cooperative member, Alam Ansari, said that profits rarely get to the weavers. 'The balance sheets are never made at the end of the financial year and the rules are openly flouted,' he said. "The reality was that Ansari businessmen with capital and connections accrued the benefits of special state provisions, for instance through the appropriation of cooperative financial benefits, thereby reinforcing their economic status. However, these gains were made at the expense of the weavers, whom the schemes were intended to help and who were subsequently further marginalised within society. It could be argued that the capacity of local socio-economically powerful actors to misappropriate state welfare provisions is just one factor contributing to wealth accumulation by some, and the reproduction, real or imagined, of their class advantage within the Muslim weaving community."[25]

The cooperative societies are anti-women. "When I was pregnant, I got no medical benefits although there is a provision for maternity benefits in the cooperative society act', said another cooperative member, Shabana. According to Zuleikha Bano, president of the Handloom Silk Cooperative Society, playpens are rare and educational facilities for the children of female workers are non-existent. But the condition of women who are not in cooperatives is even worse as they are paid less than their male counterparts. In fact, in traditional weaving families women are not paid at all although they form the backbone of the industry and work in every aspect of sari production. One local weaver, Nizamuddin, says he prefers to have nothing to do with cooperatives. Master weavers float bogus cooperatives to get raw material at subsidized rates and a platform to market the saris profitably – we get nothing."[26]

So Banaras, unlike Andhra Pradesh and Mau has a different experience of implementation of schemes. While analysing the current status of cooperatives in India A. Vaidyanathan argued that "the manner in which they are organised and function are not conducive to efficient and prudent use of the vast resources at their disposal. Mechanisms to ensure accountability for benefiting sections of the population that they are expected to cater to, are weak and ineffective. With few significant exceptions, their finance is in a chronic state of sickness and prone to recurrent crises... The legal framework in which cooperatives are to operate is framed by state governments. Responsibility for ensuring compliance with that framework also vests with them. But enforcement is notoriously lax. Violations of the letter and spirit of cooperative law regarding election of boards, maintenance of proper records and their audit, transparent and objective processes in granting loans, ensuring their proper use and recovery of dues, have been endemic features of cooperatives all over the country. Enforcing discipline through supervision of a huge number of dispersed societies is impractical. More active interventions – such as appointing government officials to manage societies or superseding elected boards – have also proved ineffective. Though most of the resources of cooperatives come from public funds, there is no mechanism to ensure prudent and efficient management of funds."[27]

In Mau all the respondents show unawareness about the government schemes for the welfare of weavers. Not only that, they claim no help reaching them from the government. Table 70 shows the varied response of Mau weavers regarding government policies and schemes.

Table 70: Weavers' awareness about the Govt. Schemes in Mau

	Response	*Total Respondents*	*Percentage*
Do You get any help from the government?	No	267	89
	Yes	33	11
	Total	**300**	**100**
Are you aware of the government welfare schemes?	No	280	93
	Yes	20	7
	Total	**300**	**100**
Who takes initiatives to resolve the problems?	(a) Trade Union	-	
	(b) Local Leaders	210	70
	(c) Government Official	-	-
	(d) None	90	30
	(e) Others	-	-

Source: Fieldwork in Mau by author in 2010.

Table 71: Allocation for Handloom Schemes in Union Budget

Allocations for Handloom Schemes in Union Budget	
Scheme	**2011-12**
Integrated Handloom Development Scheme	129.70
Handloom Weavers Comprehensive Welfare Scheme	125.00
Diversified Handloom Development Scheme	24.10
Weaver Service Centre	29.65
Mill Gate Price Scheme	55.60
Market Promotion Program	45.60
Others	21.96
Grand Total	431.61

Source: Expenditure vol. 2, Union Budget, 2012.

Critical Review of the Government Policies for the Weavers

Before embarking on a critical analysis of the policies, it is important to consider how the weavers of Banaras perceive government efforts to help distress weavers. Table 72 shows the weavers rating of government's efforts.

Table 72: Banaras Weavers' Opinion on Govt. efforts

Rating	*Total Respondents*	*Percentage of Respondents*
Good	20	6.66
Bad	220	73.33
Worst	60	20
Total	**300**	**100**

Source: Fieldwork in Banaras in 2009.

The above table shows that the weavers are not entirely satisfied with the role of the government.[28] 93.33 per cent of overwhelming population disapproves the government effort and merely 6.66 per cent feel that government is doing its bit to help the people. Thus, it could be argued that the adopted policies to uplift the status of weavers are short of vision, lack professional knowledge about the nature of work and mostly miss the target itself. Other survey results support the finding of this research. Interrogating the Muslim weavers' perception of 'welfare state' Philippa Williams (2011) argued that "...many *Ansaris* consistently levelled primary culpability for their destitute condition at the government, which they understood within a broader spectrum of neglect for their welfare.... the perception articulated by Muslim *Ansaris* in general was that the government persistently neglected their social and economic needs. Such neglect was interpreted in relative terms, contrasted with the relative advantage of the majority Hindu population, and recognised as the result of discrimination based not only on their religious identity but also their minority status. The weavers' sense of marginality and limited access to the state were also determined by socio-economic and educational status."[29] The chart[30] below is showing the entities responsible for the decline of handloom.

If we look at the Integrated Handlooms Development Scheme (IHDS), its main target is to form groups of 300-500 weavers as a part of cluster development. It's a move towards cooperatives, which were ruined by corrupt practices and control by *gaddidars* for their personal benefits. This is because of extreme dependency of weavers on the *gaddidars* and traders for raw material and wages. As a result they do not oppose any act, which could harm their interests. Secondly, the communal bias has its negative effect in the functioning of the cluster program. As most of the weavers are Muslims and live in ghettos, there is a clear lack of required facilities to make the cluster program successful. The negative attitude of the administration contributes to this state of affairs. Lenin Raghuvanshi, head of PVCHR, argued that the cluster program in Muslim ghettos is not functioning properly as compared to the cluster in the Hindu majority areas. "Administration is bias", Raghuvanshi.[31]

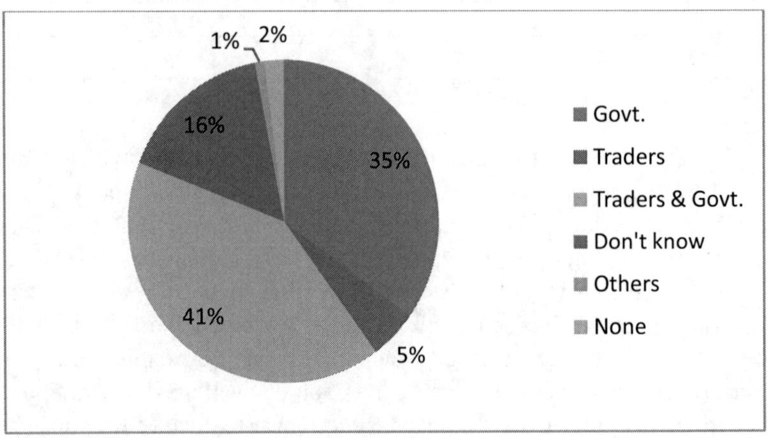

Source: Philippa Williams (2011).

Figure 5: Institutions and Non-Institutions Responsible for the decline of Handloom

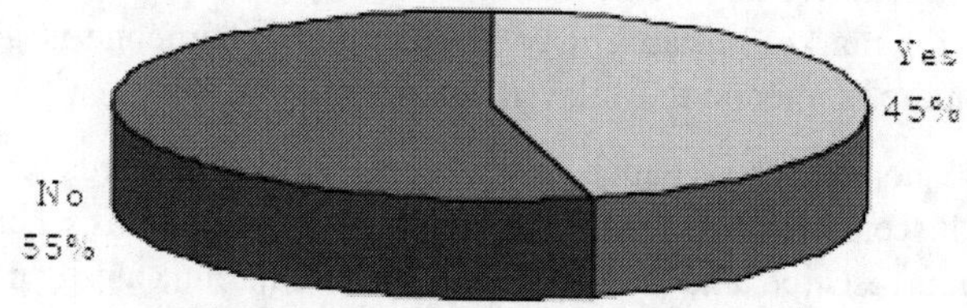

Source: Nayak, Rout and Rajanikant (2009).

Figure 6: Awareness on Weaver Service Centre[32]

The government's efforts to help weavers through agencies remain fruitless and bear no success. For example, if we look at the above chart it shows that merely 45 per cent of respondents knew about the WSC. Critical in-depth studies have proved that those who knew about the WSC are mostly upward mobile weavers. Another study by Amit Basole found that "…the Weavers' Service Center, which is supposed to be a nerve center for the design development and the training of the weavers, is deserted. In a survey done by Pandey (1981) the author found that only 5.6 per cent of Banaras weavers said that they required further training in weaving technique or repair and maintenance of looms. The author also notes that there is a weaving institute in Varanasi but hardly any weaver goes for training in that institute."[33] Amit Basole further noted down, in his thesis, the ignorance and unsupportive role of WSC which has the lead responsibility of imparting technical education to the weavers.

"While waiting to meet the Director of the Center, I introduced myself to his secretary. He asked what I was working on and I told him the political economy of weaving" and artisanal knowledge. On hearing the latter he asked what that is. The Director for his part, on hearing the same term asked you mean education? This response, though different and less derisive than the secretary's, also demonstrated the theoretical lens through which artisans are viewed by formal sector workers: as lacking in education and hence in knowledge also. The Director also complained that the weavers do not show much interest in skill development initiatives run by the Center (3 out of 20 may show further interest). By and large, he noted, they are not keen to improve."[34] The weavers, for their part, remain skeptical of the center's capacity to help them in any substantial way and resent the way they are treated there. Ateek Ansari, a powerloom weaver, journalist and long-time industry observer noted,

> It [the WSC] is a white elephant. Ordinary weavers do not benefit from it. Some more aware people may go there and get some personal

benefit. It performs the function of disbursing government aid. Foreign tours for market research may be sanctioned; someone is going to Singapore, someone to Malaysia and so on."[35]

Consequently, it has changed the weavers' attitude towards the cluster program. It seems that they are not very enthusiastic about this scheme. For instance, this research takes an analytical view of Bajardiha cluster program. Bajardiha cluster consist of 300 members, official at ADI claims. This has eight organising members with Md. Haaris Maqdoom as a President. The members meet once in a week with prior information to each one. Table 73 show the details of equipment provided as per quota by the Bajardiha cluster to the weavers. These materials are directly provided to weavers, and not to any representative. In return, weavers have to provide the purchased material cash-memo. "This leaves no room for corruption", said Sawale Ansari, a member of Bajardiha cluster.

Table 73: Equipment provided by local administration to the Weavers

Name of Equipment	*No. of Equipment*	*Price of each Equipment*	*Weavers' contribution*
Jacquard	2	6000/-	600/-
Handloom	6	8000/-	800/-
Other Technical support	5	2000/-	200/-

Source: ADI office, Banaras.

Apart from providing materials the ADI arranges tours for the 5-6 weavers to various exhibitions and expos in the country. A critical analysis of this cluster's functioning explains the detachment of poor weavers from the cluster program. For example, the touring weavers are generally rich (master) weavers in the name of real workers who made the product. Secondly, the weavers are too poor to contribute the required money for the available equipment. This gives chance to rich *gaddidars* to exploit the situation in their favour. Thirdly, if we take the face value of official numbers of 300 weavers associated with Bajardiha cluster, it is not even the fraction of total weavers' population of approximately 1.5 lakh in the area.

Similar deficiency met with the Mill Gate Price Scheme (MGPS). As noted earlier, its objective is to provide all types of yarn to the "handloom weavers' organisations" at the price at which it is available at the Mill Gate.

Now, from this research, it is confirmed that all the so called weavers' organisations are controlled by *gaddidars* and traders. Yet, the benefit of this scheme ultimately reaches those who are already rich and powerloom owners. The initial response to the implementation of GI was not very satisfactory due to lack of will to implement the policy. Dr. Lenin Raghuvanshi argued that "The situation would improve only when the programmes meant for weavers would be implemented properly and effectively."[36] HIS too came under attack from the weavers as the dealings under it were not transparent, and were marred by corruption right from the making of the card itself. "Whilst the thinking behind the HIS appeared to be sensitive to the needs of the weaving community, it seemed that the programme had so far brought little visible assistance to weavers in Madanpura, the neighbourhood where I predominantly focused research, or indeed those living in other Muslim majority neighbourhoods. Weavers were either unaware of the scheme or, months later, were still waiting to receive their cards. Those with social or political connections seemed more successful in obtaining the cards, but with no 'empanelled' hospitals in Madanpura weavers still needed to find the capital upfront to pay for their health care and claim expenses later."[37] "The healthcare is all a sham," Amir Jahan says angrily. "I was refused treatment on grounds of huge expense. I won't ever go to be humiliated again."[38]

Mohammad Ali, 25, said he was denied treatment at one of the private hospitals and ended up paying from his own pocket. Another man, Mohammad Irshad, grumbled that he couldn't get his wife covered under the same card because he couldn't provide proper identification for her. "Getting the insurance card is tedious," he says.[39] Akhtar Ali, resident of Bajardiha, points out that for getting ICICI health card, he had to pay Rs. 60 as bribe. Further, he mentioned that "After getting a health card when I went to Javed Iqbal clinic in Aurangabad, Varanasi, the doctor said, this card is useless."[40] A similar fate met Md. Ekram, resident of Lallpura, when he went to Shiv Prasad Gupta hospital for the treatment of TB. Alimul Haq of Bajardiha who holds a health card told this researcher that he had to pay bribe to get it. He informed about the corruption in issuance of health card. Abdul Salem, s/o Sobrati Khalifa, a resident of Jaitpura and member of Sankat Mochan Press club argued that corruption is the biggest issue in delivery of health card to the weavers. He expects government to give BPL card to weavers in Banaras. Nasim Ahmad of Jaitpura (House number 34/44) reported about the corruption in weavers' health card. Md. Afzal Ansari who works as a weaver reported that he had applied for health card but he did not receive it. But payment was drawn in his name. Almost all the respondents of Jaitpura, Varanasi acknowledged that there is corruption in making and delivery of health card.[41]

When Gular Ahmad, a social worker running an NGO for handicap weavers went to a hospital for 'certificate of handicap', the doctors asked for bribes. Those who pay get' certificate of total handicap'. He alleged that handicapped assistance pension of Rs. 2500 per year is not disbursed by the authorities without hassle or bribe. Many interviewees alleged a nexus between the hospital and insurance agents who counter check the medical claims by weavers. For any disease, respective hospitals demand more money than prescribed in OPD (i.e. Rs. 7,000/-) of Health Insurance Scheme. Weavers most of the time give Rs. 2000-3000 extra to the hospitals. Weavers give it thinking that they have to pay only Rs. 2000 for the bill of Rs. 9-10,000. Mr. Siddique Hasan, convener, Bunkar Dastkar Adhikar Manch (BDAM), argued that many identified hospitals in the ICICI Lombard Health Insurance Scheme, provide neither the bill nor information about expenses in the treatment of beneficiary weavers and late reimbursement (up to 3-4 months) of claims.[42]

According to the Lalmani Verma, Secretary of CPI (M), Varanasi, "We fought very hard for the health card and weavers' identity card, but today its benefit is not reaching to the desire members. Rather, big gaddidar and traders are using it for their men and family." Concurring about the widespread corruption in healthcare, the ADI head at the Rathyatra, Varanasi, said that only 30 out of 100 weavers are correct. He further claimed that while counter-checking the medical claims made by weavers, we found that 3000 out of 5000 were incorrect.[43] Table 74 shows the number of respondents possessing the health and Weavers Identity Card.

Table 74: Number of Respondents (Weavers) having Health and Identity Card

	Total Number of respondents	*Percentage of respondents*
Weavers with ID and Health Card	98	32.81
Weavers without ID and Health Card	115	**38.28**
Only Health Card	28	9.37
Only Identity Card	59	19.53

Source: Fieldwork in Banaras.

The table reveals that maximum percentage of respondents i.e. 38.28 per cent does not possess either Weavers Identity Card (WIC) or Health Card (HC). 9.37 per cent have only health card which was exposed the trumpet of government health policy in the area. Phillipa William (2011) argued that "The cumulative effects of low education levels, economic vulnerability, mistrust of the scheme and indifference towards government assistance discouraged the poorest of weavers from even applying for the Health Insurance Schemes in the first instanced."[44] Further, only 19.53 per cent possess WIC, which many respondents complain to be of no use.

If we analyse the budgetary support to handloom sector we find that it has been inadequate throughout. In 2011 total Central Budget is 12, 57,729 crores (13.4 per cent increase over previous year). Central textile budget is 5,855.75 crores. Handloom budget is 431.61 crores (16.9 per cent increase over previous year). This is 7.37 per cent of the textile budget. It is 0.03 per cent of total central budget. There are no new schemes for handloom sector. While handloom sector has been crying hoarse over rise in yarn prices, the allocation for Mill Gate price Scheme has increased by a mere 1.60 crores over the previous year allocation of 54 crores. For 2011-12, allocation is 55.60 crores. Handloom sector invests more than 25,000 crores, on silk and cotton yarn, across the country every year.

The rise in prices has increased the cost of production suddenly by 30 to 50 per cent. Mill gate price scheme, with all its lacunae, does not impact or influence the yarn prices at all. They do not reduce the burden on the handloom weaver. Government should do a scale assessment and invest more on the Mill gate price scheme (at least 1,000 crores), and correct the distortions in its delivery. The loan waivers are also turning into a futile exercise as they have targeted co-operatives, which contain only 2 per cent of weavers in Banaras. Alimul Haq of Bajardiha who has been weaving since his childhood argued that "I don't know about the co-operative things."[45]

Reduction of import duty on raw silk is not going to help handloom weavers at all because it is not going to solve the exploitative structure that has developed. Apart from it has its own operation problems this at the all India level. This is a huge reduction, which does not help domestic sericulture farmers, silk reeling and twisting industry. It also seems to be an off-hand decision, rather than a well-planned initiative, according to the interests of every stakeholder along the silk supply chain. Also, the stipulation that this reduction is only for raw (not thrown) helps only a particular section of powerloom and mill producers, who are geared for silk-based readymade garments based in UP and Tamil Nadu. This reduction would help only Chinese silk, which is not used in the form of import, by handloom weavers.

In fact, India requires about 25-30,000 metric tonnes of silk yarn for its domestic silk industry, while the production is only about 16,000 metric tonnes. Handloom sector, which is a major producer of silk saris, caters to a major part of this demand. In the last one year, silk yarn prices have shot up by more than 150 per cent. It has completely debilitated the silk-based handloom production. This shortfall is essentially because of the neglect of sericulture and diversion of lands under sericulture. Sericulture farmers do not get good market prices, and lack effective market infrastructural facilities. Silk reeling and twisting industry also has not grown because of withdrawal and reduction of government investments.

In fact, in Ramanagara area, near Benguluru, in Karnataka, more than 70 per cent of the silk reeling and twisting units have closed down, in the last five years, because of this neglect. Often, the problem is simple confusion: which department has to respond to their needs? At the central level, silk is under the Ministry of Textiles, while at the state level it is with the Agriculture department. In Andhra Pradesh, the responsibility of silk cooperatives keeps rotating between department of handlooms and textiles and department of sericulture like a football. Central Silk Board (CSB) is independent under the Ministry of Textiles, which has no field staff to respond to the needs of the industry. Also, the problem is about reduction in allocations and gross neglect of the silk supply chain, which supports more than 1 crore families. In budget 2011-12, allocation for CSB has been reduced from Rs. 453 crores to Rs. 429 crores. This would have an impact on the silk production, even taking for granted the inefficacy of CSB in responding to the needs of silk industry.

Summarising the policies and its effectiveness at the ground level Sardar Maqbool Hasan (aka bade sardar) opined in a letter addressed to the Prime Minister in March 6, 2006 that "Funds disbursed by the government for weavers through apex bodies get misappropriated. The role of these apex Bodies/All India Handloom Fabric Marketing Cooperative Society Ltd. should be directly distributed to weavers on the basis of Weavers Identity Card. Bunkar Panchayat can also be formed to achieve this objective…It is desired that an insurance policy be devised for the weavers, wherein the weavers contribution to premium will be 10 per cent the balance 90 per cent should be borne by the Central Government /LIC/ Other Development Financial Institutions. The existing weaver insurance scheme named "Mahatma Gandhi Weaver Insurance Scheme" should be materially altered as the interim or terminal benefit being offered under the scheme are of no financial significance, except for the name of our father of nation."[46] Two years later when assured of no commitment and action from the government, bade Sardar addressing a letter to the Prime Minister writes that "In all the relief-packages introduced by the government, it is a sorrowful fact that the poor and least educated deserving weavers are never at the receiving end. The entire system of distribution must be toned up to provide the weavers their due share."[47]

Presenting the analysis of government strategy to deal with the weavers' crisis Ashoke Chatterjee, former President, Craft Council of India, argued that "Indian authorities have little idea of what is going wrong or what to do about it. There is no strategy apparent, either in Varanasi or elsewhere… What we lack is any kind of political priority for handcrafts, despite the sector representing such a colossal employment factor, despite its contribution to the economy, despite the endless mantras about our ancient heritage as a vital part of our present and future."[48]

Why Government Policy has failed in Banaras

A number of factors are involved in the failure of policies in Banaras region: (a) Lack of information/Hiding information about the scheme, (b) Corruption, (c) Faulty scheme.

(a) Lack of information/hiding information by the official about the scheme: The government starts various schemes but weavers are not even aware of these schemes. Hazi Ishtiyar Ahmad said that most weavers don't even know about the existence of 5 to 6 silk yarn banks in Varanasi.[49] Mr. Siddique Hasan shared that "The office of ADI handloom does not circulates the guideline of the scheme. The office is not providing any information to the weavers and artisan except using the Right to Information Act." He also added "ADI Handicraft Mr. Mangala Singh always sits in the office in alcoholic condition." Artisans are not aware of Baba Saheb Ambedkar Hastshilp Vikas Yojana and no camp is organized for making their identity card.[50] "We heard about GI, but do not know how it could benefit us," said Affat Ansari, a weaver from Sarnath area. More or less, similar expressions came from other weavers like Suleman and Badre Alam from Lohata area and Nakhadu Ram and Shivpoojan from Harahua area. They know that something significant has happened in the interest of Banaras brocades and saris, but they have no idea about its impact.[51]

(b) Corruption: Almost all the interviewees complained about the corruption in implementation of all the schemes and all institutions marred by it. Denying the corruption in Central agencies, Deputy Director of the Weavers' Service Centre, Varanasi, A. K. Shukla explained about the corrupt practices in State agencies at various levels. He cited one example of sending weavers to various exhibitions such as Dilli Haat to prove his point. A few interviewees challenged WSC clean image. They alleged that the officials do not merely allocate slots to participate in the exhibition, but also favour rich traders and gaddidars. Using prior information sent to them, the officials select the names of men sent to them while the rest of the common weavers rarely get chance in the lottery. Thus, Mobin, Convener of Bunkar Dastkar Morcha, opposed the 'lottery' system for the selection of weavers to participate in fair. Instead he proposes that a list of weavers who applied for selection should be prepared and sent to the exhibition in a set. In another study, the charge of corruption came forth. Mira Mohsini (2011) in her ethonographic study of Old Delhi artisans recorded an interviewee perception. "Mansoor, however, refused to compete in any of these competitions. He claimed that the entire process was rife with corruption and bribery. What ends up happening, he told me, is that someone competing for one of the awards – who may or may not be a skilled artisan – will typically get the zardozi done by a skilled artisan and then strike a deal with one of the judges. If the artisan wins, then the cash prize will go to the judge and the so-called artisan will keep the government-issued certificate. Mansoor contended that the reason this deal is a win-win scenario for the people submitting zardozi pieces for an award is that having a certificate acknowledging one as a national awardee gives one unlimited access to all of the government-sponsored exhibitions around the country and sometimes abroad."[52]

(c) Faulty Scheme: Most of the schemes are meant for weavers of handloom organisations such as cooperatives and clusters and not for individual weavers. As in Banaras, merely 2 per cent weavers come under the organised category, and rest of them work independently. Rajan Behl, head, Banarasi Vastra Udyog Sangh, argued that government invests in Cooperative Societies of which 95 per cent is fake. He adds that "cluster program run by the government is strange, as sari business in Banaras is unorganised."[53] Thus, any scheme gives them a miss. Haji Ishtiyar Ahmad told that sometimes impractical schemes upset the traditional system in such a way that the weaver does not benefit from the new scheme. The faulty schemes made by the government after meeting so called the 'representatives' of weavers forget to consider the issue raised by the real weavers. Md. Sharif Ansari, resident of Bajardiha, argued that "some so-called experts and visiting senior officials do not even understand who the real weaver is. They meet traders and exporters in the name of meeting weavers and only listen to the views and opinions articulated by traders and exporters. He added that "existing co-operatives should be dissolved as now most of these are not serving the intended purpose of extending benefits and facilities to real weavers."[54]

Weavers' Response to the Crisis

The community in the focus has been going through socio-political and cultural churning under the tremendous pressure of continuous economic decline. The julaha community, in order to meet the challenges thrown by economic hardship are trying things such as: diversifying their product, using mixed yarn rather than pure silk, moving toward powerloom at the economic level, and focus on education and delay in marriages at the social level.

Weavers of Banaras famous for their delicate Banarasi sari of higher end such as *Zari* brocade, "which uses gold (meaning silver thread with gold polish) and silver threads – real or imitation – thrust either as special weft or warp to create glittering raised ornamentation"[55]. The weave- rich varieties of sari are: Banaras silk *Jamdani, Jangla, Tanchoi, Vaskat*, Cutwork, *Tishu* and *Butidar*. Banaras Silk *Jamdani*: The silk *Jamdani*, a technical variety of brocade or the figured muslin, traditionally woven in Banaras may be considered to be one of the finest products to come out of the Banarasi loom. Here silk fabric is brocaded with cotton and rarely with zari threads. *Jamdani* is woven by transfixing the pattern thread between a varying numbers of warp threads in proportion to the size of the design then throwing the shuttle to pass the regular weft. By repeating this process, where in the size and placing of the cut-thread is in accordance with the character of the pattern, *Jamdani* weaver produces a range of intricate designs. Some of the traditional motifs of *Jamdani* include *Chameli* (Jasmine), Panna hazar (Thousand emeralds), *Genda buti* (Marigold flower), *Pan buti* (Leaf form), *tircha* (diagonally striped) etc. The most attractive design feature of the *Jamdani* sari is Konia or a corner-motif having a floral mango buta. *Jangla* Sari: Brocade weavers of Banaras have often endeavored to add a sense of gaiety and festivity by brocading patterns in colourful silk threads amidst the usual gold and silver motifs; of the brocade convention. The sari is an example in which munga motifs have been laid. *Jangla* wildly scrolling and spreading vegetation motif is among the eldest in Banaras brocades. This old rose sari is embellished with beautifully contrasted gold creepers and silver flowers of the *Jangla* motif. The borders have brocaded running creepers in munga silk and gold and silver zari threads. The end panel is a combination of motifs of the borders and condensed *Jangla* of the field. Muga silk brocading enhances the beauty of the sari while reducing the cost. All over *Jal Jangla* design to get the stylish work of the saris and also used *meena* work for the decoration of the fabrics. The exclusive design sari is time-consuming skilled work. Jamwar *tanchoi* sari: Using a technique similar to that of brocade, weavers of Banaras weave sarees using colourful extra weft silk yarn for patterning. This variety is known as *Tanchoi*. This maroon coloured sari on satin weave is brocaded with elaborate motifs from the *jamawar* shawl tradition from Kashmir, the characteristic feature of which was paisley motif, often elaborated into a maze, which would look kaleidoscopic in character. The field has a densely spread minute diaper of *jamawar* style paisley. The end panel has large motifs of multiple paisley forms one growing out of the other. The border as well as the cross-borders of the end panel, has miniature paisley creepers. Tissue Sari: The tissue sari of Varanasi is unbelievably delicate, combining the use of gold and silver metallic threads. The renowned *zari* brocade weavers of Banaras have evolved a technique of weaving tissue material, which looked like golden cloth. By running zari in weft a combination of *zari* and silk in extra-weft (pattern thread) and silk in warp, the weave of this sari has densely patterned with golden lotuses floating in a glimmering pond. The drops of water are created by cutwork technique. The borders and the end panel have a diaper of diamond pattens enclosed by a border of running paisley motifs. Cutwork Sari**:** This type of sari is prepared by cut work technique on plain ground texture after removing the floated thread which are not woven (design) during the weaving process which provide good transparent look. Cutwork is the cheaper version of the *jamdani* variety. In cutwork, the pattern is made to run from selvedge to selvedge letting it hang loosely between two motifs and the extra thread is then cut manually, giving the effect of *jamdani*.

Butidar Sari: The most striking feature of this dark blue silken sari is that it is brocaded with pattern threads of gold, silver and silk. Due to darker shade of gold and lighter shade of silver this variety of patterning in brocade is conventionally known as Ganga-Jamuna, indicating the confluence of these two rivers whose waters are believed to be dark and light respectively. The end panel has a row of arches, in each of which a bouquet of flowers is placed. A slightly smaller and variegated bouquet is diapered all over the field. The butidar sari is a rich kind of the Banaras Saree in high traditional pattern motif of the design locally popularized such as *Angoor Bail*, *Gojar bail*, *Luttar Bail, Khulta Bail, Baluchar Bail, Mehrab Bail, Doller Butti, Ashraffi butti, latiffa butti, resham butti, jhummar bhutti, jhari butta, kalma butti, patti butti, lichhi butti, latiffa butta, kairy kalangathakka anchal, mehrab anchal* with the use of real gold and silver *zari* and katan silk in the weft.

However, in recent times, the handloom weavers have diversified into the following[56].

- Stole 22"*72"
- Scarf 45"*90", 36"*36", 36"*90"
- Muffler 11"*72", 10"*60"
- Mats 16"*16", 18"*18"
- Dress material (Running)
- Furnishing (Running)
- Wall Hanging Various (dimensions)
- Made ups like curtain, cushion cover, table cover, napkins, runners.

Conclusion

Though, even today sari dominates the total production in Banaras, these are not high-value products. Weavers are trying their hand at weaving cheaper saris for common consumption. "This shift from weave to non-weave ornamentation may not be temporary and poses a serious, long-term threat to the prospects of higher-end Banarasi sari."[57] Thus, to produce such sari, today, weavers are also moving away from the natural silk yarn to the synthetic material in which they have no brand name as "Banarasi Sari." This tactic has worked temporarily to sustain weavers from the onslaught of the market but in long run it damaged the reputation of Banarasi sari. On the other hand, the low-range sari weavers have to face competition from the already established powerloom products. This has pushed many weavers into the powerloom and Computer Embroidery

Machine (CEM) factory as workers in a very bad working environment. The building lacks even normal facilities. When I went to a CEM factory in Asfaq Nagar near Madanpura during my fieldwork, I found lack of minimum facilities to the worker. The building has 3-4 CEM, which are operated by mixed labour (migrant worker combine with the local). The factory remains open for 24 hours in shift. The migrant worker stays in the factory, which has terrible sanitation and ventilation. They cook inside the factory. Thus, the production structure restricts workers' movement to the maximum. The wage for the trained worker was Rs. 2,500 and Rs. 1,500 for helper.

The deplorable working environment has been captured by many investigators. For instance, Anju Grover captured the sentiment of worker about their working milieu. "Poor working conditions including insufficient ventilation and lighting have damaged our (interviewee Moinuddin) health and reduced our output. Most of us suffer from respiratory illnesses and eye problems."[58] The transformation of weavers to workers also results in using the former weavers to crush the existing traditional base of livelihood. A typical sign of capitalism taking deep root in India. On the social front many changes are taking place. One such thing is delay in the marriage of males and females. According to Hafiz Sahabuddin, "Due to poor condition of weavers, the age bar of marriage is rising within the community."[59] But the ongoing crisis has sent a strong message to the illiterate weavers that education could turn their bleak future into prosperity. Earlier, the good business was a hurdle as children left their schooling to join the family workshop or business. But, today weavers want to send their wards to school when they cannot afford education at all. What an irony? Government effort in this regard is negligible in the Muslim dominated areas of Banaras. In Lohata area, children are forced to go to community run madrasas because there is only a government primary school for a round 10,000 population, mostly of weavers. According to the rule, there should have been 33 primary and 12 upper primary schools in the locality. A similar situation is faced by the weavers of Bajardiha, where not a single anganwadi exists.

Today, most of the children go to community-run madrasas for their basic education. The weavers are also now giving priority to girl children's education. Most of these educational institutions impart modern education. The well paid job in the market is certainly pulling them against the bondage labour. Though higher education is still limited to well to do families, the essence of education has reached the girls and poor families.

Thus many of those emerging from this system are now urgently demanding the opening of more and more schools in these areas.

References

1. According to *The Gazette of India*, September 4, 2008 the eleven items reserved for the handlooms are: Sari, *Dhoti*, Towel/*Gamchha* and *Angwastram*, *Lungi, Khes*/Bedsheet/Bedcover/Furnishing, Carpet, Dress Materials, Blanket, Shawl/ Muffler, Woolen fabric, *Chadar/Mekhna*.
2. C.P.ChandraSekhar, 'Handlooms: In Survival Mode', paper presented in the Seminar on 'Growth and Prospects of the Handloom Industry', Centre for Economic and Social Studies, Hyderabad, September 23-24, 2001.
3. SRUTI, op.cit. p. 26.
4. *Ibid;* p. 27
5. *Ibid;* p. 27
6. Weavers of Banaras had refused to update with technology as it was available at the interest rate attached with principal amount. At the beginning of the 20th century, the government of the United Provinces tried to introduce improved weaving technology, but weavers who professed 'a religious prejudice against the paying as well as receiving of interest, were not responsive to this move since they would have to rely on taking loans to buy this technology.
7. Ministry of Textile, '*35th Report on General Condition of Weavers in Country – A Case Study of Sircilla Concentration Zone of Weavers*', Standing Committee Report, GoI, 2008-09, p. 7.
8. Naresh Bahadur, Deputy Secretary, Handloom Department letter to Dr. Ajay Tomar, an MLA, on March 4th 2009.
9. Craft Revival Trust, 'Recommendation for Handloom Sector Policy and Schemes', Planning Commission, Government of India, 2012, pp. 156-159.
10. *Ibid.*
11. *Ibid.*
12. *Ibid.*
13. *Ibid.*
14. Annual Report 2009-10, Textile Ministry, GoI.
15. It started in the year 2005-06. ICICI Lombard is a 74:26 joint venture between ICICI Bank Limited, India's second largest bank with $ 79 billion in assets and Fairfax Financial Holdings Limited, Canada based $26 billion diversified financial services company engaged in general insurance, reinsurance, insurance claims management and invest management.
16. www.biz.zeenews.com, April 11, 2010.
17. For detailed analysis of Banaras handloom product and its authenticity please see Amit Basole, 2011. The real Banarasi sari is a high-end fabric made of pure silk on a handloom, and has brocade embroidery. The speciality of Banaras weaving tradition is mastery of the 'extra-weft' technique. In regular weaving the weft thread passes over and under the warp thread regularly. But when brocade

design in gold, silver or silk or cotton threads are to be woven, special threads are transfixed in between by skipping the passage of the regular weft over a certain number of warp threads (depending upon the pattern).

18. Amit Basole, op. cit., p. 163.
19. Mira Mohsini, 'Engagement and disengagement from the margins: perceptions of the state by urban Muslim artisans in India', *Contemporary South Asia*, Vol. 19, No. 3, 2011, p. 282.
20. K. Mukund and B. Syamasundari, 'Doomed to Fail? 'Handloom Weavers' Co-operative in Andhra Pradesh', *Economic and Political Weekly*, Vol. 33, No. 52, Dec. 1998- Jan. 1, 1999, p. 3324.
21. Nidhi Srinivas, 'NGO Advocacy and Marketing: Handloom Weavers in India', Paper for Presentation in the Milano Wednesday Seminar Series, April 12th 2006, p. 15.
22. *Ibid;* p.10.
23. SRUTI, op. cit. pp. 43-44.
24. www.UPICA.IN
25. Philippa Williams, 'An absent presence: experience of the 'welfare state' in an Indian Muslim mohalla', *Contemporary South Asia*, 2011, Vol. 19, No.3, pp. 268-273.
26. Source: file:///I:/Anju%20Grover.htm
27. A. Vaidyanathan, 'Future of Cooperatives in India', *Economic and Political Weekly*, Vol. XLVIII, No. 18, 2013, pp. 30-32.
28. Here government include both the state and central level.
29. Philippa Williams, op. cit., pp. 268-273.
30. P. Nayak, Rout, S. Shaikh and Rajanikant, op. cit., p. 65.
31. Fieldwork Interview in Banaras.
32. *Ibid.* p. 64.
33. Amit Basole, *Knowledge, Gender and Production Relations in India's informal Economy*, Ph.D Thesis, University of Massachusettes Amherst, 2012, p. 31.
34. Fieldwork in Banaras.
35. *Ibid,* p. 97.
36. *Ibid.*
37. Philippa Williams, op. cit., p. 264.
38. Vibhuti Agarwal, Indian Weavers shun health Plan, *www.Southasia.oneworld.net*, September 10, 2009.
39. Fieldwork interview in Banaras.
40. *Ibid.*
41. *Ibid.*
42. *Ibid.*
43. *Ibid.*
44. Philippa Williams, op. cit.; p. 270.

45. Fieldwork interview.
46. Letter to the Prime Minister by the head of Bunkar Panchayat Chaudaho, March 6, 2006.
47. Letter to the Prime Minister by the head of Bunkar Panchayat Chaudaho , March 6, 2008
48. Ashoke Chatterjee, 'Handloom and Handloom Weavers', *Craft Revival Quarterly*, January 2007.
49. Bharat Dogra, 'Dispossession of Weavers in Varanasi and the need for an artisan's movement', *Frontier*, 2008.
50. www.mynews.in (Dr. Lenin Raghuvansi, *Towards the Realisation of the Scheme at grass root level*, November 3, 2009).
51. Editor, 'Benefits of GI not reaching weavers', *Times of India*, Varanasi, September 26, 2009.
52. Mohsini, op. cit., p. 292.
53. Interview with Rajan Behl on November 21, 2009.
54. *Ibid.*
55. Diagnostic Study of Handloom Silk Cluster, Varanasi, Uttar Pradesh, 2005.
56. *Ibid.,* p. 3
57. *Ibid.,* p. 5.
58. Source: file:///I:/Anju%20Grover.htm
59. I interviewed Hafiz during my fieldwork in Banaras. He is a manager in *Barelwi* madaras in Bajardiha. The social effect cannot be generalised as the question on marriage was not uniformly targeted to the respondents and not part of inquiry.

Chapter - 5

Political (de)Mobilisation of Weavers in Banaras

History of Weaver Politics in Uttar Pradesh

The previous chapter underlines the problems accentuated by economic reform, and also the government's response to the crisis through policies and programmes. Though some of the policies such as the cluster programme in Andhra Pradesh have been partially successful, they have not impacted the weavers. In this backdrop, this chapter describes how the weavers responded politically to the crisis in their own ways.

The country has been witnessing different responses to the economic and political crisis. In the late 1960, left extremism was one such political manifestation of grievances generated by the failure of the State. Later on, the 1980 and 1990 saw the rise of identity politics in response to the condition of deep rooted under-development in society. Thereby, religion, caste and region became the basis of political mobilisation. Though this phase in Indian politics is often associated with the deepening of democracy, it failed to achieve the agenda of development. Instead, it led to the fragmentation of this very agenda, and weakened the progressive and democratic forces of the country, which were required to face the challenges thrown by economic reform. This phase of the capitalist mode of production has forced the rise of poverty, unemployment and destitution. The rapid rise of the number of millionaires in India has come at the cost of the common man. According to the World Wealth Report, 2011, India has forty-seven billionaires and her position is fourth in the global ranking.[1] The number of millionaires surged to a record high of 1.53 lakh in 2010, making the country's high net worth individual (HNI) population, the 12th largest across the globe.[2] On the other hand, more and more people were forced to leave their traditional jobs, as we have seen in the case of Banaras silk handloom weavers, who took up wage labour in the unorganised sector.

The current situation in the Banaras provides a strong environment for political movement of the weavers. This chapter focuses on the strategies employed towards the organization and political mobilisation of the weavers of Banaras in response to the crisis facing them. But before that, the nature of organisation involved in such activities is focused upon. If we analyse the political history of the north-Indian weaver, we find that a majority of them live in UP. The politics of weavers started in the early 20th century on the question of constituting a separate identity of lower caste weavers against the Ashraf elite of the community, whose interests were very much different from those of the lower castes. So, the politics of weavers involved the combination of caste and class with the former playing a dominant role. Santosh Kumar Rai argued that "the nature of their demands as well as the work of these organisations focused on assertion of a distinct political and social identity for the julaha weavers. Their politics displayed a quest for an alternative worldview, seeking to challenge existing social hierarchies on the one hand and create an autonomous political space on the other."[3] The national movement, rise of awareness among the downtrodden, politics of homogenization and communal politics has shaped the politics of weavers.

The weavers' grievances appear to have been addressed by caste-based politics rather than a broader politics of social justice. For instance, "In 1933, the provincial Jamait-ul-Ansar of UP resented the non-inclusion of its representatives in the provincial Haj Committee, arguing that out of the 7.7 crore Muslim population in India, Momin Ansars were three to four crores, or nearly half."[4] The political and social battle took a toll on the fight for economic justice. Many handloom weavers were going through economic hardship due to the colonial policies and even the swadeshi movement. "Gandhi's call to boycott of English yarn made the life of *julaha* weavers more miserable as the khadi yarn was neither well-suited nor easily available for their looms. A Muslim League speaker in a meeting in Banaras in September 1938 informed the audience that due to the khadi and charkha movement, 45 million Muslims weavers had been thrown out of work."[5] But *julaha* political organizations like Momin Conference failed to raise the economic issues in a major way, thereby sidelining the issue. This can be understood from the resolutions passed in first session of All India Momin Conference at Halliday Park, Calcutta on 7-9 April 1928. The conference passed the following resolutions:

(1) It appealed to the community to use cloth manufactured by their own men, especially on festive occasions, marriage ceremonies, etc.

(2) It advised their *sardars* and ulemas to induce Momins to give up extravagant marriage and other social expenditures.

(3) A special area to be selected to organise their community and to enforce improvements. To start with Allahabad was selected as such a place.

However, once weavers' politics were articulated around the question of class, the economic issues of the weavers acquired more clarity. One such movement was led by Maulana Azad Subhani, who adopted the symbol of garha or handwoven coarse cloth produced mainly by Muslim artisans. "He saw the garha movement as a means of regenerating the depressed economic conditions of Muslim weavers and contending with what he argued were their extreme poverty and the destruction of their independent artisanal status. Subhani also made British rule squarely responsible for the decline of Muslim weavers, and urged all weavers to fight against imperialism."[6] But, even this kind of movement had a tinge of religion associated with it. In case of Maulana Azad Subhani, the weavers' struggle for the betterment of their economy was linked with a pan-Islamic movement.

It was only in the late 1940 when the struggle between the Momin Conference and the Muslim League intensified that the economic questions came to the fore. This could be possible due to the communist party acquiring social bases in the weaver-dominated areas of Eastern Uttar Pradesh, such as Azamgarh, Gorakhpur, Mau and Banaras. Since the beginning of the weavers' organized movement, it was under the control of religious leaders who picked the issues of weavers, unlike the textile trade-union politics of UP, which was more focused on mills' workers. Kanpur was the hub of textile mills. "In 1961 Kanpur was the largest city of UP with a population of one million. It grew slowly and became the supply centre of clothing and other requirements for British troops throughout India. This encouraged merchants and artisans of neighbouring districts to migrate to Kanpur for trading in grains, spices, cloth, indigo, and for service and contract in the army."[7] About 70 per cent of the workers employed in the Kanpur cotton textile mills have migrated from villages. They lack education, and are economically poor and socially backward. These workers were least interested in politics and there were factions in the trade union movement, each trying to find more support. Kanpur was the base for all the major trade-unions of the time such as Indian National Trade Union Congress (INTUC), All India Trade Union Congress (AITUC), Hind Mazdoor Sabha (HMS), Hind Mazdoor Panchayat (HMP), United Trade Union Congress (UTUC), and Bhartiya Mazdoor Sangh (BMS).[8] They continuously indulged in inter-union rivalry.[9]

Types of Organisations Working for Weavers

Sardari System

In Banaras, apart from NGOs (other voluntary organisations include various government trusts) and a frontal organisation of the Left parties, a traditional social system called Sardari was crucial for the welfare and interest of weavers. A traditional social system, the Sardari calls for a preliminary analysis. Chitra Joshi discusses the mistris system in Kanpur-a textile city of Uttar Pradesh. Mistris were the agents through which new recruitment took place in the mills. In the early years of the industry, mistris had to often go to the villages to recruit labour, though this became rare by the 1920s. Each mistri was in charge of management and supervision over a certain number of workers in the department, apart from his technical functions as a mechanic or a fitter.

According to Tirthankar Roy "*sardar* is an intermediary within the group to negotiate terms. This figure, commonly called the *sardar* (leader), and in some contexts *maistry* or *kangany*, was entrusted with the accounts and eventually with some supervision tasks at destination. He is possibly from the old batch of labour. The agency of the *sardar* is the institutional response to the late industrialization in India, most of which was still rural. The labour from rural India was familiar with the village headmen who represented them before the rent collectors. The *sardars* were analogous to this system in the cities where the labourers migrated for work. These agencies (traditional) were however gone with the maturity of industrialization."[10]

The need of labour by industries and the need of work by labour make this institution a necessary element in the production process. They were present in different industries like sugar, indigo, and tea. Though the *Sardari* institution in Banaras secured prominence during the British era, its role in the life of weavers has been much bigger than what Roy has figured out: mere taking up economic issues between weavers and owners.

The institution of the *sardar* illustrates a unique relationship within the society of weavers, which can also be understood as '*biradrana*' or '*quam*'.

Along with the commonality of occupation, the *Sardari* or *Mahto* system works as glue that holds together the social fabric of the *julaha*. In Banaras, the *Sardari* system started around 1611 AD, which had its presence in other adjoining areas like Mau.[11] It is a selective body looking after the social and economic interests of the illiterate weavers. It is interesting to analyse the historical role played by this institution in the context of weavers' welfare. Looking at the dwindling economic position of weavers in the late Mughal era and then during the British period, this research argues that the *Sardari* system failed on the economic front. According to Sardar Maqbool Hasan, this system got a strong foothold during British the period. A British official impressed by this system awarded the title of 'Khan Bahadur' to his family, which was received by Sardar Rahmatullah.

The selection procedure for the *sardar* was a simple one.[12] One head from each *muhalla*[13] was selected by people, who later on selected their head known as *Amir* (combined leader of various muhallas/chief *sardar*/ bade *sardar*). Once there was a consensus to appoint a particular individual as *sardar*, a ritual known as '*Dastaarbandi*' took place in front of huge mass gathering in an open field. In principle, anyone from any sect could become *sardar;* however, in reality, the family heads of economically strong households were better placed to become the *muhalla*'s *sardar,* and typically, he would be succeeded by his son after death.

(Bawani ke Sardar)

Bahuddin *aka* Gumann Mahto → Gulam Hussain *aka* Mangar Mahto → Shah Mohammad *aka* Mia Mahto (from his period the Bawani *Sardari* started) → Hayatullah *aka* Tali Mahto → Barkatullah Mahto → Mohammad Ayub → Abdur Rahman → Naziruddin *aka* Babu Mahto

(Baaeesi ke Sardar)

Abdus Sattar → Qazi Balaguddin aka Bhanga Mahto → Qazi Kamaluddin aka Kamal Farmani → Qazi Razab Ali Satari → Teg Ali aka Teg Mahto → Janullah aka Janu Mahto → Khano Mahto → Ismail Mahto → Sadikullah Mahto → Abdul Aziz → Mohammad Anis Mahto

Source: Shad Abbasi, *Mandanpura Ki Ansari Biradri: Samaji Pasmanzar*, Vol. 1, aranasi, 2002.

Figure 7: Genealogical Tree of two Sardars of Banaras

The *Sardari* system worked through a cabinet, which was known as 'kabina'. Initially, this institution was created to protect the newly converted Muslim weaver's interest, who generally felt neglected by the royal authority and administration. However, today, this system represents weavers belonging to both the Hindu and Muslim communities. Initially, the whole of Banaras city was divided into two parts i.e. Alaipura[14] and Madanpura - each under its respective sardar. Later on, these parts were further sub-divided as given below[15]:

(a) Alaipura

(1) 22 (*Baaeesi*) Muhallas

(2) 14 (*chaudaha*) Muhallas[16]

(3) 05 (*Pancho*) Muhallas

(b) Madanpura

(1) 52 (*Bawani*) Muhallas

(2) 18 (*Attaraho*) Muhallas

(3) 12 (*Barah*) Muhallas

(4) 22 (*Baaeesi*) Muhallas

The *Sardari* system constituted an authority over the weavers. On the *sardar*'s call, weavers respond by stopping work and gathering at particular places for various purposes. The declaration of yearly holiday of weavers known as '*Murri bandi*' is still being decided by the *sardar*. But it is in case of social practices such as marriage, divorce and material disputes between families and between weavers and owners, that the *sardar* has wider acceptance. This institution has also been successful in arresting the demand of dowry within Muslim weavers of Banaras. Regarding material disputes, the matter usually goes to the *sardar,* and his decision is able to solve the problem, even though it is not enforceable under law. This is possible perhaps because the material conditions of weavers are not good, preventing them from being aggressive towards each other. They are more focused on their livelihood and tend to avoid confrontation. The second factor could be the colonial experience of court procedures, which consumed much time and money. The people considered the British legal system as 'alien' and 'extortionist'.[17] The legal system meant for the peasants led to wastage of cultivation days, indebtedness and incessant milking of their resources. It is aptly expressed in a near contemporary poem by Sukhdevji – an obscure Bhojpuri saint poet writing sometime in mid-nineteenth century. In this poem, accountability in hell is expressed through the punitive metaphor of courts, and this underlines the perception of the new legal system as a curse for the common man:

Samujhi pari jab jaeb kachhari
...khael peeal lel del kagaj baki sab niksi
Dharmaraj jab lekha leehan loha ke sotwar mar paree
age peechhe chopdar dhai bi mugdar jam ke phans pari
agin khamb men bandhi ke rakhihen, Hajri jamini koi na kari

(You will understand once you go to the court. Whatever you have eaten or drunk will all come out – only papers would be left with you, i.e., all your riches will go and they shall be replaced by tons of useless paper. Being called to account by Dharamraj (here, judge) is like being beaten by an iron rod; the court-retainers would not let you escape from the strangulation that you will face. No one will come forward to bail you out, and you will feel as if you have been tied to the pillars of the court for ever).

Nonetheless, with the passing time, the role of this institution too changed in favour of businessmen, which further declined the status of a *sardar/mahto*. The hobnobbing of the *sardar* with the *gaddidar* or traders has taken away the in-built faith of weavers in them. Its further decline has been ensured by the growing sectarianism within the Muslim weavers. For instance, the *amir* (chief) belonging to a particular sect favours his fellow sect members during any issue, which has blurred the impartial character of the *sardar*. This is in fact a classic example of upper classes exploiting religion to further their own interests. Thirdly, trade and commerce in Banaras silk fabrics was not confined merely to wage based earning. It was dependant on but the larger marketing networks, which was beyond the reach of the local sari *mandi* (market). The institutions of *mahto* and *sardar* could not impose their jurisdiction over such a large network with complex business dealings. The regional differences among the weavers too have added to the woes of this declining institution. For instance, sharp competition between the Alaipura weavers, who are known as outsiders or '*Mauwale*', and indigenous weavers i.e. '*Banarasi*' weavers of Madanpura, was illustrated when the Alaipura Sardar gave call for three days '*Murri bandi*' in 1998 without consulting, and hence bypassing the authority of the Bawani sardar.

Voluntary Organisation or NGOs

India has seen tremendous rise in numbers of voluntary organisations in the 1980s and 1990s, which coincided with economic reform. "During 2003-04, 14,700 groups were registered with the ministry of home affairs and received foreign funds worth Rs. 4,856 crore (Rs. 48.56 billion), up from Rs. 3,403 crore in 1998-99 and Rs. 230 crore in 1986."[18] These new NGOs formed during economic reform did not only aim for "development" in partnership with foreign funds. But the capitalist funding of NGOs made it easier to establish these companies and make maximum profits with the support of volunteer organisations, which understood the social and cultural environment much better. A 1994 paper on the ADB's cooperation with NGOs states that "It (NGOs) understands clientele culture and idiom which are important social dimensions that impinge on beneficiary participation in development efforts."[19] The World Bank's Report on Development 2000-01 clearly states that "Social tensions and divisions can be eased by bringing political opponents together within the framework of formal and informal forums and by channeling their energies through political processes, rather than leaving confrontation as the only form of release."[20]

Structural adjustments have led to the retreat of State from social welfare sectors like health, education and water, bringing private players into spheres that were traditionally the preserve of the State. Commenting on the budgetary expenditure of the Union government, the CBGA argued 'it has precious little to offer for inclusive growth'. The Union government's Total Expenditure as a proportion of GDP is projected to fall from 15.4 per cent in 2010-11 (Revised Estimate) to 14 per cent in 2011-12 (Budget Estimate), which reflects that expenditure compression for reducing deficits is the overarching feature of this budget.

Table 75: Priority for Social Services in the Union Budget[21]

Year	*Expenditure from the Union Budget on Social Services (in Rs. Crore)*	*Expenditure from the Union Budget on Social Services*	
		As % of Total Expenditure from the Union Budget	*As % of GDP*
2004-05	39123	7.9	1.2
2005-06	49535	9.8	1.3
2006-07	55246	9.5	1.3
2007-08	78818	11.1	1.6
2008-09	110542	12.5	2.0
2009-10	122345	11.9	1.9
2010-11(RE)	162501	13.4	2.1
2011-12 (BE)	165975	13.2	1.8

Source: Centre for Budget and Governance Accountability, Response to Union Budget 2011-12.

Thus, this process naturally excludes many of the 'development' processes, leaving the poor to pretty much fend for themselves. To control the rising frustration and prevent its manifestation into a concrete political movement, the capitalists use volunteer organisations. So the funding has become the test of autonomous functioning of any volunteer organisation. J. Mencher found that the funding can affect the functioning of NGOs in more than one way. These are as follows:[22]

(1) They may create problems of survival for smaller NGOs and indirectly coerce the organizations to tailor make proposals. Many smaller NGOs are often placed in a difficult dilemma. They may have their own set of priorities, but if a funder (be it a government agency such as Capart, or a foreign funder, or a project that they hear about that has funds only for XYZ) has different priorities, if they are low on funds – as most are – then there is a tendency to draw up proposals to meet the funder's priorities rather than their own.

(2) Problems in how they handle divergences between their own priorities and funders' priorities – ways in which NGOs can lose their focus or become over-extended and is one of the multitudes of reasons why some projects either fail or meet only very limited objectives and never spread.

(3) Funder's priorities also create difficulties for NGOs which place their main emphasis on conscientisation and advocacy. There are many reasons for this, not the least being the difficulty in evaluating or measuring success, which may not be measurable in terms such as the number of loans, or the rate of repayment of loans, or the number of plots of land redistributed, or the number of women trained to make a product, etc.

On the whole, most donors tend to fund NGOs that are not seeking to "upset the apple cart" by confronting fundamental issues in the society. Thus, it is clear that pro-establishment NGOs tend to get the lion share of funds.[23] In the case of India where there is considerable power in the hands of each State, the state government's policies also must be taken into account. NGOs may be classified in terms of whether they are:[24]

(1) Working with local governments, and if so is it through a process of collaboration or one of co-optation?

(2) Working in the spaces left open by governments not wanting to or not able to carry out programmes, especially among the poor who have little political clout.

(3) Helping to utilize the benefits already available through government programmes,

(4) Confronting government to provide or allocate some of the help available through the government

(5) Confronting government to bring about changes in programmes and /or policies,

(6) A blend of several of these.

These organizations take up various activities in India and most of them are active in the rural areas.

Table 76: Areas of Activity by Number of Institutions[25]

Religion based	26.5
Community/social services	21.5
Education	20.4
Sports and culture	18
Health	6.6

Source: Srivastava and Tandon (2005)

The funding of NGOs by world capitalists or similar organizations affects the aims, functioning and method of advocacy of NGOs. It has been a matter of concern for the organised labour movement by Left parties, which views the NGO – a post-modernist institution - as an imperialist intrusion into the labour movement at the local level. Post-modernism argued that society is no more divided into proletariat and bourgeoisie. It talks about the emergence of many classes due to change in production process. In a sense, they were characterising the contemporary society as post-industrial society, which has no central power of oppression. So they were prescribing to look at the multiple-forces, which are dominant at different levels, causing exploitation to the people. It gives rise to identity politics causing dis-unity among the working class.

Prakash Karat, General Secretary of CPI (M), argued that "Post-modernism is a bourgeois philosophical outlook which arose as a result of the success of late 20th century capitalism and the retreat from socialism. It is antithetical to Marxism. It arose out of a profound sense that the 'Enlightenment' project is dead or exhausted. Post-modernism questioned all the enlightenment values and rejected any philosophy or politics which was 'universal' and 'totalising'. Post modernism dismissed all 'totalising' theories as so called 'meta-narratives'. Post modernism does not recognise capitalism or socialism as a structure or system. It sees knowledge and power as mediated by language and there are different ways of seeing it. History therefore can be seen only in a context and relatively. Post modernism only recognises a mosaic of identities, differences and conflicts. Hence what is possible is recognising the fragments of a particular identity. What is possible are particular struggles or autonomous social movements which are based on a fragmented politics of 'difference' and 'identity'. Post-modernism poses to be a radical social theory. But it is in reality not antithetical to capitalism. It is not an alternative to bourgeois theory and is utilised as a hostile counter theory to Marxism."[26]

NGOs in Banaras: There are many volunteer organisations working for Banaras weavers and they are as follows:

(a) Bunkar- Dastakar Adhikar Manch (BDAM, Weaver-Artisan Rights Front)

(b) PVCHR and FWRA

(c) HWA (Human Welfare Association)

(d) Bunkar Bachao Aandolan

(e) Banaras Bunkar Samiti (BBS)

(f) Purvanchal Bunkar Morcha

(g) Vanarasi Weavers Trust (VWT).

There are governments and other organisations at the national level which work among the artisans and craftsmen:

(h) Craft Council of India

(i) Craft Revival Trust

(j) Craftmark

(k) CRY and ASHA

The organisations successful in terms of intervention and hold over the weavers are those funded by either by Indian capitalists or international agencies. For instance, Bunkar-Dastkar Adhikar Manch and Banaras Bunkar Samiti are two such organisations. The figure 8 shows the funding structure of the two organisations. As we can see from the figure 8, Varanasi Weavers Trust (VWT) is funded by Asian Human Rights Commission (AHRC) through People's Vigilance Committee on Human Rights (PVCHR), which also provides funds to Bunkar Dastkar Adhikar Manch (BDAM). Bunkar Dastkar Adhikar Manch (Forum of Rights of Weavers and Artisans) was established in 2003 and elected Mr. Siddique Hasan, a weaver, as Convener of this union.

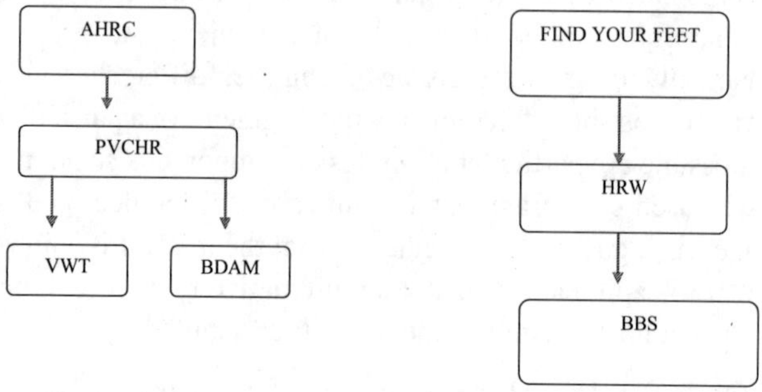

Figure 8: International Organisations link and support to the local organisation in Banaras

When PVCHR found the problem of suicide among weavers it called a meeting of a core team together to discuss the problems. It was decided to intervene in their problems. "Nearly 500 weavers came in contact with PVCHR and they decided that they were in need of a union of weavers, which would struggle to revive the handloom industry and lobby the government for better social security for weavers."[27]

BDAM uses strategy called 'folkway', a means of providing the victims an opportunity to speak of their problems, which are recorded to be utilised for the advocacy of these weavers. BDAM focuses on three main issues: right to food, right to health and revival of the handloom industry. Similarly, VWT is also run by PVCHR. VWT started by PVCHR in 2004, is based on an innovative model by Sri Lankan economist Dr. Darin Gunesekara of the Wiros Lokh Institute, the Varanasi Weavers Trust is a unique non-profit organization started with a mission to eliminate the crisis facing the weavers of Varanasi. The Varanasi Weavers Trust promises to provide the much needed impetus to the Varanasi Silk industry and a solution to uplift the weavers from their current plight. Similarly, Banaras Bunkar Samiti (BBS) is funded by 'Find Your Feet' (FYF) through Human Welfare Association (HWA). HWA is a Varanasi based NGO with the support of Find Your Feet – India. It is intensively intervening for empowering marginalized weavers through project *Tana-Bana* for the last five years. At this moment the organization has facilitated the establishment of a community-based organization of weavers called the BBS that was registered as a society last year.

"This Association is a federation of ninety-six self-help groups (1307 weavers families) with own executive board and official set ups. Now we are doing our concerted efforts to strengthen the forward and backward linkages (marketing and production) of the Association. Now, the focus is on sustainability of the weaver's association. The strategy adopted is systematic capacity building of the representatives of the Association and step by step handing over the responsibility for association's operations. The executive board members and other representatives have taken the responsibility of monitoring of saving /credit groups on routine basis, visiting groups for planning of income generating activities, scrutinizing and sanctioning of revolving fund requests, monitoring the weaving works provided by BBS and quality control of finished goods. Similarly the office bearers of association visit **BBS** office and showroom regularly to monitor the day by day activities. Bank accounts are operated by themselves and all the transactions related to revolving fund and capital loan are regulated by them. **BBS** actively participate in planning and execution of the project activities. Exposure visits and participation in outstation training programs are facilitating the process of their capacity building.

On the other end, the organization has raised the issues of handloom weavers at various national and international forums and sensitized various communities for the issues. The organization has done concerted efforts for sensitizing the government of India towards the framing of policies for uplifting the declining handloom sector. These advocacy efforts played a vital role in drawing the attention of the government, civil society groups, media, political parties, trade unions and several other organizations towards the starving situation of the handloom sector in Varanasi. Now the **BBS** jointly with HWA, from time to time, shakes up the government machinery through rallies, protest march and other non-violent direct actions for survival of the handloom industry."[28] The rest of the Banaras based NGOs are individual initiatives based on area specific mobilisation. For instance, Bunkar Bachao Andolan (Save Weavers Movement) is initiated by the Dr. Mahfooz Alam and concentrated in his locality of Ashfaq Nagar. This kind of organisation most of the time plays a secondary role to the larger mobilisation.

Left Political Parties

Bunkar-Dastkar Morcha (Weaver-Artisan Front) is a frontal organisation of the Communist Party of India (Marxist) formed in 2002. It was formed as a response to economic reform and its adverse impact on weavers in

Banaras. This is the only organisation which treats weavers as a worker and presents them within a secular framework. Com. Mobin, convener of Bunkar-Dastkar Morcha (BDM), argued that many organisations which work for the weaver do not care about those who exist in rural areas. In contrast, BDM tries to bring all the weavers together to strengthen the fight against globalisation and exploitation. It worked through the frontal organisation to get acceptability among the weavers. The rise of identity politics with the propaganda that Left Parties are atheistic made the BDM untouchable and restricted its access to the community. The left party's activists are seen as 'godless' people despite their hard work for the weavers.

Political Mobilisation of Weavers

The weavers of Banaras got their first taste of radical mobilisation in 1857 when they revolted against the British and the middlemen who were involved in their economic exploitation. Thereafter, the weavers were involved in collective action several times for various reasons. The Banaras weavers were part of the Momin Ansar Conference, which was active to reformulate the weavers' identity in the pre-independence period.

In the post-independence period, the implementation of policies under the Five Year Plans curbed the momentum for collective action by weavers. The leaders began to rely on petition and request. Initially, leaders like Z.A. Ahmad started advocating in favour of weavers' interest. He called Jawaharlal Nehru to Banaras, where he promised to set-up dyeing and chemical factories. The Congress and the Muslims of Uttar Pradesh had a patron-client relationship. To keep weavers within the party, the Congress chose Ansari as leader and allocated a post to him. Earlier, the Textile Ministry or Small-Scale Ministry was given to Ansari leaders. A.Q. Ansari (Bihar), Zia-ur-Rahman (Uttar Pradesh), Habib-ur-Rahman Numani (Mau, UP), Amin Ansari (Phoolpur, UP), Abid Ali (Lucknow, UP) etc. were some leaders who consistently advocated the cause of weavers. However, the consistent decline of the weavers' economic status gave the Communist Party an opportunity to intervene. In 1972, there was a huge mobilisation of weavers and artisans under the banner of All India Weavers' Federation, which raised the issue of supply of yarn at low cost, marketing facilities and bank loan at lower rates of interest. This agitation was able to win all their demands. Uttar Pradesh Handloom Corporation was one such organisation which came after this agitation to help out the weavers. But, with the weakening of Left parties in the state, the issues of weavers did not feature consistently in politics.

The rise of identity politics in the State undermined the scope for the secular mobilisation of workers. Most of the Left party workers and activists claim that the backward class politics of Chaudhary Charan Singh weaned away Left supporters, and dismantled the organisation.[29] In Mau, Com. Imtiaz and Com. Jalis of CPI shared their view on the rise of identity politics. The rise of Bahujan Samaj Party (BSP) gave another jolt to their base in the State. At the central level, CPI (M) sees the functioning of identity politics as a political challenge to the overall left politics. "Identity politics based on caste, religion, tribe, ethnicity and region is posing a major challenge for the Left in India. The ruling classes and imperialist finance capital find such politics eminently suitable for their interests. Fragmentation of the people on the basis of narrow identities and keeping them separate ensures that there is no threat to the rule of capital and the state. The challenge before the Left is to tackle identity politics by building common class-based movements, while at the same time, taking up the issues of caste, social and gender oppression experienced by different sections of society", said Prakash Karat.[30]

However, the Left parties, which believe in class politics also failed to recognise the democratic value of 'caste' assertion, causing much damage to the prospects of workers and weavers. By not supporting the cause of OBCs, they created the impression that Left Parties are anti-OBCs. Not only that, the upper caste dominated leadership of Left parties too created confusion among the social bases. For instance, in Bihar, almost all the posts of CPI and CPM were dominated by upper castes. CPI [1990] – The Bhumihars (Brahmana) occupied the following key positions in the state: Chutranand Sharma, leader in the RS; Ramavtar Sharma, State Party Secretary; Ramendra Kumar, leader of the party in Bihar Assembly; Parmanand Singh Madan, leader of the party in Legislative Council; Jitendra Kumar, State General Secretary of All India Youth Federation; Triveni Sharma Sudhkar, President, Kisan Sabha (CPI); Dinesh Prasad Sinha, MLC, General Secretary, Indo-Soviet Cultural Society; Shatrughan Prasad Sinha, MLC, General Secretary of the Secondary School teachers' Association, Shatrughan Prasad Singh, General Secretary, Non-Gazetted Employees Federation; Chandra Ketu Sharma, State Secretariat member and incharge of at party headquarters.[31] CPM [1990] – The Bhumihars' position in the CPM was as follows: Ganesh Shankar Vidyarthi, State Secretary of the party and leader in the Legislative Council; Vijay Kanth Thakur, Ramashray Singh and Krishna Kant Singh, members of the State Secretariat of the Party (total membership nine); Ram Pukari Devi, President of CPM women's cell; Ramashray Singh, Assembly leader of the party; Krishna Kant Singh, President, Kisan Sabha (CPM), Lallan Choudhary, DIYF general secretary; Yoginder Singh, General Secretary of the Non-Gazetted Employees Federation; Sarvodaya Sharma, incharge of Student Youth Sub-Committee.[32]

Thus, with the weakening of Left forces in the Banaras region ended the most consistent force fighting for the weavers and workers. Tokenism replaced the consistency of struggle. Once again prices of yarn shot up in the 1980s, which sparked a massive agitation in Eastern UP. However, none of the demands were met by the Chief Minister. "The agitation was sparked off by a spurt in yarn prices, from Rs. 85/kg bundle in September 1986 for the ordinary variety, to Rs. 135 in 1987, and eventually to Rs. 160 in January 1988. Since the weavers could not sell their products at prices high enough to compensate for the hike in yarn prices, their looms were forced to remain idle. The silk industry of Varanasi was paralysed because of a steep rise in yarn prices from Rs. 650 in 1987 to Rs. 1100/kg in 1988, and an acute shortage of the raw material."[33]

*Si*nce the start of economic reform, weavers have not been in a position to take the long course of agitation, as their status did not permit them to stop loom for a long time. Weavers submissively accepted the hunger, poverty, bad health and unemployment as their fate and ultimately resorted to suicide. To fill the vacuum created by retreat of Left parties, and to curb conditions favourable to rise of the Left, NGOs and volunteer organisations with foreign funding flourished in Banaras. For instance, Bunkar-Dastkar Adhikar Manch came up in competition with Bunkar-Dastkar Manch (weavers' organisation of CPI-M). As told earlier, the strategy is to absorb the weavers and prevent them from the joining the movement under the Left's organisation. Equipped with money power, which is used to employ men among the weavers to some small time gain, these NGOs are successful in halting weavers from joining the Left forces. The volunteer organizations have picked up issues ranging from wage increment to mobilisation for waivers of electricity bill. For instance, on August 04, 2004, weavers struggling for their existence through wages even demanded the scrapping of all the handloom cooperatives and enquiry into their corrupt practices. They knew that there have been on-going corrupt practices in the name of co-operatives, which have been under the big gaddidars' control.

When the UPA-I led by Congress came to power in 2004, the Banaras weavers had great expectations. They believed that the previous Brahmin-

Bania government at the Centre had overlooked them. On April 26, 2006 a number of weavers and artisans under the banner of Forum on Rights of Weaver and Artisans staged a demonstration at the district headquarters. They were demanding inclusion of Varanasi districts in National Rural Employment Scheme, issuance of red cards to the handloom weavers, exemption from electricity bills and implementation of Darin's Varanasi Weavers' Trust plan. The speakers were of the view that the government should ensure upliftment of weavers and artisans by implementing several welfare schemes. They further added that weavers and artisans were reeling under poverty and economic crisis, and were on the verge of starvation due to recession in the market. A number of weavers and artisans committed suicide due to poverty during last two years in Varanasi, they said. Further, to protect handloom from imitations and Chinese import of yarn and silk, weavers mobilised themselves on March 27, 2006 under Banaras Bunkar Samiti along with HWA. They staged a sit-in at the district headquarters on March 27, 2006 demanding registration of Banarasi sari under GI. But it seems that UPA-I too was giving a miss to weavers and not paying heed to their demands. "This infuriated weavers who on Nov 6, 2008 publicly burnt Chinese yarn and silk fabric, demanding that the government ban its import to save the handloom sector."[34] Scores of handloom weavers took to streets in Varanasi, famous for its world renowned Banarasi saris, against the cheap quality Chinese imitation products flooding the market.[35]

At the end of the UPA-I tenure, the rage was on the rise. The Central government that was solely responsible to make and implement policies regarding textiles was proving incompetent. Weavers gathered in late November 2008 at a public hearing held in village Dulaipur Satpokhri of Chandauli district, to raise their concerns over the rapid loss of work and incomes.[36] However, peeved with the non-fulfilment of their long pending demands number of weavers of 'Forum on Rights of Weaver and Artisans' have staged a *dharna* at the district headquarters on February 18, 2009. While issues like malnutrition and poverty were prominently raised during the protest, other demands like waiving off due electricity bills for hand loom and power loom weavers and fixing of subsidised electricity bills (monthly) also figured in the protest. Along with the food insecurity, the rising electricity bills and irregular supply of electricity brought weavers together.

On August 12, 2009, the weavers associated with Purvanchal Bunkar Morcha held a Bunkar Panchayat at Madarsa Faizul Uloom, Lohta to protest against excessive power cut in the weaver dominated area. "We hardly get 5-6 hours of electricity", said Faizal: It was decided in the panchayat that a delegation of weavers would call on the divisional commissioner on Thursday to apprise him of the problems being faced by the weavers due to power shortage. "We are hardly getting 5-6 hours electricity supply in Lohta, the hub of power loom industry, and adjoining areas," said Shamim Nomani, the convener of PBM. According to him, there are over 4000 units of power looms, alone in Lohta village that give employment to the many weavers of the neighbouring villages. About 16000 weavers are directly engaged on power looms in two shifts. But, the pathetic condition of power supply mars the prospect of weavers, said Nomani, adding that the power loom industry is passing through a critical phase due to poor power supply. "We need proper and regular supply of electricity for the interest of power loom weavers and their families," he said. The panchayat was attended by the gram pradhans of many villages including the gram pradhan of Lohta, Haji Salim Ansari. They submitted a memorandum of demands to the nayab tehsildar (sadar). On June 21, 2010, Subeh-e-Banaras activists burnt the effigy of power department MD to express their protest against erratic power supply at Maidagin in Varanasi on June 21, 2010.[37]

On the other hand, the Left parties, especially CPI (M) and its mass organisation BDM were the first to articulate the problems of weavers and formulate demands to bring respite to the weavers. BDM has been consistent throughout the decade in its struggle for the weaver. The problems aggravated in and around the financial crisis of 1997-98, which began to impact weavers in the years to come. With the phasing out of the MFA in the process, the cost of yarn shot up. BDM in direct collaboration with CPI (M) organised the people and demanded the lowering of yarn price. It also demanded from the administration that government should procure and provide yarn at a lower rate to the weavers, as was done earlier. In other words, it was demanding a permanent solution to yarn problems and reversal of liberalization.

The government responded to the weavers' demand by providing institutional help to the co-operative, which it is still continuing with. However, it has been said earlier that co-operatives are under the control of elite gaddidars who benefit out of such government help. BDM started addressing this problem by mobilising weavers against such fraudulent acts of co-operative societies whose demand of import of raw material under OGL was to benefit the owner of the societies. Due to increase in yarn prices and other materials, the input cost too increased, for which weavers began to take loans from local moneylenders (as shown in previous chapter). They fell into the debt trap of sahukars.

BDM demanded that government should provide soft loans to the weavers to protect them from trap. Along with that, BDM demanded that government should waive off all loans of those weavers who had taken loan from various banks. On February 12th, 2004 and again on April 4th 2004 BDM took a delegation to the district administration and submitted memorandum in this regard. The year 2004 had seen many such struggles from BDM on behalf of weavers. This established the credit of BDM among the weavers. On April 6th 2004 BDM demanded that Handloom Corporation should procure the finished product and also supply raw materials on subsidised rate. On July 3rd 2004 the organisation demanded: a) procurement of finished product through Handloom Corporation; b) supply of raw materials by govt. on subsidies rate, c) Loan up to Rs. 50,000 to weavers without interest rate, d) Waiver of all the previous debt, e) Free electricity, f) BPL card to the weavers.

After such a persistent and non-negotiable struggle, the government introduced weavers' identity card, based on which help was to be delivered. But there were two problems in the implementation of this scheme. First, the number of weavers' cards was very limited. Due to poor record of documents of indigenous banarasi weavers, they were left out. Second, there was huge corruption in the making of weavers' identity card. Influential but non-eligible gaddidars bribed officials to have the ID card.

BDM took up this case as well with the administration and started a movement for more and more IDs to the eligible weavers and removing corrupt practices in the process. On August 13th 2004, the organisation submitted a memo to the government official in Banaras. The presence of PDS is very bad especially in Banaras – the city where most weavers reside. They were not receiving anything from PDS. So on September 15th, 2004 BDM agitated to implement the policy of Rs. 2 for a kilo of wheat and Rs. 3 for a kilo of rice, and ration-cards permitting 35 kilograms of ration per family. But this did not stop weavers from enduring chronic malnutrition and distressful life, and suicide seems to be the natural choice for them. To stop them from committing suicide, BDM on May 14th, 2006 started a movement for BPL cards for weavers; waiver of electricity arrears and previous debt; direct procurement of the finished product by Handloom Corporation; providing low costs yarn; minimum of 20 hours electricity supply etc. Next year too, BDM demanded 20,000 BPL and 5,000 red-card to the poor weavers, loan on low interest rate and extending the central Govt. assistance to the individual weavers. To make government aware about the worsening situation of Banaras' julaha, the CPM wrote to Prime Minister Manmohan Singh on February 11th, 2006.

In the later phase of the movement, a regular supply of electricity on subsidised rate became a prominent issue for the handlooms of Banaras. It is also because of increased working hours of the weavers (sometimes until midnight), enforced by the competition from powerlooms. Secondly, the increasing number of powerlooms, which had absorbed displaced weavers, and looked for more production, required a regular supply of electricity. BDM along with CPM continuously fought for the regular and cheap supply of power. The year 2009 had seen a three phase movement demanding electricity. The first phase of movement against the Electricity bill payment started on November 16th, 2009 followed by November 24th, 2009 and December 2nd, 2009. Before that, on October 11th, 2009, BDM called for a consultation meeting of weavers to articulate their demands. The good thing about BDM movement is that it does not link the problems of weavers with their religious identity. Unlike other organizations, it brings forth a unified mobilisation of weavers and aids the system that is in place to further the weavers' interests. Apart from the noted record of BDM, it works to raise the issues of daily importance for the weavers. First, it mobilises people on issue basis and sensitise them to work for their own betterment. BDM selects the most articulate and regular participants and organises them into a group. This process involves ideological and manpower support for the furtherance of the demand. No money is involved at any level of mobilisation. This is the most authentic process of political mobilisation provided by Left.

One such example of mobilisation was seen by a researcher during his stay for fieldwork. BDM through its local committee tried to organised weavers for the water problem in Razanagar, a locality of Bajardiha. On October 18th 2009, at a meeting of weavers, it was decided that a delegation will go to meet Jal Nigam officer to place a demand for safe drinking water and issuance of hand-pipe for the locality. On October 22nd, 2009, a delegation comprising of local committee members along with Com. Mobin *reached the Jal Nigam office. The officer was initially rude; however, th*e logical intervention of Com. Mobin toned him down. Later on he agreed to send a team of technicians for the inspection of the area and promised to set-up a hand-pipe as per requirement.

The mobilisation of weavers against hiked electricity bills and its irregular supply forced regional parties like Samajwadi party (known to appeal to Muslims) to include this in the election manifesto of the party in 2012 assembly elections. Under the heading 'Protection of minorities' interest' the party promised to provide financial support to the cottage industries such as lock, bangle, hand loom, carpet, handicraft, zardozi etc. It also promised to waive off electricity bills and supply free electricity to the weavers. However, the problems of hand loom industry are treated as the minorities' problem rather than broader industrial challenges. Hand loom is missing from the industrial section. This approach missed the link between the industrial policy and handloom sector, instead linking the latter to a particular community. Thus the charity approach of regional political parties continued unabated.

Despite a continuous fight for the rights of weavers, the Left parties have negligible presence among the weavers. The reason which stopped the labour movement from succeeding in Banaras was the caste and religious solidarity between the exploiters and exploited. The poor weavers and the rich men in the business belong to the same caste and religion. The poor weavers could not separate themselves from the rich even though they were exploited. No one could dare to call or participate in a strike against the rich. The other reason could be the poverty itself and the hand-to-mouth situation of weavers, which stopped them from being productive for long periods. Thirdly, weavers are dependent on the rich Muslim gaddidars for their raw materials, works, wages and advances.

Hence, J.M.F.Wood concluded that in Varanasi, protest is for the privileged. She argues that, "those groups with fewer economic resources have weaker, more loosely established associations and have a more difficult time mobilising members of their occupational group to participate in time-consuming and expensive strikes and demonstrations. Strikes are particularly costly and almost impossibly so for most lower-class worker such as handloom weaver and boatmen. However, middle-class occupational groups in (Banaras) have the necessary resource to build up powerful associations and indulge in contentious politics to get their demands fulfilled."[38] J.M.F.Wood argued against the theoretical framework of Sudipta Kaviraj, John Harris and Partha Chatterjee who define civil society as a small elite gathering not involved in political participation.

Table 77: Reports of Contentious public action by occupational associations in Varanasi, 1998-2008

Year	*Traders*	*Lawyers*	*Boatmen*	*Weaver*	
				Handloom or Unknown	*Powerloom*
1998	5	4	0	3	3
1999	9	5	0	0	0
2000	18	17	0	2	2
2001	9	18	0	5	0
2002	21	8	0	2	0
2003	58	11	0	10	14
2004	14	11	0	17	0
2005	55	7	2	6	1
2006	19	7	1	7	0
2007	26	21	1	5	0
2008	27	6	18	1	0
Total	**261**	**115**	**22**	**58**	**20**

Source: J.M.F.Wood, Contentious Politics and Civil Society in Varanasi, p. 101

"Most of the handloom weavers '58 contentious actions represented above was small, brief rallies organised by outside activists, NGOs, and political parties on the handloom weavers' behalf."[39] Most of the actions organised by powerloom weavers were costly, lengthy strikes and major demonstrations.

Analysis of Political Mobilisation

Of the entire organisation at work for the weavers, the Sardari/mahto system is the weakest one. It plays practically no role in political mobilisation except showing its presence in other mobilisations. However, its claim over the weavers is large and it believes in its sole prerogative to handle any kind of issue within the community. So it does not like any other organisation taking over the leadership. It uses a religious rhetoric to reject the communist movement and does not recognise the tokenism of NGOs with the weavers. A meeting attended by Syeda Hamid, member of Planning Commission, on November 18th 2009, to know the problems faced by weavers, turned ugly as clash of leadership between NGOs and traditional social leaders came out in public.[40] Table 78 shows the weavers' attitude toward the sardar/mahto and its system.

Table 78: Sardar's role in Social and Economic affairs in Banaras

	Sardar's role in Social Affairs			*Sardar's role in Economic Affairs*		
	Effective	*Ineffective*	*Total*	*Effective*	*Ineffective*	*Total*
Number of Respondents	257	43	300	21	279	300
% of Respondents	85.71	14.28	100	7.14	92.85	100

Source: Fieldwork in Banaras

Note: number of respondents and percentage are given in round figure.

Most of the respondents (85.72 per cent) think that sardar/mahto is effective and plays a major role in resolving social issues, whereas same respondents feel that this system has failed to take care of economic issues. It has been argued that the destruction of the handloom industry in Banaras makes it favourable for political movement. Karl Marx notes "So long as, in a given branch of industry, the factory system extends itself at the expense of the old handicrafts or of manufacture, the result is as sure as is the result of an encounter between an army furnished with breach-loaders, and one armed with bows and arrows.' [41] But, interestingly there is no such sign in the near future. Many factors are at work to halt the gathering of momentum for any political movement viz. lack of political leadership, role of religion, role of NGOs, dismissive role of social head etc. The current situation also defies the theoretical premise that poverty and economic distress leads any group, in this case Muslim weavers, towards extremism. Muslim julaha of Banaras is rather peace-loving and averse to the idea of violence.[42] Perhaps, this is so because julaha communities of Banaras have evolved themselves psychologically against the ups and down of the market.[43] Migration and shift to other jobs have been part of a survival strategy. But the current crisis prolonged over two decades, has taken their suffering one step ahead, leading the weavers to commit suicide. Even then it did not push weavers for strong agitation. However, this doesn't mean that there is no anxiousness and will to fight for their rights; however, the lack of support and tokenism has taken the hope away from the weavers and pushed them to accept the situation as 'Allah's will'.

Role of Religion: Most of the weavers believe that the silk handloom business prospers on two things: their labour and Allah's blessing. They try to co-relate the two elements and wrap it in religious colour. It is labour that Allah loves and blesses with prosperity. Surprisingly, nobody ever questions the poor living conditions, which have only worsened despite hard work and longer working hours for even the women and children. The religious overtone helps to bypass the corrupt practices of officials, gaddidars and traders as well as wrong policies of the government. Weavers think that the crisis is due to their own fault (sin), and so on the call of their respective sardar/mahto, they gather to 'kulpadhaiya' or 'duakhani' outside the city for three days in an open field for prayer. Perhaps, this is why Marx called religion as 'opium'.

Role of the Social head (Sardar/Mahto): The sardars are considered as the representative of the weavers, who takes care of their economic and social problems. However, most of the sardars are illiterate themselves and unable to comprehend the fast changing situation after economic reform. But as they are linked with weavers and themselves in the business, they understand that something is ailing in the industry. Thus, they hope for change by appealing to the corrupt officials at the local level and ideological shift of policies, which has thrown weak industry into the competition at the international stage. Asked in an interview during the fieldwork about the nature of political agitation, bade sardar told that "We generally appeal to the government. But, we never go into mobilising weavers for strong political movement against the wrong policies of the government."

Lack of Political Leadership: It seems that social heads are not ready to accept the new role of political leadership, as they think that these are the role of professional politicians, once sprouted by political parties from the Ansari community. They argue that Ansari community's lack of political leadership has two connotations: forgetting their own potential of mobilisation or reluctance to get involved with issues. Along with the bourgeoisie politics, Banaras weavers have also experienced a strong Communist movement in post-independent period. In 1950 and 1960 CPI tried to organise labour movement among the weavers of Banaras. Though, it had only a marginal effect on the weavers' prospects, the party got support of weavers from both parts of the city (north and South) during municipal and legislative elections. Rustum Saiting (a Parsee), was elected, and became minister as well. Under his tenure many CPI supporters became big corporators. Once Communist Party divided into CPI and Communist Party of India (Marxist), (CPI-M), supporters also got divided. Thereafter, Marxists were never able to gain momentum though they raised number of issues during the on-going crisis period.

Division among the Organisation: There is stark division among the various types of organisations that have been at work to uplift the status of weavers. The division is not only ideological in nature but also regarding assuming leadership of weavers. The traditional leadership is unable to comprehend the changing situation after economic reform. So they are unable to device any strategy to counter it. At the same time they are not allowing others to lead the weavers. On the other hand, the politics of voluntary organisations is to minimise the frustration of weavers, but they usually do not think of challenging the government's policy of economic reform, which has been the root of problems. Their nature of working depends much on the funding from capitalist sources, which ultimately discourage them to take up such issues.

Conclusion

The advent of an aggressive finance driven capitalist globalisation and the weakening of socialism have set the background for the rise of identity politics. Globalised finance capital finds it convenient to deal with the people fragmented on the basis of multiple identities. It makes it easier to penetrate the market and take control. Consumerism and the market cater to all the disparate groups, but their fragmentation into innumerable identities prevents their coming together to challenge the exploitation of capital and its domination of the market.

The capitalist State under imperialism is dealing with competing groups – who make claims for access to the social surplus and economic goods. Multiple but discrete (separate) groups are better for the ruling classes than a universal solidarity forged across communities and groups who resort to radical politics and demand equality in distribution of the economic goods/surplus. The theoretical support to identity politics is being provided by post-modernism. Post modernism is a bourgeois philosophical outlook which arose as a result of the success of late 20th century capitalism and the retreat from socialism. It is antithetical to Marxism. It arose out of a profound sense that the 'Enlightenment' project is dead or exhausted. The Enlightenment which began in Europe in the 18th century and became firmly established in the 19th century espoused universal values of individual freedom, progress and rationalism.

"Post modernism only recognizes a mosaic of identities, differences and conflicts. Hence what is possible is recognising the fragments of a particular identity. What is possible are particular struggles or autonomous social movements which are based on fragmented politics of 'difference' and 'identity'."[44] Hence, what we see today in Banaras is a working class movement under the influence of NGOs and bourgeoisie politicians, who support the division of working class. *In other words,* by providing liberal funds to these groups, imperialism has created avenues to penetrate vital sections of the Indian society, and simultaneously use this movement as a vehicle to counter and disrupt the potential of the left movement. Economic aid, the instrument of multinationals for perpetuating subjugation and cultural penetration has become the mainstay of the modern new-colonialist strategy of imperialism. It is in this scenario that we have to observe the capitalist penetration and strategy in utilizing charitable agencies / action groups in countries like India. The utilization of this network of agencies has become a new factor in imperialist strategy.

On the other hand, the SCR and the Rangnath Mishra Committee Report on Muslims' backwardness in the national context captured the attention of the policy makers. These reports highlighted the lack of inclusiveness of Muslims in the developmental process in various States ruled by parties of different ideological hues. It forced Muslims to believe that no political party is good enough to deal with their grievances. Consequently, they argued for a separate party for Muslims. Hence, the period after the release of the reports has witnessed the mushrooming of Muslim-centric political parties. Peace party of India (2008), Welfare Party of India (2011), Popular Front of India (2006), Rashtriya Ulema Council (2008), People's Democratic Conference of India are some of them. The leadership of these parties is under Muslims. They are articulating the community anger and strengthening their bargaining power. But the approach of Muslim political parties is mostly communitarian, which gives little scope for the weavers' politics per se. Thus, it is up to the Left parties to mobilise and provide the leadership to weavers of Banaras and working classes of the nation. Their weakness means weakness to the workers and peasants.

Reference

1. USA heads the list with 396 billionaires followed by China (72), and Russia (58). India followed by Germany (43), UK (42), Hong Kong (29), Switzerland (27), Japan (23) and Canada (22).
2. According to Swiss wealth manager India would double its number of millionaires by 2015. However, according to Mr. P.Chidambaram, the Finance Minister of India, 2013-14 budget speech there are only 48,000 billionaires in India.
3. S.K. Rai, 'Muslim Weavers' Politics in Early 20th Century Northern India: Locating an Identity', *Economic and Political Weekly*, Vol. XLVII, NO. 15, April 14, 2012, pp.61-62.
4. *Ibid.* p. 62.
5. *Ibid.* p. 63.

6. *Ibid.,* p. 63.
7. S.M.Pandey, 'Rival Unionism in an Industrial Centre: A Study of Kanpur', *Indian Journal of Industrial Relations*, Vol. 3, No. 2, pp. 138-159.
8. *Ibid.,* p 143.
9. *Ibid.,* p. 157. The phenomenon of inter-union rivalry has been aided and sustained by: (i) The patterns of past events which has created an environment of splits and intense inter-and intra-union rivalries; (ii) The desire of the political parties to have their bases among the industrial workers and to lead the labour movement in the "right" direction; (iii) Present personal-cum-factional politics of the local union leaders whose low level of tolerance causes frequent conflicts among them; (iv) Dominance of the unions by "outsider" leaders who are primarily interested in accumulating more power and influence both within and outside of the labour movement; (v) Attitude of the management who are unwilling to grant recognition to a representative union as defined in the Code of Discipline, and who encourage the formation of rival unions; (vi) The existing legal framework which offers no incentives for the development of a strong and united trade union organization; and (vii) The nature of the workforce whose low level of participation in union activities and frustration and discontent offer a favorable climate for the "outsider" leader to indulge in militant rival unionism. The above factors are not independent of each other, and act in combination.
10. Thirthankar Roy, 'Sardars, Jobbers Kanganies: The Labour Contractor and Indian Economic History', *Modern Asian Studies*, Vol. 42, No. (5), 2008, pp. 971-998.
11. As told by bade Sardar – Sardar Maqbool Hasan – in an interview during my fieldwork. He seems passionate about the welfare of the weavers but could not able to improve the deteriorating economic condition of weaving.
12. Fieldwork interview.
13. It means a ward or street.
14. This is named after Hazrat Malik Afazal Alawi. Malik Afazal Alawi was Sayyad Salar Masud's sipah salar ("general"), hence the muhalla Salarpura. The group of muhallas in the north called Alwipura, which is supposedly populated by his descendants.
15. It is not necessary that the given number show the exact number of muhallas under it. As population has been on increase the muhallas too get enlarged.
16. Chaudaha muhallas today contains eighty four muhallas and at least 400 years old.
17. P. Raj, op. cit., p. 118.
18. Nilanjana Biswas, 'On Funding and NGO Sector', *Economic and Political Weekly*, October 21, 2006.
19. *Ibid.* p. 4408.
20. *Ibid.* p. 4408.
21. Centre for Budget and Governance Accountability, '*Response to Union Budget 2011-12*', page no. 9, 2011, New Delhi.
22. J. Mencher, 'NGOs – Are they a force of Social Change', *Economic and Political Weekly*, July 24, 1999, p. 2083.

23. *Ibid.*
24. *Ibid.* p. 2084.
25. S.S. Shrivastva and R. Tandon, 'How Large is India's Non-Profit Sector', *Economic and Political Weekly*, May 7, 2005, p. 1949.
26. Prakash Karat, 'The Challanges of Identity Politics', *The Marxist*, Vol. XXVII 1-2, January-June 2011, pp. 40-41.
27. Prashant Bhagat, *Home-Based Weavers in Varanasi From a Union in the Struggle to preserve their culture and Livelihood*, Oct. 15, 2008, Asia Monitor Resource Centre.
28. www. HWA.org.
29. During my fieldwork, I interviewed many activists of CPI and CPM in Banaras Zone, who opined the same view.
30. Prakash Karat, 'Political Challenges Confronting the Left', Council for Social Development, August 12, 2012.
31. K.C.Yadav and R. Singh, *India's Unequal Citizen: A Study of Other Backward Classes*, Manohar Publication, New Delhi, 1994, p. 120.
32. *Ibid.*
33. SRUTI, op. cit.
34. www.thehindu.com
35. www.thaindian.com
36. *Ibid.*
37. www.Varanasview.blogspot.com
38. J.M.F.Wood, Contentious Politics and Civil Society in Varanasi, in Ajay Gudavarthy (ed.), *Re-framing Democracy and Agency in India: Interrogating Political Society*, Anthem Press, Delhi, 2012.
39. J.M.F.Wood, "White-Collar Agitation, No-Collar Complaince", Ph.D., University of texas, 2010, p. 57.
40. The meeting was organised by BDAM and PVCHR on the issue of education and development of Muslim weavers in the context of Sachar Committee Report.
41. Karl Marx, *Capital*, vol. I, p.424.
42. Last time weavers took up arms against the ruler, it was during 1857 revolt.
43. Banaras handloom weavers have been facing the fluctuating market since long time. Their experiences shows that bad condition for business has been short lived. Good time always come back.
44. Prakash Karat, "The Challanges of Identity Politics", *The Marxist*, Vol. Xxvii, No. 1-2, 2011, p. 41.

Chapter - 6

Muslim *Julaha*, Hindu traders and Communalism in Banaras

History of Communalism in Banaras

Communal riots in general and Hindu-Muslim communal violence in particular have been endemic to Indian society for centuries. Incidents of communal strife have been recorded since the early eighteen century. "There was a riot in Ahmedabad in 1714, centring round Holi celebrations and cow slaughter questions. There was a Hindu-Muslim riot in Kashmir in 1719-20, in Delhi in 1729, in Vidarbha region of Maharashtra in 1786, occasioned by an attack on a religious procession."[1] Why do communal riots occur? What purposes, if any, do they serve? What conditions aggravate communal strife? These are some pertinent questions upon which social scientists have pondered extensively.

Banaras had witnessed its first major communal riot in the year 1809 over the issue of '*Lat Bhairava*'[2] when the Hindus had attempted to construct a Hanuman shrine on the neutral ground between the Gyan Vapi Mosque and the Vishwanatha Temple.[3] It occurred in the backdrop of declining Mughal rule over Banaras, and rise to power, of the *bhumihar* (caste) zamindar clan at the local level under the complete patronage of the British. The rajas of Banaras, in order to create and sustain the new political identity of the new class, played a major role in rejuvenating a distinct cultural milieu through patronage. This research argued that 1809 and the riots thereafter in Banaras were illustrations of the process of establishment of the new socio-political identity for emerging classes.

Christopher Bailey, in his study of the evolution of the north Indian economy and society in the late eighteen and nineteenth centuries, has described the emergence of powerful Hindu mercantile classes, the development of Hindu corporate towns, and the consequent transformation of north Indian urban political culture and social ethos. Nandini Gooptu in her paper 'Urban Poor and Militant Hinduism in Early Twentieth-Century Uttar Pradesh' tried to explain how the urban poor creatively appropriated and interpreted on their own terms, the ideas and ideologies generated by the affluent, the educated or the politically powerful. The agrarian distress in 1920s and rise of '*Bazar*' industry in urban areas initiated two things: migration of mostly lower castes Hindu population from rural to urban areas, which swelled the urban underclass workers; this underclass faced economic instability and entered into direct competition with other marginalised sections of population i.e. Dalits and Muslims.

Prior to that, the revenue-obligations pattern of zamindars and farmers in four parganas shows the decline in Mughal control over the resources in the Banaras region. Muslim zamindars and farmers held merely 13 per cent and 24 per cent of total revenue respectively as shown in table 79 and 80. Parallel to the decline of Mughal rulers, rajas of Banaras were busy in formulating a Hindu identity. Balwant Singh, though spent most of his time in consolidation of his authority over Banaras, found some time to raise his social status. In 1756, he began the construction of Ramnagar fort on the river bank, which was giving a commanding view of the city. He created many a shrine of which the shrine of Mahadeva was prominent. He also patronised the brahbhasa. However, Balwant Singh wasn't considered overtly a patron of Hindu religion and culture. He also patronised Sheikh Hazim, a Persian poet.

The next ruler was Raja Chet Singh (1770-81), who had the legacy of synchronized court culture of his father. But, Raja Chet Singh lavishly spent on Durga and Gopal Lal Ji temple in Ramnagar. He also associated with Hindu fairs and festivals freely, which actually confirmed his authority over the Hindu mass. However, there were episodes which heralded the changed power conditions, and documented the awareness of the Hindu population of the territories that the political power of the nawab had passed into the hands of a Hindu king, who could be pressurised into offering the special protection to Hindu religious activities, which herewith acquired political dimensions as well.[4] Once, on learning the Hindus suffering at the hand of Muslims in a riot, the Raja was 'perplexed and annoyed' and sent Jaykarn Chaudhuri to investigate the matter. Afterwards, the Muslims remained under surveillance for three months, after which they were fined and let off. Further, Raja Chet Singh ordered to destroy a mosque in Jaunpur.[5]

Table 79: Castes of *zamindars* and their revenue obligations in four parganas, 1793-94

Caste	Saktigarh			Narwan			Dhoos			Chausa			All Parganas		
	No.	Revenue in Rs.	% of rev.	No.	Revenue in Rs.	% of rev.	No.	Revenue in Rs.	% of rev.	No.	Revenue in Rs.	% of rev.	No.	Revenue in Rs.	% of rev.
Rajput	11	3,600	24	31	16,900	62	7	7,600	40	20	7,200	32	69	35,300	42
Brahman	8,	2,000	13	28	3,400	12	4	2,700	14	32	4,100	18	72	12,200	15
Bhumihar	2	600	4	10	5,500	20	1	100	-	32	9,200	41	45	15,400	18
Muslim	2	300	2	2	1,200	4	8	8,400	44	3	1,100	5	15	11,000	13
Kurmki	5	2,900	20	-	-	-	-	-	-	-	-	-	5	2,900	3
Other Hindu	24	5,600	37	5	400	2	3	300	2	7	900	4	39	7,200	4
Total	52	15,000	100	76	27,400	100	23	19,100	100	94	22,500	100	245	84,000	100

Source: Bernard. S. Cohn (1962)

Table 80: Caste of revenue *farmers* and their revenueobligations in four parganas, 1793-4

Caste	Saktigarh			Narwan			Dhoos			Chausa			All Parganas		
	No.	Revenue in Rs.	% of rev.	No.	Revenue in Rs.	% of rev.	No.	Revenue in Rs.	% of rev.	No.	Revenue in Rs.	% of rev.	No.	Revenue in Rs.	% of rev.
Rajput	-	-	-	9	14,300	61	-	-	-	12	6,700	37	21	21,00	46
Brahman	-	-	-	1	300	1	3	1,800	40	8	1,700	9	12	3,800	8
Bhumihar	-	-	-	-	-	-	-	-	-	5	200	1	5	200	-
Muslim	-	-	-	-	-	-	3	2,300	51	7	8,500	48	10	10,800	24
Other Hindu	-	-	-	5	9,000	38	1	400	9	5	900	5	11	10,300	22
Total	-	-	-	15	23,600	100	7	4,500	100	37	18,000	100	59	46,100	100

Source: Bernard. S. Cohn (1962)

However, it was during the reign of Udit Narayan Singh (1795-1835), who was offered full protection by the British while being entirely relieved of any administrative duties, period that the religious and cultural life of the city began to take shape. Udit Narayan Singh, though devotee of goddess *Durga* and god *Shiva*, blended himself into the local cultural atmosphere in such a way that he became the meeting ground of *vaishnavites* and *shaivites,* and other Hindu cultures, thus truly representing Hindu king. Udit Narayan Singh incorporated the Rama epic into his own territories. The Raja played a large role in Ramlila and represented himself as Shiva. This tradition was maintained by Ishwari Narayan Singh (1835-89). It was in the long titular reign of Ishwari that the culture of the court had leisure to evolve in a style which was by now self-consciously Hindu, though it absorbed influences from many directions. By now it seemed natural for the Raja to slip into the role of the protector of Hinduism. Ishwari was also patronising Sanskrit learning and employed a number of pandits. The court, as also the affluent merchant in the city, was beginning to attract musician from other centres in the north. The *Tarikh* (219) mentions that Udit Narayan Singh had become interested in learning the sitar and had become the pupil of the famous *binkar* Nisar Jan. Ishwari liked to figure as a patron of paintings as well.

Colonial Distortion of the Banaras History

Simultaneously, at the central level, power was passing into the hands of the British who took the help of the Raja of Banaras as they were more interested in solidifying their position in north India. Thus, the British Raj and Rajas of Banaras with the exception of Chet Singh had found allies in each other. The East India Company got supported by Raja Balwant Singh in the battle of Buxur in 1764. In return, the Company pressurized the Nawab for the retainment of zamindari of Balwant Singh.

The good and friendly relationship which had developed between the Bengal Council and Raja is best illustrated in the following letter of Governor Cartier to Balwant Singh in February 1770: "I am confident you need no fresh assurances from me to certify you of the favour in which you stand with the English Serdars (gentlemen), neither have I the smallest apprehension that we shall, at any time, repent of our protection or you of your attachment. In these days when engagements and treaties have become the sport of capricious minds and friendship is a name found without principle and violated without reserve, our connection is a rare and perhaps a single instance where no suspicion lurks."

Not only that, influential people like Raja of Banaras; Deo Narain Singh; Surat Singh; Gokal Chand and others neither took part in the revolt of 1857 nor provided any kind of substantial co-operation to the rebelling masses. Rather they helped the British in suppressing the rebellion. "To tackle the dispersed rebellion, martial laws were proclaimed on June 9 throughout the Varanasi division. The military officers were hunting down all sorts of people and hanging them as if they were pariah dogs, jackals or vermin."[6] In Banaras city permanent gallows were erected which took the toll of many lives. So many people were thrown into the city jail that they could hardly be contained within its walls and the authorities resorted to meting out punishment with the lash instead of by imprisonment.

At the same time the new Hindu merchant class of Banaras, which had subordinate role to play in Mughal period, strengthened their position and pushed Muslim merchants, who once dominated maritime trade from Surat, to the margin. They began to play a prominent role in the creation of the older public arena with their patronage of public festivities organised by the Raja. The economic antagonism between the upper class of the two communities developed during this period, which later on resulted in communal polarisation. Nonetheless, colonial ethnographers of the administration and Oriental scholars penned down the temporary communal strife in such a way that they established the image of two communities unable to co-exist owing to vast religious and social differences.

For instance, Katherine Prior argued that consolidation of identity had already taken place before the 1809 riot. "It is crucial to my understanding of religious disputes in the late-eighteenth and the nineteenth centuries that Hindus and Muslims could and did think of themselves as Hindus and Muslims and not just in circumscribed terms of locality, sect or profession. There seems to be no other way of explaining why, even if a dispute was primarily between a town's Ahirs and butchers, say, that the protagonists would petition the colonial authorities as 'the Hindus' and 'the Muslims' of that town.

If we look at the aftermath of the 1809 Benares riots we find that the Muslims, although variously identified by the British and the Hindus as weavers, butchers or members of the 'influential' classes, petitioned the Magistrate as one body with a uniformly-applicable grievance. Likewise the Hindus, despite their obvious internal differences, presented their case to the British with one voice; if there were dissenters they did not publicly express their disagreement, given the inter-communal nature of the conflict.

This adoption of a broad and inclusive religious identity did not preclude the formation of identities based on other shared experiences, such as residence in Benares or work as an artisan, but it was nevertheless a legitimate and sometimes powerful form of association."[7]

Speaking at various points of time about the official records of the 1809 riot in Banaras, Gyanendra Pandey noted that each official record is full of discrepancies despite citing 'authentic reports'. For instance, colonial government records of 1809-10 showed that 28-29 people were killed and 70 wounded while Gazetteer (1907) records the killing of several hundred.[8] This colonial construction of 'communalism' had immense impact on the psyche of post-independent India. After independence, in Banaras, the colonial readings of 'communalism' found space in school text books while dealing with Aurangzeb, Salar Masud Ghazi (aka *Ghazi Mian*) or Mahmud Ghazni. As pointed out by Mary Searle-Chatterjee, how the text book opined the majoritarian view while neglecting the lesser one has been instrumental in creating religious division. The variants of the Ghazi[9]/ Ghaznavi corpus of symbolic narrative was summarised by Mary Searle-Chatterjee as follow:[10]

Version	***Proponents***
(a) Wicked Muslim King attacked Innocent Hindus, destroyed Somnath/Siva Temple (national reference)	Local school history books Local conversation of literate Hindus
(b) Muslim warrior overthrew evil Hindu who was oppressing Hindus in the Somnath/Shiva temple (local reference)	Local-level Muslims

Table 81: Communal Violence in Banaras since 1927-2008

Year	*Month*	*Day*	*Reported Killing*	*Reported injured*	*Duration*
1927	8	11		6	
1931	2	11	26	210	2
1938	3	-	10	-	-
1939	3	4	35	200	3
1939	3	4	46	200	3
1946	11	7	-	-	-
1947	3	-	-	-	-
1947	4				
1952	3	23	0	0	1
1967	4	21	4	55	3
1969	12	2	3	15	2
1972	6	16	9	68	4
1977	10	23	8	60	1
1977	11	2	-	-	1
1986	2	17	1	-	2
1989	8	13	-	6	1
1991	11	8	17	26	6
1992	12	28	-	-	1
1992	12	-	-	-	1
1995	7	31	0	50	1
1996					
1997					
1998					
1999					
2000	4				
2008	3		3		

Source: S.I. Wilkinson

Other Factors Contributed to Social Tension in Banaras

Apart from the colonial construction of separate religious identities, there were a number of other factors which contributed to the separation between Hindus and Muslims of Banaras. Equally important were the tensions within the Hindu community and specific changes that occurred at this time. A circumstance for Hindu revival was the emergence of its mercantile culture in north India in the early nineteenth century. Post-1857 revolt, not only was there a rapid expansion of all means of transport and telegraphic communications, but also a sharp increase in new professions, law courts, the number of lawyers, schools and colleges, public bodies and libraries, publishing houses, press and vernacular newspapers in the

Gangetic plains. The Hindu middle classes, though influenced by the lifestyles of the Europe, also resisted them, and sought an independent shared identity: temples mushroomed, novel processions appeared on the streets and the cow attained a new prominence as a focus of the Hindu community.

Table 82: Number of District affected by Communal Violence in Uttar Pradesh, 1961-70

State	*1961*	*1962*	*1963*	*1964*	*1965*	*1966*	*1967*	*1968*	*1969*	*1970*	*Total no. of district*	*Total no. of istricts affected*
Uttar Pradesh	13	11	6	9	12	9	10	14	9	16	54	31
India	61	47	40	71	77	58	63	79	94	116	316	216

Source: S.I. Wilkinson (ed.) Religious Politics and Communal Violence, pp. 155.

There were also growing economic insecurities among the Hindus as the colonial onslaught posed a serious challenge to many of the traditional occupations, and dislocated existing social and economic relations. For example, the working of the 1900 Municipalities Act in UP reveals the intervention of colonial authorities in almost all occupations and customary rights of various classes, at least at the level of regulations. However, the actual implementation of these acts was largely in Indian hands, which increased the potential for tyrannies and rivalries between middle-class Hindus and Muslims. Various facets of everyday existence such as what food to sell and where to sell it; where, when and how to bathe, wash and reside; issues regarding vehicles, streets, lights, drains, filth, prostitutes, noise, scavenging, and the like – became contentious. At the same time, in UP towns, Muslims were relatively advanced in literacy and employment, which led to a feeling among many Hindus that Muslims were usurping their jobs.

Table 83: Communal Violence in Uttar Pradesh, 1961-70 rural/urban distribution

Year		*Uttar Pradesh*	*India*
1961	Rural	15	153
	Urban	76	286
1962	Rural	14	110
	Urban	17	101
1963	Rural	7	68
	Urban	5	70

(*Contd...*)

1964	Rural Urban	14 7	872 1243
1965	Rural Urban	12 27	141 346
1966	Rural Urban	8 121	75 498
1967	Rural Urban	21 26	395 1076
1968	Rural Urban	10 147	122 353
1969	Rural Urban	11 18	253 873
1970	Rural Urban	15 38	403 526
Total	Rural Urban	**127** **482**	2592 5372

Source: S.I. Wilkinson (ed.) Religious Politics and Communal Violence, pp. 56.

By 1935, the problem of unemployment had become extremely acute in UP. Through the figure of the Hindu woman, certain menial jobs and professions in which Muslims were employed were specially attacked. By asking her to keep away from Muslim menials, an opportunity was created for Hindu males to venture into those occupations instead. Thus, in the realm of the everyday, Muslims were often seen as bigger threats than the British. Many of the lower and intermediate Hindu castes were feeling the anxiety of extreme economic insecurity, and taking an oppositional discourse against the Muslims, were therefore seen as economically advantageous.

Table 84: Causes of Communal Violence in Uttar Pradesh, 1961-70

State	*Cow Slaughter*	*Desecration of religious places*	*Festivity/ celebrations*	*Graveyards*	*Total*	*Chain incidents*
Uttar Pradesh	17	4	27	3	51	425

Source: S.I. Wilkinson (ed.) Religious Politics and Communal Violence, pp. 163.

Communal Polarization in Modern Banaras

In case of Banaras, the religious division and consequent tensions along with communal division of labour that is poor weavers belonging to the Muslims community and businessmen and traders financially controlling the silk handloom industry has been Hindus, existed for centuries and the ruling class has exploited that division, when necessary to further fortify their position. Until 1970 the class contestation had been in the premise of communal division of labour. It means, the principal issue at the time was rich Hindu businessmen exploiting poor Muslim weavers, and whenever poor silk workers tried to raise their genuine demands, communal tension was escalated. However, after 1970, good business turnovers and substantial investment in real estate benefited the master weavers, who along with owners of the large number of handlooms, emerged as the neo-rich upper class among Muslims.

Harish Damodaran noted that "The *Ansaris* are traditionally weavers, many of whom, to escape retribution following the failed 1857 revolt, moved from the Indo-Gangetic plain to settle along towns on the Agra-Mumbai's textile mills. From the 1960s, this spurred the growth of a decentralised power loom industry to meet the demand for grey fabric, and created a class of master weavers turned- power loom owners in Bhiwandi, Malegoan and other peripheral urban clusters of Maharashtra. The *Ansari*, today not only controls a large chunk of the business in the major power loom centres, but have since around the late 1970s also made in roads as middlemen and wholesale traders in the Varanasi-Mau handloom belt of Uttar Pradesh. Needless to say the emergence of this new, often assertive, Muslim bourgeoisie has fuelled business rivalries with established Hindu mercantile interests. These tensions have often assumed communal overtone, making the likes of Bhiwandi, Malegoan, and Mau sensitive trouble spots. Also, unlike the old Muslim gentry, the leadership of the new bourgeoisies has tended to back non-congress formation like the Samajwadi party or built independent power bases."[11]

High standards of living in very beautiful mansions outside the city have become the physical marker of upper class amomg weavers. Earlier old residential houses were a place where weavers were dealt with to supply raw material and to collect the finished product. With the increase in usage of power loom and later on CEM in 1970, there have been changes in the production process and profit turn over. This gave the nature of communal relationship at least two new turns. With the rise of new businessmen and traders from the weaver community, the Hindu counterparts sensed fear of losing to them. This business rivalry between the two groups often took a communal turn as both of them mobilised their religious brethren in their support.[12]

The riot in 1977 was the example of intra-class rivalry rising out of economic tension between the established Hindu elite and emerging Muslim upper class. The pretext of the riot was very simple: a territorial quarrel between some students of the Anglo-Bengali College and some Muslim weavers extending their yarns into the school grounds, reportedly taking up space for playing. However, the micro analysis of that riot revealed that a rising upper class among the Muslims was the factor, which was seen by Hindus as an economic challenge to their long domination. They wanted to crush the 'Muslim economic assertion' at the onset. Hence, they funded the riots. Marzia Casolari notes that "Hindu dealers provided some funds to organise the riots and to support the men who had to create the violence against the Muslims. Evidence that economic competition was the real reason for the riots is provided by the fact that a large number of shops, factories and properties belonging to the Muslims were looted and destroyed. It is clear that Hindu dealers aimed at confining their Muslim rivals to a subaltern role."[13]

Nonetheless, with time this bitterness between Hindu and Muslim traders and businessmen has gone down, and the neo-rich Muslims have been accepted in elite circles to avoid confrontation for common benefits. Now the organisations like 'Banarasi Vastra Udyog Sangh' and 'Reshmi Taga Sangh' which were earlier dominated by the right wing, now included Muslim gaddidars as members. These kinds of organisations have their own policy regarding silk yarn, purchase of finished product, wages, cuts etc. These have wide ramifications upon the *Banarasi* silk product. This class act is aimed against the working class and prevents them from making profit. In an interview, owner of Banaras Sari Factory, a major manufacturer of *Banarasi* saris, Shyam Kumar Pandey (Om Dutt) summarized the whole argument as - "There are only two kinds of people in the sari business here – the rich and the poor. That's all."[14]

A weaver's delicate silk product can fetch Rs 30,000 in retail, but could get merely Rs. 100-120 for the same. Even the rise of communal politics in 1990s did not disturb the class relationship. Class cooperation among the Hindus and Muslim businessmen and *gaddidar* remained intact. Riots and communal tension were used to corner the maximum benefit from wage cuts and under payment to the weavers. In fact, any kind of disturbance, whether it is communal tension or economic slowdown, has been used by traders to garner benefits. M. Showeb, while mapping the behavioural changes between the *gaddidars* and weavers noted that it underwent unusual changes after the Ayodhya controversy. He wrote that "Whenever the Ayodhya crisis deepens, the behaviour of the *kothidars/ gaddidars* becomes rather unusual. The procurement of silk fabrics becomes low, the price of the raw material soars high and payment to weavers/master weavers becomes jittery and haphazard. Apart from this, the behaviour at the personal level also becomes tainted with a tinge of communal touch."[15] But nowhere M. Showeb talks about the positive change in behaviour of Muslim *gaddidars* in favour of poor weavers while delivering wage or yarn. They get away with the excuse of disturbance in areas.

However, the two recent riots that had occurred in the year 2000 and 2008 shows the existence of inter-class antagonism and intra-class based communal riots. Riot in the year 2000 was the example of intra-class rivalry taking communal turn. The background of the riot is the development and growth of Madanpura as a major business centre replacing tradition marketing places like Golghar and Kunjgali of Chowk areas. According to a fact finding report brought out by the Saajjha Sanskriti Manch (United Cultural Forum) that visited the riot-affected areas, events were the 'unfortunate result of business rivalry and unchecked police cruelty against the minority.'[16] However, the March 2008 riot in Bajardiha area was the result of inter-class antagonism i.e. between the rich traders and poor weavers. Banaras has seen the increment of wage demand for the past one year. The demand has been constructed by left party's mass organisation which percolates down to the masses facing the price hike of all the necessary commodities. This issue along with the other demands began to attract the masses, and huge rallies and meetings were organised. Taking it as an attack on the profit, traders and *gaddidars* put forth the counter-argument of economic recession. On the other hand, the approaching general election of 2009 brought about the much awaited opportunity of communal polarisation with a dual intent: to break the weavers' unity on the issue of wage increment and political benefit for the right-wing candidates - Murli Manohar Joshi of BJP against Mukhtar Ansari of BSP. The strategy worked as intended. The unity broke down and all the genuine demands of weavers were rolled back.

Actors and Agents in Communal Violence in Banaras

Paul Brass has highlighted the significance of agency, that is, the capability of actors 'to make a difference', to exercise some sort of power. By studying the occurrence of riots, Brass necessarily focuses on the destructive capacity of agency. He argued that agents do not operate in a vacuum; rather their actions are enabled and constrained by different layers of social structure. During the whole discussion on communal violence, the role played by various organisations and institutions, which set up the stage of communal flare through their propaganda, instigation, raising hatred or sometime direct involvement, is due. In the above discussion it has come out that 'distorted' historical facts were mainly presented by Hindu right wing organisations and biased school texts to polarise and separate Hindus and Muslims psychologically. For instance, local legend within Hindu community treats '*Ghazi*' as a 'Wicked Muslim King, who attacked Banaras, killed Raja Banar and innocent Hindus'.

However, Muslims have their own legend regarding *Ghazi mian*, whom they see as a revered '*pir*' (saint) who helped both Hindus and Muslims, in time of necessity. The local informant in Mary Searle-Chatterjee's account described the munificent Ghazi via several versions. Some of these are as follows: "Ghazi Mian, otherwise known as Saiyad Salar Masood, was the nephew of Mahmud Ghaznavi, the first invader of India in the eleventh century. Ghazi was a great and good man who helped both Hindus and Muslims in trouble. He made seven unsuccessful attempts to marry. Each time he was prevented by some untoward event. On one occasion the bride-to-be died, on another there was a violent thunderstorm, on other Ghazi had to be involved in battles. He had miraculous powers."[17] Another version associated with the Ghazi story widely circulated among the lower class/castes Muslims and some Hindus as well is that "On one occasion he (Ghazi) came to the help of a Hindu woman whom he found weeping hysterically. She told him that every day in Banaras one person was sacrificed by lot at the temple of Somnath where sorcery was used. The lot had fallen on her only son. It was his wedding day. Ghazi at once offered to stand in as a substitute. He took a bath in the Ganges to purify himself. Then he put one foot inside the temple. As he did so, the floor fell in beneath the image and only the head remained visible with its tuft of hair. Ghazi grabbed the tuft and kicked the head. The image disappeared below the ground. Ghazi threw the tuft as far as he could. Wherever it fell there grew a type of grass used for making stools."[18]

The benevolent face of Ghazi has been shared and passed from one generation to another as 'collective memory'. Whether this image was produced in past to counter the right wing propaganda that Muslims rulers were necessarily brutal, is not dealt by Mary Searle-Chatterjee. Nonetheless, family and 'religious public gathering' act as a carrier of this myth. But this research finds that the shared myth never was cited by respondents as a part of memory while recalling the cause of communal tension. Most of the respondents across the variables remembered immediate communal occurrence effecting Hindu-Muslim relationship in Banaras as shown in table 85.

Table 85: Class-wise response of Weavers about the incidents effecting Social Harmony in Banaras

Incidents	*Economic Status*			*Occupation*
	*Poor (83)**	*Middle Class (3)*	*Upper Class (4)*	
Babri-Masjid as watershed	78	2	2	Weaver
Prior to Babri Masjid	5	1	2	Weaver

Source: Field Work in Banaras during October, 2009.
* Figure in parenthesis represents total number of respondent

Here, literacy and age have become very important factors as far as remembering communal riots in Banaras are concerned. As most of the respondents in this research were young, they cited Babri Masjid incidents as the starting point of their communal memory and thus hold BJP responsible for communal riots. However, old upper class respondents feel that it is politicians (of all sorts) who are responsible for it. This is the understanding of communalism among Muslim weavers of Banaras. What is interesting is that while tracing the communal organisation of Muslims, which ignite or may causes communal riots, this research found not a single organisation propagating anti-Hindu feelings. However, the presence of large number of faith based organisations working among Muslims at the religious level do indirectly help in creating sustained divisions between the two communities reminding its member about the religion or sect which they belong to.

Table 86: Agents responsible for the Communal Riots in Banaras

Who are Responsible for the Riots in the city	*Economic Status*			*Occupation*
	*Poor (83)**	*Middle Class (3)*	*Upper Class (4)*	
BJP	78	2	2	Weaver
Politicians	5	1	2	Weaver

Source: Field Work in Banaras in 2010.

According to a study by Mahfooz Alam, it is found that sectarian Muslim organizations have contributed to the religious consciousness among Muslims. Though the research work is focused on Muslim majority area of Banaras, some generalisations could be possible. However, if we combined the first and third factors (Table 87); on the whole they contribute 38.67 per cent. The reason for combining the two factors is their institutionalised character. The spread of Islamic education is not an individual effort. It runs through various sectarian institutions working in the district. Similarly, the religious missionary is also an institutionalised sectarian effort.

Table 87: Institution helping in the rise of religious consciousness among Banaras' Muslims

Sl. No.	*Factors contributing to religious consciousness*	*Per cent*
1.	Spread of Islamic education	18.00
2.	Role of media in propagating the message of Islam	12.33
3.	Role of religious missionary work	20.67
4.	Growing affluence in the community	11.00
5.	The cultural shock and Political setback	21.67
6.	Not Applicable	16.33
	Total	**100.00**

Source: Mahfooz Alam, Continuity and Change among the Muslims, Unpublished Ph.D Thesis, 2001, BHU.

Thus most of these organisations work within the sectarian boundaries of the communities, which instead of uniting Muslims under one banner to fight for the rights of weavers, necessarily work to divide them into many sects. Today, sectarian competition within the Muslim weavers of Banaras is on the rise. Mary Searle-Chatterjee has rejected the popular feeling that "Islamization process in Banaras is influenced by its trade, pilgrimage and migrant workers' contact with Arab countries. Rather, she found local socio-economic factors as a sufficient explanation for the cultural changes that are occurring in Banaras. The rise of the Ahl-e-Hadith sect in Banaras is not, however, she argued, a defiant reaction against the dominating presence of Hinduism. Instead, it is the product of conflicts and competition among local Muslims. It attempts to displace older elite, not by a process of cultural emulation, but by the challenge of a rival type of cultural practice."[19] Thus, it makes Muslim weavers of Banaras practically inappropriate for communal misadventure. On the other hand, Hindus of Banaras are well knitted around the cultural and religious activities organised by different religious trust and *mandir* controlled mostly by right wing forces. A large number of festivals, the list of which is given below, manifests the Hindu dominant position and projects the city as the 'centre of Hinduism'.

Table 88: List of Fairs and Festivals in Banaras

Chaitra:-	**Bhadra:-**
New-year(Vikram), Navratri Started	Bheemchandi Darshan, Vishwalakshi Yatra
GunGaur, Matasyavtar	Kajari Teel Bahula Chautha(manasa Devi Puja)
Ram Raja Mahotsav	Lalahi Chhatha, Halkhashthi-Balram Mahotsav
Suryakhashthi, Skandkhashthi	Krishna Janashtami okulashtami, Nandotav, Durvashtami
Oli(Jain)	Barah Awtar, Hartalika Teej, Barah Jainti
Ramnavami	Thelwa Chautha, Ganesh utsaw
Mahavir Jainti (Jain)	Rishi panchami, Bhartendu Jainti,
Hanuman Jainti	Lolarak Khashthi, Dev Khashthi, Krikunda Kajari Fair
Bashakh:-	Sarohiya Fair, Sri Chadra Jainti, Dashawer vrata
Panchkroshi Yatra	Vaman Dradawsi
Kachchap Jainti	Annat Chaturdasi, Ramleela Started, Ratan Trayvrata
Maha Prabhu Ballabhacharya Jainti	Nanadi Sradh, Lokpal Puja, UmaMaheshwer Vrata,
Amavas Satudan	Pritpaksh, Vishwakarma Puja, Lalita devi Yatra,
Chhatrapati Shiva Ji Jainti	Jeevit Putrika Vrata, Maha Lakshmi Darshan, Matri Navami,
Akshay Tritiya, Parshuram Jainti, Jhanjhaer Kshata Dan	Pritra visarjan, Mhalaya
Adi Shankeracharya Jainti	**Aswan:-**
Ramanuja Charya Jainti	Shardiya Navratri Started, shailputri Darshan,
Ganga Spatami, Shahanai Dangal	Braham Charani Darshan, ChitraGhanta Darshan,
Janki Jainti, Kuwer Singh Jainti	Kushmada Darshan.
Narsingh Chaturdashi	Skanda Mata Darshan, Upang Lalita Vrata,
Badhha Jainti, Kurma Jainti, Sarnath-Fair, Buddha Purmina	Katyayani Darshan, Akal Bodhan Puja, Kal Ratri darshan,
Jyeshtha:-	Durga-Puja Utsav, Mahanisha Puja, Maha Gauri Darsha,
Fair- Jangi Miya	Durga-ji Fair, Sindha Puja, Sidhidhtri Darshan Mahanavami
But-Savitri, Briksh Puja, Badasait Vrata	Vrata, Vijaya Dashami, Nilkantha darshan Shashtra Puja,
Ganga Dashahara, Birthday of Gaga, Gudia Visarjan	Shami puja, Ravan Badh, Durga Pratima Visarjan,
Nirjal Akadashi, Gangotsav, Deepotsav, Nakali Lathi Yudha	Madhwacharya Jainti, Dashahara, Bharatmelap
Bheemaseni (chhata, Juta, phal, Patra Dan)	Kojagari, Maharas, Kaumuri Mahotsav, Sharad Puja,
Sant Kabir Jainti	Balmiki Jainti, Lakshami Kuber Pujan.
Ashath:-	**Kartik:-**
Rathyatra -Fair, Shankudhara-Fair	Karva Chautha, Nakkataiya (chetganj), Ahoi Ashtami,
Vishnu Shayani, Ekadashi, Guru Purima, Vedbyas darshan,	Radha Jainti, Krinshna Lela At Assi Ghat, Goverdhan Puja,
Shivashayanotsav.	Dhanterash, Dhanwantri Jsinti, Kameshwer Jainti,

(*Contd...*)

Shravan:-	Samundra Manthan, Narak Chaturdashi, Kali Chaturdashi,
Thakurain Teej	Hanumant Jainti, Kedar Gauri Vrata, Devali, Lakshami Puja,
NagPanchami	Mahavir Nirvan Divas, Annakuta Goverdhan Puja,
Balmik Jainti	Ramdwitiya, Bhaiyaduja, Chitragupta Puja, Suryakhashthi
Tulsi Jainti, Putra Akadashi, Jhulontsav	Dala Chhatha, Nag-nathaiya at Tulsi ghat, Gopashtami,
Kajali Purima, Rakshabandhan,	Akshya Navami(kahada Dan), Nagar Prikarama, Tulsi Byah,
Sarnath-Fair, Durga Ji-Fair	Hari Prabodhani Akadashi, Devuthauni, Bhisham Panchak,
Marg-Shirsha:-	Mahavinshnu Puja, Kartik Purima, Tripurotsav, GuruNanak
Guru Tej Bahadur Sahadat, Ram Vivah, Skand Khashthi,	Jainti, Rath-yatra(Jain), Mukki Dangal, Devdevali.
Champa Khashthi, Mitra Spatami, Surya Sptami, Nanda	**Falgun:-**
Navami, Gita Jainti, Lata Bhanta Fair, Dattatray Jainti,	Maha Shivratri, Rangbhari Ekadashi, Swarn Annapurna
Panchkroshi Yatra, Nagar Prikarma	Darshan, Govid Drawadashi, Holika Dahan, Holi Yatra,
Pausha:-	**Chaita:-**
Parshwanath Jainti, Guru Govinda Sigh Jainti, Shakambhari	Dhul Vandan, Holi, Chausathi Darsan, Rang Panchami,
Jainti, Badri Narayan Puja, Veda byas Fair, Ganesh Chautha	Buthawa Mangal Fair, Gulab Vari Chaiti Mahotsav,
Bada Ganesh Fair, Ramanucharya Jainti, Vivekanand Jainti.	Vahji Fair-Varuni, Mahavirji, Maha Maha Varuni
Mauni Amawsaya.	
Magh:-	
Kunr Chauth, Timul Chauth, Basant Panchami, Sri Panchami	
Serswati Puja, Takshak Puja, Basantotsav, Ratikamotsav,	
Vagishweri Jainti, Achala, Spatmi, Rath Sptami,Bhanu Sptami	
Maha Nanda Navmi, Hersubarm Fair, Lala Rajpath Rai Jainti	
Guru Ravidass Ji Jainti, Maghi Purima, Kalpvas	

Source: Varanasi.nic.in

This religious assertion has overshadowed the presence of social divisions within the Hindu social structure. Stefan Schutte exposed the lowly social position of *Dhobi* (washerman), a Dalit caste, in Banaras' social life. He noted down that though they (*dhobi*) belong to Scheduled

Castes, they are not subjected to untouchability today. "...But, even after efforts in education, no more than 8 per cent of the total *Dhobi* population in Uttar Pradesh has found an occupation outside the washing business. They have been governed by '*Tat*' system continuing since 19th century. The '*Tat*' system works as an extensive social institution – its various councils define rules, obligations, codes of conduct and measures of social control for the community members in the sphere of social and professional life."[20] Another study on Banaras boatman known as *mallah*, again a Scheduled Castes, pointed out the servile social position of boatman. "Brahmins give a limited recognition to the boatmen's ritual capacities likening them to 'needles' by comparison with their own capacities as 'swords', but denying to them the honorific title, which the boatmen claim of being Gangaputras, i.e. 'sons of the Ganges.'"[21]

Further this study found that "During Ganga Action Plan (GAP) Brahmans or *Panda* of Banaras found allies in environmentalists to assert their castes domination over the *kewat* (fisherman/*mallah*)."[22] "You see, the Brahmins who hold knowledge of the Purans try to cover up the story of *kewat* and Rama because they want to continue to exploit us and treat us like dirt, but now the truth is being revealed...Brahmans argue that *mallahs* try to prove their relationship with Rama and force people to believe it, but to us (Brahmins) they will never say they are Gangaputra because we know they are not. But to those who don't know the truth, that is what they claim."[23]

Further, to maintain the status-quo in power relations, Brahmans invented many of the above mentioned festivals. According to a study by Michael S. Dodson "there were, in fact, numerous new festivals conceived and practised over the course of the 19th century. The prevalence of these is testified to by a resident missionary, M.A.Sherring, who recorded some forty festivals that occurred throughout the year in Banaras. Sherring also noted the changing and adaptive nature of many of these public celebrations. He described this, for example, with respect to the '*Ganga-Saptami mela*' held on the banks of the Ganges, on the 7th day of *Jeth* in which formally, the idol representing the goddess was simply worshipped; but, in later years, a *mela* has been held accompanied by *nach* or dancing. Other fairs were also newly invented, such as the *Dangal mela*, held on the day after the *Burhwa Mangal festival* when 'singing parties proceed to the temple, accompanied by crowds of listeners and boats, laden with people.

It is attended by singing and dancing girls, rowing on the river, proceeding as far as Ramnagar."[24] And this strong assertion of Hinduism and its imprint all over the area divide Banaras society into the binary of a Hindu-Muslim framework. Such a situation along with religious work creates a perfect breeding ground for the right wing forces. In the shroud of cultural and religious functions, the continuous propaganda throughout the year goes on with an ease.

Occupational category		*Function*	*General caste category*
1. *PANDA*	*Tirth-purohit*	pilgrimage priest	BRAHMAN
	Gumasta	agent of *tirth-purohit*	
	Ghatiya	supervises bathers; performs minor rituals on the *ghats*	
	Joshi-Bhandar	pilgrim guide	
	Temple Priests		
2. *KARM KANDI*		specialist ritual technician	
3. MAHABRAHMAN		funeral priest	
4. MAHABAPPA		funeral priest to Mahabrahmans	
5. NAU		barber; funeral priest to low castes	middle order clean caste
6. MALLAH		boatman	
7. *OJHA*		spirit medium	not caste specific but generally low
8. DOM		funeral attendant	UNTOUCHABLE

Source: Jonathan Parry, *Ghosts, Greed and Sin: The Occupational Identity of Benares Funeral Priests,* Man (New Series), Vol. 15, No. 1, 1980, p. 91.

Figure 9: Occupational Specialists with a role at Death in Banaras.

The National Textile Policies of 1985 and 1991 (after liberalization) affected weavers very badly, resulting in closure of large numbers of handlooms. The worst hit was the lower Hindu castes such as *chamar*, the late entrant into the business.[25] Many of them left weaving and shifted to other menial occupations. But Muslim weavers showed some resilience by shifting their base from urban to rural areas. They began to sell their land in the city, and permanently shift to rural places, which earned them some capital to start their weaving in the hinterland. It also gave some respite from the urban expensive life style.[26]

As in the case of communal disturbance during 1930, when right wings played with the insecurity of middle castes, Dalits played the role of foot-soldier in communal violence of the 1990. The right wing forces associated with R.S.S. were able to fully utilise the situation and mobilise poor weavers along with other sections of Hindus. The national atmosphere too fuelled the communal flare in the district. The BJP had resorted to a naked and vicious communal propaganda in the May 1991 elections. It was bent on capturing power by making use of the powerful religious symbol of *Ram Janmabhoomi*. Thus the November 1991 riots in Banaras took place against the background of by-elections.[27] Shirish Chandra Dixit subsequently won the Lok Sabha seat. Vasanthi Raman reported that "About 564 people were arrested under the Indian Penal Code (IPC) and other prohibitory measures, which included 340 Hindus and 214 Muslims. It has been estimated that Hindus lost property worth Rs. 4,00,000 and Muslims worth Rs. 6,00,000."[28]

The role of the administration has been in favour of Hindu fundamentalists throughout the history of communal violence in Banaras. The November 1991 riots were no exception. A. A. Engineer noted the role of administration as follows: "It was quite lax. There was no proper police *'bandobust'* when the Kali procession was passing through Madanpura. The District Magistrate (DM) maintains that adequate police was not available. The question is did the administration not know that the Kali procession was to be taken out. Also, on November 8, people in Godowlia were killed in the presence of the police including the burning alive of two persons. On November 13 too, when the Muslims were on a killing spree, the police did not do a thing. The administration did not take any step to quash rumors. While it permitted S. C. Dixit of the BJP to roam around freely in the riot affected areas, other prominent politicians and social workers including V. P. Singh were not allowed to visit these areas. It speaks volumes for the objectivity of the administration."[29]

In the riot that took place in the year 2000, the story was similar. After a small skirmish between the two communities on April 16, 2000, the Section officer of Adampur police station, M.P. Singh, was behind the major acts of violence leading his police team against the Muslim residents. United Cultural Forum recorded that "Forty-year old Haji Vakil Ahmad, sitting on a wooden cot with a child was beaten up by the police as was 80 year-old, Sardar Fateh Mohammed, a much respected leader and representative of five Muslim communities. His son was also beaten and a four-year old girl, sitting on the upper floor of her home, was flung down the staircase of her home by the police... When Muslims came out to protest against the police atrocities, the administration refused to take cognisance of the protestors."[30]

Conclusion

Communalism is an old Indian problem that time does little to solve. Analyses of Home Ministry data on communal riots since 1954 to 1964 (year Nehru died) reveals that as many as 1,690 incidents took place in which 2,310 were dead and 7,318 hurt. However, the post-Nehru era differs only in terms of frequency of riots. So right-wing political mobilisation, anti-minority campaign and physical violence have been parts of Indian politics and it influences Banaras, a Hindu religious centre and important pilgrimage, as well. The economic contestation between Muslim *gaddidar* and Hindu traders and various demands of weavers potentially creates the communal polarisation. To incur maximum profit from the trading of handloom products, traders and *gaddidar* use un-fair means to cut the wages, increase the prices of yarn, charge huge interst rates on loan, claim defects in the products to cut the price etc. This increased the frustration of weavers which act as a catalyst for communal polarisation. The unfair trade has to stop. Second, something like the Prevention of Communal and Targeted Violence (Access to Justice and Reparations) Bill, 2011 is long overdue to prevent violence against the minority and weaker section of the society.

On the positive side of this bill, it has clear and broader provisions against the sexual assault on women. From rape, gang rape and mass rape to exposing one's sexual organs in front of any person, any act which causes sexual indignity to others are to be considered as sexual act. Its implementation will really deter communalists at the ground level. Compensation and resettlement too are merits of the bill. "Hostile Environment against a Group" in chapter one and "Hate Propaganda" in the following chapter gives ample scope to quell the communalism prior to physical violence. However, the proposed bill, apart from a number of minor problems, has two main problems. Firstly, the government proposal to declare certain areas as "communally disturbed" may create a permanent situation like north-east in minorities dominated areas. Given the fact that most of the Muslims' areas today are pointed out by bank and administration as sensitive areas, they are deprived of many facilities, which a normal citizen gets. Hitherto almost all the riots took place near minorities' dwelling and it is very natural that every time communal riots flare up, their ghettos will be declared as communally disturbed. And if we consider the frequency of communal riots in the country, minority areas will be 'communally disturbed' each day. It would be a frightening situation for the minorities. Each time, in the name of protection, minority areas will be under a curfew-like situation. With the right-wing at the helm of affairs, both at the centre and in the states, the law will be manipulated to suit the communal elements.

Further, this bill gives the District Magistrate (DM), the powers to take preventive measures when there is an apprehension or breach of peace or creation of discord between members of different religious groups. It is provided that he may, by order in writing, prohibit any act which in his opinion is likely to cause apprehension in the minds of another community or caste or group that it is directed to intimidate, threaten or otherwise promote ill will against that community or caste or group. This provision is generating a fear in the mind of the minorities, especially Muslims.

Continuous eruption of pre-planned communal riot has jolted the base of secularism in India. Religion has proved to be potent for communal mobilisation, and lethal when mixed with politics to gain politically. In recent times, religion has come in handy to capture political power. The Kalyan Singh government in Uttar Pradesh, Narendra Modi's rule in Gujarat, Shiv Sena government in Maharashtra, and 1998-2004 NDA (led by BJP) rule are examples of politicisation of religion. Today, right-wing forces are crippled with factionalism and loss of face due to non-fulfilment of communal agenda they promised before coming to power. But even then one cannot rule out their comeback. It is not necessary that the right-wing always captures state power by the use of religion. They also come through the promise of corruption free administration, better development alternatives and security of nation from external and internal threats. Once they come to power, the hidden agenda of segregation takes place.

Hence, Communal Violence Bill is necessary to protect minorities from communal riots, but it is not sufficient. The bill has its own weakness as argued above. Further, this bill is tilted more in favour of post-violence scenarios and less on preventing communalism. May be the bill has a limited purpose to serve. Thus to protect minorities, secularism needs more than a law. It needs a democratic and secular politics in praxis and consistent opposition to communalism in society.

Reference

1. Gopal Krishna, 'Communal Violence in India' in S.I.Wilkinson (ed.) *Religious Politics and Communal Violence*, OUP, New Delhi, 2005, p. 149..
2. Lat Bhairava means "staff" of Bhairava (it is popularly known as the police chief of sacred Kashi). It is located on the northern fringe of Banaras where the road to Sarnath intersects the Grand Trunk Road. Lat Bahirava is known to the

Puranas as Kapali Bhairava. This image of Bhairava is a pillar, encased in copper, and smeared with vermilion. The pillar is very old and perhaps the Puranic Mahashmashana Stambha, the "Pillar of the Great Cremation Ground," or the Kula Stambha, the "Pillar of the Race." It was here they said that Bhairava would administer his punishment, the *bhairavi Yatana*, as a moment's prelude to liberation.

3. According to the Hindu belief Aurangzeb had broken the temple to construct the Muslim tomb site. However, when Sherring examined the site in 1860, he was convinced that the most ancient remains there were not those of the Hindu temple, but of a much earlier Buddhist complex, and that the Lat itself was really an Ashokan pillar, with just the dimensions of the Ashokan pillar found at Sarnath a few miles to the north.
4. Vasudha Dalmia, *The Nationalisation of Hindu Tradition: Bhartendu Harishchandra and Nineteenth Century Banaras*, New Delhi, OUP, 1997.
5. *Ibid.*
6. G.B. Malleson and J. Kaye, *The Indian Mutiny*, London, Vol. ii, 1889, p.176.
7. Katherine Prior, Making History: The State's Intervention in Urban Religious Disputes in the North-Western Provinces in the Early Nineteenth Century, *Modern Asian Study*, 27 (1), 1993, p. 183.
8. R.Guha, ed., *Subaltern Studies* VI, Delhi, OUP, 1989.
9. There is no authentic document available which shows that Salar Masud Ghazi had ever visited Banaras. However, the replica of Ghazi's tomb, *yadgah*, in Banaras in Jaitpura, a densely Muslim populated area near the old city centre, draws large crowds annually for the symbolic enactment of the wedding of Ghazi.
10. B.R.Hertel, ed., *Living Banaras: Hindu Religion in Cultural Context*, New Delhi, Manohar, 1998.
11. Harish Damodaran, *India's New Capitalists: Caste, Business and Industry in a Modern Nation*, Palgrave Macmillan, New York, 2008.
12. Muslims *gaddidars* and businessmen mobilized their poor weaver, whereas Hindus counterpart brings in local Hindus population with the help of communal active organisation. Muslim *gaddidars* or businessmen are able to rally his poor community members because he is their employer, belong to the same caste and religion and professionally once both were same.
13. Marzia Casolari, 'Role of Benaras in Constructing Hindu Identity', *Economic and Political Weekly*, Vol. 37, No. 15, 2002.
14. *Hindustan Times*, Banarasi Sari weaves Hindus and Muslims, April 13th, 2007.
15. M. Showeb, *A study of Socio-Economic problems of weavers*, Ganga-Kaveri Publishing House, Varanasi, 1994.
16. Communalism Combat, July 2000, p. 30.
17. Mary Searle-Chatterjee, Religious Division and the Mythology of the Past, in B.R.Hertel (ed.) *Living Banaras: Hindu Religion in Cultural Context*, New Delhi, Manohar, 1998, p.149.
18. *Ibid,* pp. 147-48

19. Mary Searle-Chatterjee, 'Wahabi sectarianism among Muslims of Banaras', *Contemporary South Asia*, Vol. 3, No. 21994.
20. Martin Gaenszle and Jorg Gengnagel (2006).
21. Assa Doron (2008), p. X.
22. *Ibid;* p. 60.
23. *Ibid;* p. 68 and 133.
24. Michael S. Dodson (2012), p 20.
25. The caste *chamar* entered into the weaving profession by 1930s in and around the rural areas of Banaras as apprentice to the Muslim master weavers. However, the new masters could have as much economically exploitative, but for *chamar* weaver it was like freedom from caste hierarchy and unclean jobs they earlier used to do. At the same time, Banaras had seen rise in communal violence during 1930s when middle castes (*Shudra*) workers face economic competition from Muslims and Dalits urban poor. Hindu merchant favored to have Hindu workers in their factory.
26. These things came up in many interviews that I had conducted during the fieldwork.
27. Former DG Police Mr. S.C. Dixit contested on BJP ticket and won. Dixit was also connected with the VHP.
28. Vasanthi Raman, Op. cit. p. 136.
29. Asghar A. Engineer, Benaras Rocked by Communal Violence, *Economic and Political Weekly*, vol. 27, No. 10/11, 1992, pp. 509-511.
30. *Communalism Combat*, July, 2000, p. 30.

Conclusion

Despite the warning from many economists, intellectuals and pro-people political parties liberalization was introduced in India. Joseph Stiglitz argued that if India liberalised its capital markets 'rapidly, it would expose itself to the kind of volatility" which led to downturn and instability in Latin America. He felt that the external liberalization had "exposed India to inequalities of the global trading system.' Unlike Ejaz Ghani, World Bank Economic Advisor for the South Asia Region, claim that globalisation has advanced the South Asian economy a report entitled 'Human Development in South Asia' from Pakistan noted that "at least half a billion people in South Asia have experienced a decline in their real incomes.

"The costs in this period of globalisation have been almost entirely borne by the poor. It is a matter of serious concern that the number of people living in poverty has increased and the levels of human development, which had improved after the 1960, have started to stagnate and even decline. The levelling of incomes that was supposed to occur with the rise in productivity, reforms and an increase in the country's shares in global trade, finance and services, has not taken place. With markets having been liberalised, domestic industries have been thrown open to global competition, which has led to the closure of several industries. The report revealed the fact that reforms that were conducted in the last one and a half decades have not really led to an acceleration of growth rates. Among the South Asian countries, while Bangladesh and Nepal had modest growth rates, the growth rate faltered in the case of Sri Lanka in the second half of the 1990s while it declined in the case of Pakistan. Only India has been able to achieve a growth rate of above 6 per cent."[1] However India success story is too much credited to the external liberalization rather to the shift in the policies - from anti-market to pro-market, argues Stiglitz.

Opening of the market brought formidable competition to India's textile industry in general and to the handloom sector in particular. Globalisation has affected different units of textile in different ways. Mills has its own problems. It is facing competition from powerlooms; cut in subsidies from government, non-availability of raw materials, apparel dumping, technologically poor machine having less efficiency etc. Recently mills stopped working for one day to register their protest against the cut in subsidies and ban on export of cotton yarn. The strike was announced by the Confederation of Indian Textile Industry (CITI). Recently government has raised the excise duty of 10.3 per cent on the garment industry in this year's budget and the legal action against hundreds of dyeing units in Tirupur had created serious problems for the industry. In turn, this was affecting the consumption of both yarn and fabrics. The cumulative effect of all these are closure of mills – Spinning and Composite.

Table 89: Total numbers of mills closed down

As on	*No. of Mills*			*No. of Mills Closed*		
	Spinning	*Composite*	*Total*	*Spinning*	*Composite*	*Total*
31.03.02	1579	281	1860	295	126	421
31.03.03	1599	276	1875	350	134	484
31.03.04	1564	223	1787	374	94	468
31.03.05	1566	223	1789	379	99	478
31.03.06	1570	210	1780	387	96	483
31.03.07	1608	200	1808	381	87	468
31.03.08	1597	176	1773	318	63	381
31.03.09	1653	177	1830	340	65	405
31.03.10	1673	180	1853	365	68	433
30.04.11	1766	185	1951	471	81	552

Source: www.texmin.nic.in

Total 552 closed textile mills had an installed capacity of 9.84 million spindles, 1.31 lakh rotors, 0.37 lakh looms and 3.05 lakh workers on roll as on 30/04/2011. Out of 552 closed mills, 40 mills are under Official Liquidator. Recent study on Mumbai textile mills shows that "Of the 58 textile mills in Mumbai, 32 are privately owned, 25 are owned by the National Textile Corporation, and one by Maharashtra State Textile Corporation. Century Mills was the last one to close down in the year 2006. At present, only two textile mills (Tata Mills and Poddar Mills) owned and managed by the National Textile Corporation (NTC), Government of India, are functioning partially. In these mills the workers are employed (or re-employed after retrenchment) on a contractual basis.

On 16 November 2007, DNA: Daily News and Analysis reported that the NTC had entered into a joint venture with a private corporation called Pantaloons. However, when this work was about to begin on 21 January 2010, a Hindustan Times correspondent reported that the mill was set on fire. This has raised doubts as to whether the state is willing to restart any mill given the massive real estate value of the mill land."[2] L. Gayer and C. Jaffrelot argued that the mechanisation and increasingly competitive nature of sectors such as meat, leather or textile export, in the context of neo-liberal and export-oriented economic policies in India and beyond, have had a cost for small entrepreneurs hailing from traditionally marginal communities. These changes have condemned the least capital-intensive producing units to disappear, as exemplified by the crisis of the handloom industry in Varanasi, which affected around 500,000 weavers in and around the city.

Meanwhile CITI has reported that out of 287 companies listed in the Bombay stock exchange 122 companies have reported net losses in Q1 of 2011-12 and 166 companies have shown poorer results compared to previous year. The highest price volatility in cotton prices in the past 150 years followed by a collapse in April, 2011, had immediate repercussions in the domestic market. Cotton yarn production is down by 15 per cent and fabric production is down by 19 per cent in the April-October 2011 period over the previous year. Textile Mills faced with high priced cotton inventories could not pass through the prices into yarn and fabrics as the price decline came suddenly in the month of April, 2011. This led to a slowdown in production and reduced utilization capacity.

The Ministry of Finance constituted a committee under the Chairmanship of Shri M.D. Mallya, Chairman Bank of Baroda for examining the textile restructuring proposals. The Committee identified a sizable exposure to the textiles sector of Rs. 146885 crores. The Report of the Committee recommended a restructuring package that sought relaxation in prudential norms by RBI for banks to restructure working capital and term loans. Government has not sought international collaboration for investments; foreign investments are on automaticroute for textile sector. Similarly powerloom too has its own problems: competition from CEM, competition from Chinese apparel, government negligence etc. But handloom sector is worst effected among all.

Unfortunately, most of them have been compelled to switch over from the handlooms to the powerlooms. The rising costs and absence of government policy for craft protection in India, has resulted in the decline and the craftsmen's shift to other professions. The mechanisation and increasingly competition, in the context of neo-liberal and export oriented economic policies in India and beyond, have had a cost for *julaha*. These changes have condemned the least capital intensive producing units to disappear, as exemplified by the crisis of the handloom industry in Varanasi, which affected weavers in and around the city. Most of the weavers, today, worked as a daily wager taking raw material from *gaddidars*. Their wage has gone down with the increase in working hour. The casualisation of work, shift to other jobs, low income, increased working hour and absence of holiday (*sair*) marks their transformation from independent artisan to a labourer.

Opening of the market, which flooded the market with cheap finished product and withdrawal of subsidies from raw materials on which handloom had been depending, created a condition extremely unfavourable to the Banaras silk handloom and left a deep mark on the *julaha* community. Government has introduced various programmes as a panacea to all the problems. However, the field survey debunked the myth of government claim. Government efforts are half measure, ill-planned and uninformed. For instance, government has major relief and subsidies sanctioned for cooperative sector. But, in Banaras less than two per cent of weavers fall under this category. Not only that, it has followed a homogenised approach for overall industry. To cope with the situation, weavers are turning to cheap material to produce a sari with low input cost. But this takes away the elegant craftmenship and aesthetic claim that a *Banarasi* sari represents. Apart from that, weavers are diversifying their production as well.

However, there are some positive outcomes of this crisis. The crisis has sent a strong message to the uneducated weavers that education could turn their bleak future into prosperity. Earlier, the good business was a hurdle as children left their schooling to join the family workshop or business. But, today weavers want to send their ward to school when they cannot afford education at all.

There are many pro-weavers organization which are articulating their problems. This study has categorised various pro-weavers organisations into three parts: traditional, non-governmental and political organisation. They have organized weavers around the issues of weavers' identity card, health card, un-interrupted supply of electricity etc. The role of Left parties' mass organization needed special mention as they have been most consistent force fighting for the welfare of the weavers in Banaras. However, weavers, not seeing any way out of globalisation, are less in demand of complete change of policies. What they are asking for are some welfare measures to ease past the crisis. Weavers raised many demands, which they thought would smooth the functioning of business and their life. The demands are that government should provide yarn by rejuvenating the districts offices which were responsible for it; government local offices should also procure the finished products; supply of electricity at cheaper rate; health/medical facilities for the weavers' family; educational institutions for their children in their localities; supply of easy credit; proper implementation of Handloom Reservation Acts. Surprisingly, there was no demand for reservations in the educational institutions and government jobs.

Apart from this, there are many experts on handloom and sympathisers' who want to protect this traditional craft have their own suggestions to protect it. Jaya Jaitly, well-known expert of artisan-related issues, said that during freedom movement Khadi (hand-spinning and weaving) had become an integral part of the freedom struggle, but in recent times government policies have been moving away from genuine help to handloom weavers. However demand for the quality products of handloom weavers certainly exist, and there must be a way to link this demand to protecting the livelihood of handloom weavers. One practical suggestion she gave was that representatives of weavers working here should visit other big handloom weaving centres like Andhra Pradesh, West Bengal and Assam particularly to learn how they are coping with existing problems and particularly to link up with the wider struggles and initiatives of handloom weavers in the country. She said that attention should be given to some problems arising from existing government schemes. Earlier the government had several schemes to help handloom weavers some of which have been scrapped. The key words for the govt. are 'cluster', 'value-added' and 'exports'. But due to the over-emphasis on exports, some small-scale weavers working independently could be left out of govt. schemes to help handlooms. The scheme to mark or certify handloom products could be problematic if a big fee has to be given for this, as this too will leave out the small-scale independent weavers. Powerlooms may be creating problems for handlooms, but in some areas and for some demands there can be joint efforts. She said Varanasi needs a *haat* where weavers can sell their products directly to customers. Till this is provided weavers should try selling their products on footpath.

Human Welfare Association with reference to Banaras weavers argued that the condition of silk handloom weavers is fast deteriorating and as many as 6,000 of them have been forced to migrate in a single year to cities like Surat, Mumbai and Kolkata. One reason for this is the WTO trade regime under which silk cloth imports have increased very fast. Another threat is from powerloom owners who have been producing cheap imitation products at various places, helped by computer-assisted copying of designs and selling the cheap imitation products as the famous Benarsi saree. The government has not even carried out a proper survey to get a reliable estimate of how many looms and weavers still survive. Eight-year old data which is no longer relevant is still being used so that available statistics do not reflect the real crisis. During this period of crisis some relief was provided when many women could take up zardoji ernbroidery work but this livelihood too has been snatched by indiscriminate mechanisation, particularly Chinese machines that Dr Rajnikant called the "Chinese Dragon."

Another expert, Nesar Ahmed, who prepared a report on Banaras weavers, suggested that the *Banarasi* silk sari has three unique features which distinguish it from other saris. First, the yarn it uses is high quality silk yarn from Karnataka. Though now the Chinese imported silk is also being used they are not of the same quality. Secondly, weavers claim that the saris woven on handlooms are of much better quality, not only in terms of design and motif but also in terms of weaving quality and durability, than those that are copied on powerloom. And, third and the most important, the artistry of Varanasi weavers in designing the saris is unique to the cluster. The challenge is to present these saris as a brand, highlighting these three features. The efforts to put labels like Silk Mark and Handloom Mark, if implemented properly, can help to establish the distinctive identity of the *Banarasi* saris in mainstream markets. However, effort to promote *Banarasi* saris as unique products has to involve all the stakeholders in the cluster collectively. Lack of ownership amongst stakeholders is a significant bottleneck. Though the traders are making profits selling *Banarasi* Saris, they do not seem to invest in improving production in the area. For them running their business and getting orders is what matters most. Most of them deal in a range of textile products (powerloom products, handloom products, made-ups etc. of both silk and non-silk yarn) and have inadequate incentive to invest in improving handloom quality and production to regain lost market share.

The weavers, who are the real stakeholders and take ownership of the weaving occupation ("our forefathers have been doing it, how can we leave it" or "it is our forefathers' occupation"), are into weaving more by compulsion than choice. Additionally, these poor weavers are cut-off from the market and are too unorganized to make any difference. They lack resources, access to market, credit and raw material and any form of organization to have an effect on the market. The need is to create and promote structures that organize the weavers to collectively engage with the market; provide them with quality raw materials and other facilities; and consequently, enhancing their bargaining power in the production process. Initiating and identifying and promoting such existing organizations should be given the greatest priority. The value addition in form of embroidery work (*zaridozi*) seems to be providing opportunity for diversifying and generating employment. "As a trader from Madanpura said the Banarasi saris with zaridozi work is more in demand now than the ones without *zaridozi* work. There is a need to identify such trends and encourage production to take advantage of it".[3]

Such collectives would also enhance the ability of weavers to access market information. Diversification into other products is taking place mostly into the powerloom products. Diversification by the handloom weavers is very limited and is mostly by compulsion and not by choice or any sustained market strategy. There is a need to create structures that enable weavers to access market trends and respond to them accordingly. At the policy level, the industry needs protection from the cheap import of silk fabric and from the powerloom sector. The act prohibiting powerlooms from manufacturing saris and other items entails to be implemented more seriously.

References

1. T.K.Rajalakshmi, 'Globalisation in South Asia', *Frontline*, Vol. 19, Issue 9, 2002.
2. Sumeet Mhaskar, 'Indian Muslims in a Global City: Socio-Political Effects on Economic Preferences in Contemporary Mumbai', Working Paper, Max Planck Institute for the Study of Religious and Ethnic Diversity, Gottingen, 2013, p. 12.
3. Nesar Ahmad, "Globalisation and the indegineous Artisan Economy", cribe.com. Also see Craftrevical.org.

Bibliography

Abdul, Noorbasha. 1996, 'Handlooms in Distress', *Economic and Political Weekly*, Vol. 31, No.23.

Aiyar, S.A. 2012, 'Rapid GDP Growth – Best Anti-dote for Poverty', *Economic Times*, 28th March.

Alam, Mahfuz. 2001, *Continuity and Change among the Muslims*, Ph.D Thesis, BHU, Varanasi.

Anjali, T.M. and Sergeti, E. J. 2010, 'Economic Growth and Ethnic Violence: An Empirical investigation of Hindu-Muslim riots in India', *Journal of Peace Research*, Vol. 47, No. 5.

Annapurna, M. 2006, 'Transitioning Markets: Transcending Consumption', *Economic and Political Weekly*, Vol. XLI, No. 31.

Anonymous, 2005. '*Diagnostic study of handloom silk cluster Varanasi* (Uttar Pradesh)', Ministry of Textiles, Govt. of India, New Delhi.

Ansari, Ashfaq Hussain. (ed.) 2007, *Basic Problems of OBC and Dalit Muslims*, Serial Publication, New Delhi.

Ansari, Hasan N. 1982, 'Socio-economic Status and Conditions of the Momins under British Rule', *Journal of Bihar Research Society*, Vol. 47-48.

Ansari, Ibadurrahman. 1971, *Varanasi men Banarasi Saree Udyoga: Ek arthik Sarvekshan*, Kashi Vidyapith, Varanasi.

Antze, Emily Christine. 2011, They Should Stand on their own feet: Mothers' Accounts of Education, School choice and their children's uncertain futures in Varanasi, India, Ph.D Thesis, University of Toronto. Aruna, M. 2006, 'Urmul: Weaving Self-Reliance', *Economic and Political Weekly*, Vol.XLI, No. 31.

Bagchi, Amiya Kumar. 1999, 'Globalisation, Liberalization and Vulnerability: India and Third World', *Economic and Political Weekly*, Vol. 34, No. 45.

Bagchi, Jayanta. 2008, *Indian Textile Industry: Liberalization and World Market*, Samskriti Publication, New Delhi.

Baker. D. Epstein, G. and Pollin. Robert (ed.). 1998, *Globalisation and Progressive Economic Policy*, Cambridge University Press, United Kingdom.

Basole, Amit. 2012, *Knowledge, Gender and Production Relations in India's informal Economy*, Ph.D, University of Massachusettes Amherst.

Bhagwati, Jagdish. 2001, 'Growth, Poverty and Reforms', *Economic and Political Weekly*, March 10, Vol. XXXVI, No. 10.

Bhanumurthy, N.R. and Mitra, Arup, 2002, 'Economic Growth, Poverty and Reforms in Indian States in the Pre-Reform and Reform Periods', *Asian Development Review*, 21(2), 2004, Philippines.

Bose, Tarun K. 2007, *Globalisation Pushes Varanasi Weavers to hunger and Death*, Actionaid, Varanasi.

Callewaert, W.M. and Schilder, Robert. 2000, *Banaras: Visions of a living ancient tradition*, Hemkunt Publishers, New Delhi.

Casolari, Marzia. 2002, 'Role of Benaras in Constructing Hindu Identity', *Economic and Political Weekly*, Vol. 37, No. 15.

CBGA, 2010, 'Response to Union Budget, New Delhi.

Chadha, G.K. and Sahu, P.P. 2002, Post-Reform setbacks in Rural Employment: Issues that need further scrutiny, *Economic and Political Weekly*, May 25, Vol. 37, No. 21.

Chandrasekhar, C.P and Ghosh J. 2001, 'In Defense of Handloom', *Business Line*, Oct.2.

Chaudhary, Asiya. 2011, 'Changing Structure of Indian Textile Industry After MFA (Multi-Fibre Agreement) phase out: A Global Perspective', *Far East Journal of Psychology and Business*, Vol. 2, No. 2.

Ciotti, Manuela. 2007, 'Ethnohistories behind local and global bazaars: Chronicle of a Chamar weaving community in the Banaras region', *Contribution to Indian Sociology*, Vol.41, No.3.

Dalmia, Vasudha. 1997, *The Nationalisation of Hindu Tradition: Bhartendu Harishchandra and Nineteenth Century Banaras*, Oxford University Press, New Delhi.

Damodaran, Harish. 2008, *India's New Capitalists: Caste, Business and Industry in a Modern Nation*, Palgrave Macmillan, New York.

Dastkar Andhra, 2010, '*Study for Scheme for Handloom Weavers Outside Cooperative Fold'*, Commissioned by the Office of the Commissioner for Handlooms and Director of Handlooms and Textiles, Government of Andhra Pradesh.

Datta, R.K. and Nanavaty, M. 2007, *Global Silk Industry: A Complete Source Book*, APH Publishing Corporation, New Delhi.

Dhas, A.C. and Helen, M. J. 2008, 'Impact of Globalisation and Economic Reforms on Employment in India', *Munich Personal RePEc Archive*, Paper No. 9597, Germany.

Directorate, 2009, *Handloom and textile Industry Director*, Kanpur, Uttar Pradesh.

Diwakar, D.M. and Nayak, Snatan (ed.). 2007, *Development Challenges: Afflicting Uttar Pradesh*, Manak Publication, New Delhi.

Doron, Assa. 2008, *Caste, Occupation and Politics on the Ganges: Passages of Resistance*, Ashgate Publishing, England.

Durkhiem, Emile. 1950, *Suicide: A Sociological Study*, Routledge, New York.

Engineer, Asghar A. 1992, 'Benaras Rocked by Communal Violence', *Economic and Political Weekly*, vol. 27, No. 10/11.

Eslake, Saul. 2002, *The Driver of Globalisation*, ANZ Banking Group, Melboune.

Fetterman, D.M. 1998, *Ethnography: Step by Step*, Thousands Oaks, California.

Fowler, Floyd. J. 1985, *Survey Research Methods*, Applied Social Research Methods Series, Sage Publications, New Delhi.

Francis, Lenin (Ed.). 2005, *Handloom has become live grave for weavers*, PVCHR and FWRA, Varanasi.

Frank, Thomas. 2001, *One Market under God: Extreme Capitalism, Market Populism and the End of Economic Democracy*, Secker and Warburg, London.

Freitag, Sandria B. (ed.) 1989, *Culture and Power in Banaras – Community, Performance and Environment, 1800-1980*, University of California Press, Berkeley.

Friedman, Thomas. 1998, *The Lexus and the Olive Tree*, Strauss and Giroux, New York.

Gaenszle, Martin and Gengnagel, Jorg. 2008, *Visualizing Space in Banaras: Images, Maps, and the Practices of Representation*, Oxford University Press, New Delhi.

Gaenszle, Martin. and Gengnagel, Jorg. (ed.) 2006, *Visualising Space in Banaras – Images, Maps and the practice of Representation*, Otto Harrass Owitz Publication, Germany.

Ghosh, Soumya Kanti. 2004, 'The Apparel Exports in Post-MFA', *Economic and Political Weekly*, Vol. 39, No. 17.

Gooptu, N. 2001, *The Politics of the Urban Poor in Early 20th Century India*, Cambridge University Press, Cambridge.

Government of India, 1995. '*Census of Handloom in Uttar Pradesh 1994-95*', Govt. press, New Delhi.

Government of Uttar Pradesh. 1965, Varanasi District Gazetteer, Allahabad.

Gupta, Charu S. 1996, 'Caste among the Muslim Zardoz of Delhi', *Man in India*, Vol.76, No.2, pp.103-13.

Gurtoo, Anjula and Pandey, Rahul. 2001, 'Power Sector in Uttar Pradesh: Past Problems and Initial Phase of Reform, *Economic and Political Weekly*, Vol. 36, No. 31.

Hammersley, M. and Atkinson, P. 2007, *Ethnography: Principles in Practice*, Routledge, London.

Handloom Census of India: 2009-10, National Council for Applied Economic Research, Ministry of Textile, Government of India.

Haneef, M. Aslam. 2001, 'Islam and Economic Development in Malaysia: A reappraisal, *Journal of Islamic Studies*, September, Vol. 12, No. 3.

Hasan, Mushirul. 2008, *Living with Secularism: The Destiny of India's Muslims*, Manohar Publication, New Delhi.

Hashi, D.A. 2005, 'Post-MFA: Making the textile and garment', *Economic and Political Weekly*, January, Vol. 40, No. 2.

Haynes, Jeff. 1999. *Religion, Globalization and Political Culture in the 3rd world*, MacMillan Press, London.

Hertel, B.R. (ed.). 1998, *Living Banaras: Hindu Religion in Cultural Context*, Manohar Publications, New Delhi.

Ibrahim, K.M. Sajad. 2000, 'Islam, Fundamentalism and the Challenges to Nation building in India', *India Quarterly*, July-Dec. Vol. 56, No. 3-4.

Issac, M.T. 1982, 'Class Struggle and Structural Changes: Coir Mat and Matting Industry in Kerala', *Economic and Political Weekly*, Vol. 17, No. 1.

Jain, L.C. 1985, 'New Textile Policy: End of Handlooms', *Economic and Political Weekly*, Vol.20, No. 27.

Jain, L.C. 1986, 'A Heritage to Keep: The Handicraft Industry, 1955-85', *Economic and Political Weekly*, pp.873-887.

Jenkins, Rob. 2002, *The Ideologically Embedded Market: Political Legitimation and Economic Reform in India*, Unpublished work.

John, M.E. Jha, P.K. and Jodhka, S.S. 2006, *Contested Transformations: Changing Economies and Identities in Contemporary India*, Tulika Books, Delhi.

Joshi, Seema. 2006, 'Impact of Economic Reforms on Social Sector Expenditure in India', *Economic and Political Weekly*, Jan. 28, Vol. 41, No. 4.

Joshi, Vijay and Little, I.M.D. 1997, India's *Economic Reforms 1991-2001*, Oxford University Press, Delhi.

Kapila, Raj and Kapila, Uma. 2002, *India's Economy in the 21st Century*, Academic Foundation, New Delhi.

Karat, Brinda. 2010, 'Towards Intensified Struggles for Adivasi Rights', *The Marxists*, Vol. XXVI, No. 3.

Karat, Prakash. 2011, 'The Challenges of Identity Politics', *The Marxist*, Vol. XXVII, No. 1-2.

Khan, Atiq. 2006, 'Handloom Fall Silent here, Weavers leave Varanasi', *The Hindu*.

Kidder, L.H. and Judd, Charles, M. 1989, *Research Methods in Social Relations*, SPSSI, New York.

Kinnvall, Catarina. 2008, *Globalization and Religious Nationalism in India: The Search for ontological security*, Routledge, London.

Kitiarsa, Pattana. 2008, *Religious Commodifications in Asia: Marketing Gods*, Routledge, London.

Kohli, Atul. 2006, 'Politics of Economic Growth in India: 1980-2006', *Economic and Political Weekly*, April 6, Vol. XLI, No. 14.

Koshy, Abraham. 1991, 'Malfunctioning of Public Distribution System: An Empirical Analysis', *Vikalpa*, Vol. 16, No.1.

Koshy, T.D. 1997, 'Banaras Silk : A Delicacy', *Indian Silk*, Vol. 35, No. 10.

Kothari, Rajni. 1988, 'Class and Communalism', *Economic and Political Weekly*, Vol. XXIII, No.49.

Krishna, Gopal. 2005, 'Communal Violence in India' in S.I.Wilkinson (ed.) *Religious Politics and Communal Violence*, OUP, New Delhi.

Krishna, R.A. and Krishna, V. 1966. 'Banaras Brocades', *Craft Museum*, New Delhi.

Krishnakumar, Asha. 2001, 'Perilous Policies', *Frontline*, Vol. 18, Issue 8.

Kumar, B.R. and Nerli, S.K.A. 2001. 'Role of designer in silk industry', *Indian Silk*, Vol. 40, No. 4.

Kumar, Nita. 1995, *The Artisans of Banaras: Popular Culture and Identity, 1880-1986*, Orient Longman, New Delhi.

Maarif, A.Syafii. 2002, 'Islam and the Challenge of Managing Globalization', *Indonesian Quarterly*, Dec. Vol. 30, No. 2.

Malleson, G.B. and Kaye, J. 1889, *The Indian Mutiny*, London, Vol. ii.

Mamatha, A. and Naik, S.D. 1997, 'Problems of handlooms', *The Indian Tex. J.,* Vol. 107, No. 11.

Mamidipudi, A. Syamasundari B., Bijker, W. 2012, 'Mobilising Discourses: Handloom as a Sustainable Socio-Technology', *Economic and Political Weekly*, Vol. xlvii, No. 25.

Mamidipudi, Annapurna. Syamasundari, B and Bijker, Wiebe. 2012, 'Mobilising Discourse – Handloom as Sustainable Socio-Technology', *Economic and Political Weekly*, Vol. XLVII, No. 25.

Mansfels, R. Colloredo. 2002, 'An Ethnography of Neoliberalism – Understanding Competition in Artisan Economies', *Current Anthropology*, Feb. Vol. 43, No. 1.

Meher, Rajkishor. 1995, 'The Handloom Industry and the Socio-Economic conditions of weavers in Orissa', *Journal of Rural Development*, Vol. 14, No. 3.

Mehta, Deepak. 1992, 'The Semiotics of Weaving: A Case Study', *Contribution to Indian Sociology*, Vol. 26, No. 1.

Mencher, J. 1999, 'NGOs – Are they a force of Change', *Economic and Political Weekly*, Vol. 34, No. 30.

Ministry of Textile, 2009-10, *Handloom Census of India*, Government of India, New Delhi.

Minz, Boniface. 1982, *Weaving then and Now: A tale of declining village industry in Chhottanagpur*, Vikas Maitri Publication, Ranchi.

Mishra, K.P. 1975, *Banaras in transition: 1738-1795, a socio-economic Study*, Munshiram Manoharlal Publishers, New Delhi.

Mishra, S.N. 1981, *Banaras*, Roli Books International, New Delhi.

Mishra, Sanjay. 1993, *India's Textile Sector: A Policy Analysis*, Sage Publication, New Delhi.

Mishra, V.N. and Rao, M.G. 2003, 'Trade Policy, Agricultural Growth, Rural Poor: 1978-79 to 2000', *Economic and Political Weekly*, Vol. 38, No. 43.

Modak, Savita. 2006, 'Fabindia: Weaving Customers' Dreams', *Economic and Political Weekly*, Vol.XLI, No. 31.

Mukund, K. and Syama Sundari, B. 1998, 'Doomed to fail? 'Handloom weavers; cooperatives in Andhra Pradesh', *Economic and Political Weekly,* Vol. 38, No. 52, pp. 3323–3335.

Mukund, K. and Syamasundari, B. Dec. 1998- Jan. 1, 1999, 'Doomed to Fail? 'Handloom Weavers' Co-operative in Andhra Pradesh', *Economic and Political Weekly*, Vol. 33, No. 52.

Murray, Charles. 1997, *What it means to be a Libertarian*, Broadway Books, New York.

Nagaraju, B. 2003, 'Impact of reform on Handlooms', *Journal of rural Development*, July-Sept., Vol. 22, No. 3, pp. 345-62.

Naik, S.D. 1996, '*Traditional embroideries of India*', APH Publishing Co., New Delhi.

Nandan, A.P. 1991, 'Momin, Traditional Weaver', *Journal of the Anthropological Survey of India*, Vol.40 (3-4).

Nandan, A.P., Das, S.R. and Das, B.K. 1991, 'The Momin, traditional weaver; a brief account of their economic subsistence, *Journal Anthropology Survey of India*, Vol. 40.

Narasaiah, M.L. 1999, *Crisis of Handloom Industry*, Discovery Publishing House, New Delhi.

Nayak, P. Rout, Shaikh, S. and Rajnikant. 2007, 'Dream *of Weaving: Study and Documentation of Banaras Sarees and Brocades'*, Textile Committee, Ministry of Commerce, GoI, New Delhi.

Nayar B.R. 1998, 'Political Structure and India's Economic Reforms of the 1990s', *Pacific Affairs*, Vol. 71, No. 3, Canada.

Nayar, Baldev Raj. 1997, 'Globalisation, Nationalism and Economic Policy Reform', *Economic and Political Weekly*, Vol. 32, No. 30.

Nesar, Ahmad. 2006, *Globalization and the Indigenous Artisan Economy: A case Study of the Varanasi Silk Sari industry*, AIACA.

Niranjana, S. 2001, 'Appraising the Indian Handloom Industry', *Economic and Political Weekly*, Vol. 36, No. 45.

Offredi, Mariola. 1996, 'The Muslim Weavers of Banaras and Mau in the Seventies', *Eurasiaica*, Vol. 40, pp.303-336.

Omvedt, Gail. 2008, 'Capitalism and Globalisation and Dalits and Adivasis', *Economic and Political Weekly,* Vol. 40, No. 47.

Pandey, S.M. 1967, 'Rival Unionism in an Industrial Centre: A Study of Kanpur', *Indian Journal of Industrial Relations*, Vol. 3, No. 2.

Pant, K.C. 2003, *India's Development Scenario: Next Decade and Beyond*, Academic Foundation, New Delhi.

Paranjape, H.K. 1991, 'New Industrial Policy – A Capitalist Manifesto', *Economic and Political Weekly*, Vol. 26, No. 43.

Parry, Jonathan. 1980, 'Ghosts, Greed and Sin – The Occupational Identity of the Benaras Funeral Priests', *Man (New Series)*, Vol. 15, No. 1.

Parthasarathy, G. 2003, *Economic reforms and Rural Development*, Hard Back Book, New Delhi.

Pathak, S., Sambhulingappa, Nagabhushanaiah, Y.N. and Nadigar G.S. 1993, 'Varanasi silk industry - A survey', *Indian Silk*, Vol. 31, No. 12, pp. 6-10.

Pathan, Sufiya. 2009, *A Historical and Theoretical Investigation into 'Communalism'*, Manipal University, Bangalore.

Petras, James and Polycroniou, C. 1997, 'Critical Reflection on Globalisation', *Economic and Political Weekly*, Vol. XXXII, No. 36.

Pria, Devi. 1982, *Master Weavers*, Royal College of Arts, Festival of India in Britain, London.

Prior, Katherine. 1993, 'Making History: The State's Intervention in Urban Religious Disputes in the North-Western Provinces in the Early Nineteenth Century', *Modern Asian Study*, Vol. 27, No. 1.

Raghuvanshi, Lenin and Nagvanshi, Shruti. 2005, '*Banarasi Saree Weaving Sector of Varanasi: A study of the working conditions of the unorganised workers of these sectors*', Unpublished monograph, Peoples' Vigilance Committee on Human Rights, Varanasi.

Rai, Dhananjay. 2010, 'Dalits, Globalisation and Economism', *Think India Quarterly*, Vol. 13, No. 3.

Rai, Santosh Kumar. 2011, 'Becoming a Grihasta – Hierarchies of work among Handloom Weavers in Early Twentieth Century United Provinces, India', in Rana Behal, Alice Mah and Babacar Fall, (ed.) '*Rethinking Work: Global Historical and Sociological Perspectives*', Tulika, Delhi, pp. 73-82.

Rai, Santosh Kumar. 2012, 'Muslim Weavers' Politics in Early 20th Century Northern India', *Economic and Political Weekly*, Vol. XLVII, No. 15.

Raman, Vasanthi. 2010, 'The *Julaha* – Momin Ansaris of Banaras: A Socio-historical Trajectory', *Voice of Dalit*, 3(2), 2010.

Raman, Vasanthi. 2010, *The Warp and the Weft: Community and Gender Identity among Banaras Weavers*, Routledge, New Delhi.

Ramaswamy, V. 2006, *Textile and Weavers in South India*, Oxford University Publication, New Delhi.

Ranga, N.G. 1930, *The Economies of Handloom*, Taraporewala Sons, Bombay.

Rangarajan, K. 2005, 'International Trade in Textiles and Clothing', *Foreign Trade Review*, Jan-March, Vol. 39, No. 4.

Ranjan, Sharad. 2009. 'Growth of Rural Non-Farm Employment in Uttar Pradesh: Reflections from Recent Data', *Economic and Political Weekly*, Vol. 44, No. 4.

Reddy, S.N. and Jayaram, H. 2001, 'Performance of primary silk handloom weavers cooperative societies in Andhra Pradesh – A financial evaluation', *Indian Silk*, Vol. 40, No. 3, pp. 28-31.

Roy, T. (April 18 R) 1998, 'Development or Distortion: 1950-1997', *Economic and Political Weekly,* April 18, Vol. 33, No.16.

Roy, T. 1998, 'Economic Reforms and Textile Industry in India, *Economic and Political Weekly*,

Roychaudhri, S. 1996, *Handlooms versus Powerlooms: Two Case Studies of Silk Weaving in Karnataka*, Association of Asian Studies Meeting, Washington.

Scholte, Jan Aart. 2002, *What is globalisation? The Definitional Issue – Again*, CSGR, Working Paper, University of Warwick, United Kingdom.

Sengupta, Arjun. 2001, *Reform, Equity and IMF*, Har-Anand Publication, Delhi.

Seth, S.C. 2000, *Communalism – A Socio-political Study*, Gyan Publishing House, New Delhi.

Shankar, Kripa. 2002, 'Deeper into the Debt Trap', *Economic and Political Weekly*, Vol. XXXVII, No. 49.

Sharma, K.L. 2003, 'The Social Organisation of Urban Space: A case study of Chanderi, a small town in central India', *Contribution to Indian Sociology*, Vol. 37, No. 3.

Sharma, Sameer. 2004, 'Entrepreneurship Development in Networks of Weaver Cluster of Pochampalli', *Journal of Rural Development,* Vol. 23(3).

Sharma, Ursula. and Chatterjee, M. S. (ed.) 1994, *Contextualising Caste: Post-Dumontian Approaches*, Blackwell Publisher, Oxford.

Showeb, M. 1993, *Muslim Handloom Weavers in Varanasi: Problems and Remedial measures*, Gandhian Institute of Social Studies, Varanasi.

Showeb, M. 1994, *A study of Socio-Economic problems of weavers*, Ganga-Kaveri Publishing House, Varanasi.

Showeb, M. 1994, *Silk Handloom Industry of Varanasi: A Study of Socio-economic Problems of Weavers*, Ganga-Kaveri Publishing House, Varanasi.

Shrivastva, S.S. and Tandon, R. 2005, 'How Large is India's Non-Profit Sector', *Economic and Political Weekly*, Vol. 40, No. 19.

Siddiqui, Mohd Asim. 2006, The Wretched of the Earth: A Representation of the Life of the Weavers of Banaras in Abdul Bismillah's Jhini Jhini Bini Chadria, in Adbul Waheed (ed.), *Muslim Artisans, Craftmen and Traders: Issues in Entrepreneurship*, Icon Publication, New Delhi.

Singh, Amrita. 2008, '*A Profile of Banaras Silk Sarees*', Department of Textiles and Apparel Designing College of Rural Home Science, Karnataka.

Singh, Bhagwati Prasad. 1977, *Banaras ke Vwaysayi*, Laxmi Narayan Press, Varanasi.

Singh, Rana P.B. and Rana, P.S. 2002, *Banaras Region: A spiritual and cultural guide*, Indica books, Varanasi.

Singh, Rana P.B. 1989, *Where Cultural Images meet: Literary images of Varanasi*, Tata Book Agency, Varanasi.

Singh, Yogindra. 2000, *Culture change in India: Identity and Globalization*, Rawat Publication, Jaipur.

Sinha, R.K. 1998, 'Brocades of Banaras – A luminous chapter in Indian fabric', *Indian Silk*, Vol. 37, No. 5, pp. 5-14.

Soares, B.F. 2006, 'Islam in Mali in the neo-liberal era, *African Affairs*, Jan., Vol. 105, No. 40.

Srinivasulu, K. 1997, 'High Powered Committee, Low Voltage Report: Mira Seth report on Handlooms', *Economic and Political Weekly*, 14-20 June, Vol. 32, No. 24.

Sudhakar Rao, B. Puroshotam, P. and Sudhakar Reddy, E. 1990, 'Employment, poverty and levels of living among the handloom weavers in Andhra Pradesh'. *Journal of Rural Development*, Vol. 9, No. 6.

Sushma. 1981, 'The Unorganized Weaving Sector: Problems and Prospects', *The Economic Times*, May 23.

Syamasundari, B and Niranjana, S. 2006, 'Mangalagiri: Case Study of Master Weavers', *Economic and Political Weekly*, Vol. XLI, No. 31.

Taylor, Stephanie. (ed.) 2005, *Ethnographic Research: A Reader*, Sage Publications, New Delhi.

Teltumbde, Anand. 2011, 'Dalit Capitalism and Pseudo Dalitism', *Economic and Political Weekly*, Vol. XLVI, No. 10.

Times, Hindustan. 2007, *Varanasi's Silk Sari-Weavers face bleak, hungry future*, July 04, Varanasi.

Vaidyanathan, A. 2013, 'Future of Cooperatives in India', *Economic and Political Weekly*, Vol. XLVIII, No. 18.

Varma, Pawan Kumar. 1998, *The Great Indian Middle Class*, Viking, New Delhi.

Verma, A.K. 2006, 'Formation of Muslim Political Front', *Economic and Political Weekly*, Vol. XLI, No. 40.

Verma, R.I. and Bhatnagar, P.P. (ed.) 1965, '*Cotton Textiles industry in U.P. with special reference to Maunath Bhanjan, Azamgarh*', Manager of Publication, Delhi.

Vijayagoplan, S. 1993, *Economic Status of Handicraft Artisans*, National Council for Applied Economic Research, New Delhi.

Virmani, Arvind. 2002, 'A New Development Paradigm – Employment, Entitlement and Empowerment', *Economic and Political Weekly*, June 1, Vol. XXXVIII, No. 22.

Waheed, Abdul. 2006, *Muslim Artisans, Craftsmen and Traders: Issues in Entrepreneurship*, Icon Press, New Delhi.

White-Harris, B. and Janakarajan, S. 2004, *Rural India facing the 21st Century: Essays on Long Term village change and recent development policy*, Anthem Press, London.

Wilkinson, S.I. (ed.). 2007, *Religious Politics and Communal Violence*, Oxford University Press, New Delhi.

Williams, Philippa. 2007, 'Hindu-Muslim Brotherhood: Exploring the Dynamics of communal Relations in Varanasi, North India', *Journal of South Asian Development*, Vol. 2, No. 2.

Williams, Philippa. 2011, 'An absent presence: experience of the 'welfare state' in an Indian Muslim mohalla', *Contemporary South Asia*, 2011, Vol. 19, No. 3.

Wood, J.M.F. 2012, 'Contentious Politics and Civil Society in Varanasi', in Ajay Gudavarthy (ed.), *Re-framing Democracy and Agency in India: Interrogating Political Society*, Anthem Press, Delhi.

Yadav, K.C. and Singh, R. 1994, *India's Unequal Citizen: A Study of Other Backward Classes*, Manohar Publication, New Delhi.

Annexure - 1

Data from Third Handloom Census (2009-10)

1.1 Distribution of Handloom Worker Households by Social Groups

Social Groups	*Number of Households*			*Per cent Distribution*		
	Rural	*Urban*	*Total*	*Rural*	*Urban*	*Total*
SCs	236,188	36,868	272,056	9.8	10.2	9.8
STs	598,574	16,703	615,277	24.7	4.6	22.1
OBCs	928,613	210,332	1,138,954	38.4	58.1	40.9
Others	657,742	98,251	755,993	27.2	27.1	27.2
Total	2,421,117	362,154	2,783,271	100.0	100.0	100.0

1.2 Distribution of Adult (18 years and above) Handloom workers by Social Groups

Social Groups	*Number of Households*			*Per cent Distribution*		
	Rural	*Urban*	*Total*	*Rural*	*Urban*	*Total*
SCs	331,994	58,439	390,433	10.3	9.5	10.1
STs	678,165	18,767	696,932	21.0	3.1	18.1
OBCs	1,359,355	378,188	1,737,543	42.1	61.5	45.2
Others	862,711	159,216	1,021,927	26.7	25.9	26.6
Total	3,232,225	614,610	3,846,835	100.0	100.0	100.0

1.3 State-wise Distribution of Handloom Worker Household

States/UTs	*Total handloom worker households ('000)*	*Per cent distribution*	*Share (%) to total households in state*
Assam	1,241	44.58	21.7
West Bengal	407	14.61	2.1
Tamil Nadu	189	6.79	1.2
Manipur	179	6.43	33.7
Andhra Pradesh	177	6.36	1.0
Tripura	121	4.33	17.6

(*Contd...*)

Uttar Pradesh	111	3.97	0.4
Nagaland	61	2.19	9.7
Orissa	41	1.46	0.5
Mizoram	39	1.42	18.9
Karnataka	38	1.35	0.3
Arunachal Pradesh	30	1.09	12.7
Bihar	25	0.92	0.2
Rajasthan	23	0.81	0.2
Jammu and Kashmir	17	0.62	0.8
Jharkhand	14	0.51	0.3
Kerala	12	0.42	0.1
Meghalaya	11	0.41	2.3
Uttaranchal	11	0.38	0.6
Madhya Pradesh	9	0.31	0.1
Himachal Pradesh	7	0.25	0.5
Haryana	6	0.23	0.1
Gujarat	4	0.13	0.0
Chhattisgarh	3	0.10	0.1
Punjab	2	0.09	0.0
Maharashtra	2	0.07	0.0
Delhi	2	0.07	0.0
Puducherry	2	0.06	0.7
Sikkim	1	0.02	0.5
All India	**2,783**	**100.0**	**1.26**

1.4 Techniques adopted in important centres of northern region

Brocade Weaving Techniques in Northern Region

Centres	**Techniques Adopted**															
	Fekwa	**Kardhwan**	**Katrawan**	**Cotton**	**Silk**	**Rayon**	**Wool**	**Staple**	**Jari**	**Jari Manufacture**	**Treadles & Healds**	**Adai**	**Jala**	**Jungu**	**Jacquard Machine**	**Dobby Machine**
Banaras	●	●	●		●				●	●	●		●		●	
Chanderi	●	●		●	●				●		●		●		●	●
Tanda	●	●		●							●					
Surat	●	●			●	●		●	●	●	●		●		●	
Aurangabad	●	●		●				●			●		●			

Annexure - 2

Financing of Handloom and Weavers related Schemes

2.1: Allocation of funds for the last three years and the current year is given below

Sl. No	*Name of Scheme*	*2008-09*		*2009-10*		*2010-11*		*2011-12 (up to 9.3.12)*	
		Funds allocated	***Funds released***	***Funds allocated***	***Funds released***	***Funds allocated***	***Funds released***	***Funds allocated***	***Funds released***
1.	Integrated Handloom Development Scheme	108.98	108.98	125.00	115.57	172.05	168.00	164.70	135.09
2.	Marketing and Export Promotion Scheme	46.00	45.00	50.00	49.60	61.00	58.59	55.60	36.83
3.	Handloom Weavers Comprehensive Welfare Scheme	125.17	124.87	120.00	119.80	170.00	116.14	119	60.22
4.	Mill Gate Price Scheme	29.59	29.59	30.60	30.60	65.00	65.00	55.60	37.94
5.	Diversified Handloom Development Scheme	16.24	16.00	15.78	13.72	20.00	17.78	24.10	12.62

Source: Ministry of Textile, PIB, GoI, 26th March, 2012.

2.2 Statement showing State-wise funds released and utilized during the last three years and current year under Integrated Handlooms Development Scheme (IHDS).

Sl. No.	Name of the State	2008-09	2009-10	2010-11	2011-12 (as on 15.3.2012)	Total	Total amount utilized
1.	2.	3.	4.	5.	6.	7.	8.
	General States						
1.	Andhra Pradesh	622.49	1110.70	1392.77	922.43	4048.38	1930.75
2.	Bihar	104.26		178.30	104.93	387.49	64.92
3.	Chhattisgarh	61.33		259.08	93.90	414.31	237.43
4.	Delhi	0	16.36	301.47	16.83	334.66	301.47
5.	Gujarat	74.61	97.05	77.06	200.13	448.85	187.78
6.	Haryana	0	43.28	46.56	7.63	97.47	41.93
7.	Himachal Pradesh	75.90	138.74	244.09	181.42	640.16	298.85
8.	Jammu and Kashmir	142.64	132.15	191.64	35.10	501.52	202.95
9.	Jharkhand	283.48	410.88	384.32	661.78	1740.46	935.98
10.	Karnataka	573.84	73.57	172.56	462.36	1282.33	500.26
11.	Kerala	642.62	229.93	124.32	526.74	1523.61	1024.8
12.	Madhya Pradesh	212.55	54.41	308.56	166.74	742.25	481.97
13.	Maharashtra	0.00	16.22	310.52	221.79	548.52	232.69
14.	Orissa	569.57	527.36	712.54	1323.19	3132.67	1356.37
15.	Rajasthan	53.74	14.95	171.93	40.05	280.67	77.23
16.	Tamilnadu	4175.44	5015.01	4867.84	5369.65	19427.94	13122.52
17.	Uttar Pradesh	428.39	305.58	1305.56	1201.16	3240.69	883.61
18.	Uttarakhand	157.32	15.19	306.04	0.00	478.54	162.54
19.	West Bengal	500.70	293.94	901.67	958.04	2654.35	1620.6
	NER States						
1.	ArunachalPradesh	320.83	175.99	187.54	425.36	1109.72	515.44
2.	Assam	311.83	453.91	1024.58	347.16	2137.48	766.35
3.	Manipur	286.29		616.76	1182.75	2085.79	884.21
4.	Meghalaya	54.98	342.04	260.73	246.59	904.34	657.75
5.	Mizoram	0.00	89.69	197.50	60.22	347.41	287.19
6.	Nagaland	242.70	1058.46	802.34	1541.33	3644.83	2045.92
7.	Sikkim	36.94		47.12	59.48	143.54	36.94
8.	Tripura	128.42	84.93	298.56	345.47	857.37	483.07

Source: Ministry of Textile, PIB, GoI, 26th March, 2012.

2.3 Statement showing Statewise releases made during 2008-09 to 2011-12 (as on 29.2.2012) and funds utilized under the Marketing and Export Promotion Scheme (Rs. in Crores)

Sl. No.	Name of the State	Marketing and Export Promotion Scheme					
		2008-09	2009-10	2010-11	2011-12	TOTAL	Amount utilized
1.	Andhra Pradesh	1.87	2.10	2.04	2.07	8.08	7.95
2.	ArunachalPradesh	0.02	0.00	1.75	0.07	1.84	1.80
3.	Assam	2.10	4.11	5.73	2.13	14.07	13.57
4.	Bihar	0.02	0.05	0.04	0.28	0.39	0.30
5.	Chhattisgarh	0.17	0.37	1.12	1.10	2.76	2.70
6.	Delhi	0.37	0.61	0.16	0.09	1.23	1.22
7.	Goa	0.00	0.00	0.00	0.00	0.00	0.00
8.	Gujarat	0.26	0.76	0.27	1.03	2.32	2.00
9.	Haryana	0.37	0.28	0.33	0.10	1.08	1.04
10.	Himachal Pradesh	0.26	0.51	0.61	0.59	1.97	1.90
11.	JandK	0.00	0.00	0.28	0.23	0.51	0.51
12.	Jharkhand	0.04	0.02	0.18	0.00	0.24	0.24
13.	Karnataka	1.44	1.20	1.37	1.26	5.27	5.24
14.	Kerala	0.23	0.00	0.00	0.21	0.44	0.40
15.	Madhya Pradesh	0.12	0.68	0.93	0.52	2.25	2.20
16.	Maharashtra	1.89	1.37	0.99	1.89	6.14	6.10
17.	Manipur	0.35	0.47	1.64	1.58	4.04	3.98
18.	Meghalaya	0.06	0.89	0.42	0.32	1.69	1.60
19.	Mizoram	0.34	0.00	0.05	0.11	0.50	0.45
20.	Nagaland	2.06	3.73	2.33	2.16	10.28	10.23
21.	Orissa	1.07	0.74	1.09	0.54	3.44	3.40
22.	Pondicherry	0.00	0.00	0.00	0.00	0.00	0.00
23.	Punjab	0.00	0.00	0.00	0.00	0.00	0.00
24.	Rajasthan	0.44	0.73	0.38	0.03	1.58	1.40
25.	Sikkim	0.03	0.04	0.13	0.21	0.41	0.40
26.	Tamil Nadu	1.54	0.80	1.44	1.34	5.12	5.00
27.	Tripura	0.09	0.36	0.44	0.61	1.50	1.40
28.	Uttar Pradesh	2.36	1.73	2.09	2.09	8.27	8.12
29.	Uttrakhand	0.46	0.45	0.43	0.30	1.64	1.50
30.	West Bengal	1.06	0.60	1.80	0.35	3.81	3.62

Source: Ministry of Textile, PIB, GoI, 26th March, 2012.

Annexure - 3

Data from Third Handloom Census (2009-10) on Handloom and Weavers in Uttar Pradesh

3.1 Distribution of Handloom Workers by age in Uttar Pradesh

Union/State	*Total Work force (Lakh)*	*Percentage Distribution*		*Total*
		Less than 18 years	*Adult Workers (18 years and above)*	
India	43.3	11.2	88.8	100
Uttar Pradesh	2.6	15.8	84.2	100

3.2 Distribution of Adult Handloom workers (18 years and above) by social Groups

Union/State	*Percentage Distribution*				*Total*	*Number of Adult Workers (Lakh)*
	SCs	*STs*	*OBCs*	*Others*		
India	10.1	18.1	45.2	26.6	100	38.47
Uttar Pradesh	7.6	0.9	83.3	8.2	100	2.17

3.3 Regional Distribution of Weaver households by using various types of Yarn (%)

Yarn	*All-India*	*Uttar Pradesh*
Cotton (1-20)	9.5	22.6
Cotton (21-40)	41.8	19.8
Cotton (41-80)	38.1	2.9
Cotton (above 80)	35.2	0.8
Viscose and Blends	3.0	4.3
Muga Silk	2.6	0.7
Eri Silk	1.4	2.6
Mulberry Silk	3.9	5.7
Other Silk	4.4	34.8
Wool	22.1	1.5
Polyester and Blends	7.7	3.1

3.4 Percentage of weaver Households producing major fabrics in Uttar Pradesh

Major Fabrics	*All-India*	*Uttar Pradesh*
Gamchas/angavastram	40.38	6.74
Mekhla Chaddar	38.52	0.11
Sarong	14.15	0.05
Sari	14.20	47.95
Shawls	6.29	0.36
Towel/napkin	5.99	1.68
Bedsheets	5.58	15.88
Lungi	4.61	0.09
Dhoti	2.04	0.38

3.5 Purpose of Loan by Weavers

Union/State	*Distribution by Purpose of Loan (%)*			*Total*
	Handloom	*Non-Handloom*	*Both*	
India	19.7	72.8	7.4	100
Uttar Pradesh	27.0	53.4	16.0	100

3.6 Number of Handloom Worker Households by Social Groups (2009-10)

State	*Location*	*SCs*	*STs*	*OBCs*	*Other*	*Total*
Uttar Pradesh	Rural	5622	980	49895	6459	62956
	Urban	5360	374	37081	4771	47586
	Total	10982	1354	86976	11230	110542

3.7 Distribution of Handloom Worker Households by Major Sources of Loan (%)

Source of Loan	*All India*	*Uttar Pradesh*
Moneylender	13.4	7.4
Master Weavers	44.6	58.7
Friends/Relatives	4.9	13.0
Cooperative Societies	5.9	1.9
Commercial Banks	14.8	13.9
SHGs	5.0	0.1
Traders	4.3	4.0
Others	7.2	0.9
Total	100	100

3.8 Number of Handloom Worker Households by type of Ration Card

Union/ State	*Location*	*AAY*	*BPL*	*APL*	*No Ration Card*	*Total*
All India	Rural	253110	843040	844656	480311	2421117
	Urban	17805	183656	114631	46062	362154
	Total	270915	1026696	959287	526373	2783271
UP	Rural	4747	11414	41704	5091	62956
	Urban	1489	3930	38832	3335	47586
	Total	6236	15344	80536	8426	110542

3.9 Number of Adult (18 years and above) Handloom Workers by Employment Status

Union/State	*Location*	*Independent*	*Under Master Weavers*	*Under SHDC*	*Under KVIC*	*Under Co-operative Societies*	*Under Private Owner*	*Total*
All- India	Rural	2173343	689694	15048	20960	115019	218161	3232225
	Urban	178279	348912	3614	5323	36248	42234	614610
	Total	2351622	1038606	18662	26283	151267	269395	3846835
Uttar Pradesh	Rural	45987	67622	373	169	301	542	114994
	Urban	9344	91559	577	7	237	297	102021
	Total	55331	159181	950	176	538	839	217015

3. 10 Number of Weaver Co-operative Societies (Active/Total)

Sr. No.	Cluster	Active	Total
1.	Varanasi	473	635*
2.	Mau	221	221
3.	Gorakhpur	72	599
4.	Faizabad	71	71
5.	Lacknow	176	176
6.	Kanpur	47	423
7.	Aligarh	39	238
8.	Barelly	65	99
9.	Moradabad	294	603
10.	Meerut	53	472
11.	Etawah	99	249
12.	Jhansi	62	121
	Total	1672	3272

Source: Weavers Service Centre, Varanasi

3.11 Number of handloom weavers in Co-operative fold

Sr. No.	Cluster	Male	Female	Total
1.	Varanasi	32,366	2,815	35,181
2.	Mau	31,500	3,500	35,000
3.	Gorakhpur	15,200	6,826	22,026
4.	Faizabad	2,865	716	3,581
5.	Lacknow	10,674	7358	18,032
6.	Kanpur	8,233	910	9,143
7.	Aligarh	6,493	2783	9,276
8.	Barelly	3771	1020	4791
9.	Meerut	5040	1260	6300
10.	Etawah	2140	660	2800
11.	Jhansi	12000	3000	15000
	Total	130,282	30,848	161,130

Source: Weavers Service Centre, Varanasi.

3.12 Number of Handloom weavers in Non Co-operative fold

Sr. No.	Cluster	Male	Female	Total
1.	Varanasi	92270	20254	112524
2.	Mau	60885	6800	67685
3.	Gorakhpur	900	482	1382
4.	Faizabad	3284	1407	4691
5.	Lacknow	56933	23450	80383
6.	Kanpur	880	120	1000
7.	Aligarh	9994	2783	12777
8.	Barelly	2240	610	2850
9.	Muradbad	424122	15878	440000
10.	Meerut	39350	16150	55500
11.	Etawah	1200	600	1800
12.	Jhansi	8000	2000	10000
	Total	700058	90534	790592

Source: Weavers Service Centre, Varanasi.

3.13 Raw Material required for different types of Banaras Silk Saris

Sl. No.	Saree type	Yarn type			Yarn count/ N			Silk yarn and Zari (g)		
		Warp way	Weft way	Extra weft	Warp way	Weft way	Extra weft	Warp way	Weft way	Extra weft
1	Brocade saree	Bangalore silk	Bangalore silk	Zari	16/18	16/18	3700	400	250	650
2	Chiffon Jamdani saree	Chinese silk	Chinese silk	Chinese silk & zari	14/16	14/16	3700	300	250	200 150
3	Jamdani saree	Bangalore silk	Bangalore silk	Bangalore silk	16/18	20/22	16/18	350	300	250
4	Jangla saree	Bangalore silk	Bangalore silk	Zari	16/18	20/22	1200	400	350	500
5	Kora cutwork saree	Chinese silk	Chinese silk	Cotton	-	14/16	100s/ 120s	200	250	350
6	Resham butti saree	Bangalore silk	Bangalore silk	Bangalore silk and/or zari	16/18	16/18	16/18 1600	350	250	250 400

(*Contd...*)

7	Satin border saree	Bangalore silk	Bangalore silk	Bangalore silk and/or zari	14/16	14/16	14/16 1600	350	250	150 200
8	Satin embossed saree	Bangalore silk	Bangalore silk & zari	Bangalore silk & zari	20/22	20/22 3700	20/22 1400	350	200 250	200 200
9	Tanchoi saree	Bangalore silk	Bangalore silk	Bangalore silk	14/16	14/16	14/16	400	250	250
10	Tissue saree	Bangalore silk	Zari	Bangalore silk & zari	16/18	3700	16/18 3700	300	500	100 200

Source: Amrita Singh, *A Profile of Banaras Silk Sarees*, Dept. of Textiles and Apparel Designing College of Rural Home Science, Dharwad, University of Agricultural Sciences, July 2008, p. 33.

3.14 Progress of 20 clusters sanctioned under IHCD schemes in Uttar Pradesh: Status of SHGs and Credit Linkage till March 2011

Sr. No.	*Name of the Cluster*	*SHGs formed (No.)*	*Weavers covered*	*Bank A/C open*	*Credit Amount (Rs Lakh)*
1.	Mubarakpur	70	758	65	No Linkage
2.	Barabanki	51	810	49	9.10
3.	Banaras	145	1731	135	102.23

Annexure - 4

4.1 State wise Handloom Mark Registration upto 29.02.2012

S.No.	State	Registration State wise								
		IW	MW	Coop	AHS	RT	MANE	MENE	OTH	Total
1.	Andhra Pradesh	37	21	604	2	6	1	0	0	**671**
2.	Assam	0	0	3	1	0	1	0	0	**5**
3.	Bihar	6	8	54	0	0	1	0	26	**95**
4.	Chhattisgarh	0	3	50	1	0	0	0	1	**55**
5.	Gujarat	38	10	8	2	0	0	0	0	**58**
6.	Haryana	6	0	0	0	0	28	2	0	**36**
7.	Himachal Pradesh	3	9	7	2	0	1	0	0	**22**
8.	Jammu and Kashmir	0	3	7	1	1	0	0	0	**12**
9.	Jharkhand	0	0	1	2	0	0	0	0	**3**
10.	Karnataka	2	4	15	1	1	4	5	1	**33**
11.	Kerala	29	0	204	2	3	1	2	0	**241**
12.	Madhya Pradesh	3	16	16	1	0	0	0	0	**36**
13.	Maharashtra	3	5	5	1	1	0	5	3	**23**
14.	Nagaland	0	0	0	1	0	0	0	0	**1**
15.	Manipur	0	0	0	1	0	0	0	0	**1**
16.	New Delhi	1	1	1	0	2	5	2	1	**13**
17.	Orissa	103	28	38	3	2	0	0	5	**179**
18.	Punjab	0	0	0	0	0	2	0	0	**2**
19.	Pondicherry	0	0	1	1	0	0	0	0	**2**
20.	Rajasthan	12	6	0	1	0	0	0	0	**19**
21.	Tamilnadu	5132	55	908	2	27	24	3	1	**6152**
22.	Tripura	0	0	1	0	0	0	0	0	**1**
23.	Uttar Pradesh	567	10	101	5	3	5	2	5	**698**
24.	West Bengal	6	0	347	1	0	1	2	100	**457**
	Total	**5948**	**179**	**2371**	**31**	**46**	**74**	**23**	**143**	**8815**

Note: IW: Individual Weaver; MW: Waster Weaver; Coop: Primary Cooperative Society; AHS: Apex Handloom Society; RT: Retailer and Traders; MANE: Manufacturer Exporter; MERE: Merchant Exporter; OTH: Others.

Annexure - 5

Twelfth Five Year Plan and Handloom Industry

5.1 Year-wise details of marketing events organized during the year 2007-08 to 2010-11

Sl. No	Name of State	2007-08			2008-09			2009-10			2010-11		
		NHE	SHE	DLE	NHE	SHE	DLE	NHE	SHE	DLE	NHE	SHE	DLE
01	2.	3.	4.	*5*	*6*	7	8	9	10	11	12	13	14
01	Andhra Pradesh	-	08	30	-	07	35	01	14	44	2	13	55
02	Arunachal Pradesh	-	-	03	-	-	02	-	-	01	-	-	06
03	Assam	02	07	27	02	13	30	05	22	49	07	18	57
04	Bihar	-	-	-	-	-	-	-	-	-	-	01	05
05	Chhattisgarh	-	-	03	01	03	03	01	04	07	03	03	06
06	Delhi	-	-	08	-	-	-	-	-	03	-	-	08
07	Goa	-	-	-	-	-	-	-	-	-	-	-	-
08	Gujarat	01	-	-	01	-	08	01	-	-	01	01	07
09	Haryana	-	-	08	-	-	02	-	01	03	-	01	05
10	Himachal Prad.	-	-	10	-	-	13	-	02	25	-	02	30
11	J & K	-	-	-	-	-	-	-	-	-	01	01	03
12	Jharkhand	-	-	-	-	-	-	-	-	06	-	-	07
13	Karnataka	01	01	15	01	02	19	01	06	25	01	06	25
14	Kerala	-	01	03	-	03	03	-	02	03	-	02	02
15	Madhya Pradesh	01	01	08	-	-	10	01	03	13	01	02	12
16	Maharashtra	02	03	05	02	05	09	02	06	15	02	02	15
17	Manipur	-	01	01	-	04	05	-	05	05	01	03	10
18	Meghalaya	-	01	03	-	-	07	-	01	04	-	02	05
19	Mizoram	-	02	08	-	02	10	-	-	07	-	03	10
20	Nagaland	01	03	19	04	10	20	06	15	36	06	04	40
21	Orissa	01	01	20	01	01	24	01	01	23	01	03	23
22	Pondicherry	-	-	-	-	-	-	-	-	-			
23.	Punjab	-	-	-	-	-	01	-	-	-			
24.	Rajasthan	01	-	03	01	-	06	01	-	10	01	-	10
25	Sikkim	-	-	02	-	-	02	-	-	03	-	01	03
26	Tamilnadu	01	01	22	01	02	28	01	02	43	01	11	55
27	Tripura	-	-	-	-	01	04	-	-	09	01	04	15
28	Uttarakhand	01	-	03	01	01	08	01	02	10	01	02	10
29	Uttar Pradesh	-	-	30	01	-	36	01	-	48	01	08	48
30	West Bengal	-	01	16	-	02	16	-	02	19	-	09	22
31	NHDC	-	09	-	-	12	-	-	16	-	01	23	-
32	ACASH	01	06	-	01	06	-	03	13	-	05	19	-
33	*Craft Mela*			*07*			*07*			*07*	04		
34	Others (NEHHDC)	-	-	-	-	-	-	-	-	-		01	-
	Total	**13**	**46**	**254**	**17**	**74**	**308**	**26**	**117**	**418**	**37+4**	**145**	**494**

Source: Report of the Working Group on Handloom for 12th Five year Plan (2012-17)

5.2 Statement showing State-wise number of Clusters and Group Approach Projects sanctioned during 2007-08 to 2010-11 under IHDS

Sl. No.	Name of the State	Clusters				Group Approach		
		2007-08	2008-09	2009-10	2010-11	2008-09	2009-10	2010-11
General								
1	Andhra Prd.	26	11	2	13	127	135	90
2	Bihar	9	5			6		
3	Chhattisgarh	5	3		2	6		24
4	Delhi	0		1				
5	Gujarat	5	4					
6	Haryana	0			1		12	9
7	Himachal Prd.	2		2	3	7	33	17
8	Jammu & Kashmir	0	8		2		11	6
9	Jharkhand	10	11	5	9	23	19	48
10	Karnataka	13	5		5	18		
11	Kerala	19	5			21		
12	Madhya Prd.	10	1	4	2	7		
13	Maharashtra	0			6			54
14	Orissa	16	7	8	5	46	30	16
15	Punjab	0						
16	Rajasthan	2	0	1	3	6		10
17	Tamilnadu	27	10		12	74	45	152
18	Uttar Pradesh	21	14	8	7	76	58	200
19	Uttarakhand	5	1		2	22		22
20	West Bengal	25	9		5	36		29
	Total	**195**	**94**	**31**	**77**	**475**	**343**	**677**
NER								
1	Arunachal Prd.	8	4	3		20	11	14
2	Assam	10	5		12	14	14	33
3	Manipur	19	14		6			
4	Meghalaya	4	1	2		3	14	14
5	Mizoram			1	1		13	23
6	Nagaland	5	9	10	5	4	16	11
7	Sikkim	0				15		15
8	Tripura	10	4	5	6	17		42
Total		**56**	**37**	**21**	**30**	**73**	**68**	**152**
Grand Total		**251**	**131**	**52**	**107**	**548**	**411**	**829**

Source: Report of the Working Group on Handloom for 12th Five year Plan (2012-17)

5.3 The State-wise supply of yarn under MGPS during the year 2007-08 to 2010-11 and State-wise position of operational yarn depots

(Qty. in Lakh Kgs. and Value in Lakh Rs)

S. No	Name of the States	2007-2008		2008-09		2009-10		2010-11		2011-12 (As on July, 2011)		Yarn Depot (As on July 2011)
		Qty.	Value	Qty.	Value	Qty.	Value	Qty.	Value	Qty.	Value	
1	Andhra Pradesh	34.83	4679.9	47.132	5204.29	54.487	6813.13	42.431	7528.55	13.723	3173.27	96
2	Arunachal Pradesh	0.076	16.43	0.056	12.84	0.119	26.14	0.060	18.26	0.013	4.11	10
3	Assam	0.498	124.01	0.506	196.13	1.103	351.45	0.633	491.68	0.149	68.75	42
4	Bihar	4.577	299.95	4.912	433.21	2.998	358.85	1.417	235.17	0.046	12.81	5
5	Chhattisgarh	6..326	876.67	10.592	917.13	10.144	1233.96	13.664	2189.30	7.957	1537.81	6
6	Delhi	0	0	0.004	0.33	0.004	0.42	0.016	2.36	0.000	0.00	1
7	Gujarat	0.146	31.78	0.72	96.6	1.441	192.55	0.194	78.01	1.591	341.81	6
8	Haryana	136.87	8130	218.52	14180.53	465.340	30904.83	540.865	37560.86	111.042	8969.17	51
9	Himachal Pradesh	0.017	7.44	0.46	297.74	0.577	358.44	2.978	525.44	3.325	291.76	8
10	Jammu & Kashmir	0.107	25.86	0.09	43.19	0.341	64.16	7.666	480.61	2.945	184.23	4
11	Jharkhand	0.582	60.27	0.868	102.51	0.816	226.32	0.561	267.02	0.656	208.54	7
12	Karnataka	13.519	1647.2	16.043	2237.66	15.609	2429.89	13.377	2814.24	4.923	1269.06	19
13	Kerala	81.025	3207.6	67.005	3182.01	68.227	3760.09	60.167	4123.66	19.495	1314.57	30
14	Madhya Pradesh	2.654	326.45	1.598	233.77	4.308	620.76	2.540	758.33	1.364	370.89	13
15	Maharashtra	0.574	51.56	0.726	90.52	0.780	106.31	0.730	126.96	0.183	34.78	4
16	Manipur	0.317	72.33	0.468	112.87	0.546	163.73	0.487	180.30	0.332	124.88	37
17	Meghalaya	0.048	25.63	0.114	32.23	0.035	14.57	0.052	20.98	0.022	9.18	6
18	Mizoram	0.723	159.94	0.708	162.93	0.991	231.33	0.932	267.45	0.211	66.87	7
19	Nagaland	0.07	13.12	0.079	16.63	0.081	19.15	0.053	15.45	0.012	3.69	10
20	Orissa	0.671	319.42	1.049	444.57	1.540	665.22	1.113	735.96	0.291	197.18	30
21	Poodicherry	1.566	186.16	2.069	252.7	2.456	332.53	1.812	305.72	0.334	70.12	2
22	Punjab	0.01	0.49	0.02	1.03	14.557	814.48	37.177	2081.73	6.069	330.18	2
23	Rajasthan	1.335	53.55	1.255	53.96	1.610	85.37	2.229	118.20	0.399	23.95	4
24	Sikkim	0	0	0	0	0.013	2.57	0.000	0.00	0.006	1.97	1
25	Tamil Nadu	334.02	31122	422.695	45061.36	385.779	43245.43	337.523	53056.53	59.968	12494.21	187
26	Tripura	0.865	103.63	0.513	99.14	0.730	130.89	0.421	116.63	0.036	8.64	14
27	Uttar Pradesh	50.484	3887.6	53.273	5256.62	42.996	4737.88	34.603	4465.18	3.485	692.19	92
28	Uttaranchal	0.051	3.95	0.051	5.09	0.118	12.29	0.095	10.63	0.090	10.17	5
29	West Bengal	6.246	872.6	3.594	649.99	3.214	808.41	2.164	979.87	0.498	287.75	51
GRAND TOTAL		678.2	56305.2	855.116	79377.57	1080.959	98711.15	1105.962	119555.08	239.165	32102.54	750

Source: Report of the Working Group on Handloom for 12th Five year Plan (2012-17).

5.4 Diversified Handloom Development Scheme (DHDS): Outlay and Expenditure during 11th plan

(Rs. in Crore)

S. No.		11th Plan (2007-12)	Expenditure				2011-12	
			2007-08	2008-09	2009-10	2010-11	BE	Exp. up to 5.8.11
1.	Design Exhibition cum Dyeing workshop	1.21	0.24	0.22	0.25	0.30	0.30	0.10
2.	Training of WSC staff	0.42	0.04	0.10	0.12	0	0.018	0
3.	IIHT.Bargarh (OC)	0	0	0.10	1.263	0.18	0.20	0.108
4.	IIHT.Bargarh	39.79	0	0.77	5.00	1.09	1.335	0.361
5.	Infrastructure for WSCs/IIHTs	14.63	3.13	2.50	0.98	10.35	19.10	10.00
6.	NCTD	3.42	0.22	0.80	0.81	0.85	0.85	0.150
7.	J&K Wool Project	0.89	0	0.70	0.10	1.00		
8.	R&D	0.96	0.14	0.20	0.15	0.14	0.75	0
9.	WSCs in Central Sector	0.06	0	0.02	0.25	0.00	0.547	
10.	Continuation of IIHT. Jodhpur	0.55	0.55	Transferred to Non-plan since 2008-09				
11.	Continuation of WSC. Srinagar	0.33	0.33					
12.	IIHT in State Sector (Champa)	1.05	0	0.01	0	0.00	1.00	0
13.	New IIHTs/WSC under State Sector	3.06	0	0	0	0	0	0
14.	Handloom Census/ Identity Cards	20.36	4.42	10.85	4.75	3.86	0	0
	Total	86.73	9.07	16.25	13.67	17.77	24.10	10.719

Source: Report of the Working Group on Handloom for 12th Five year Plan (2012-17)

5.5 Mandate Recommendations for Weavers Service Centres/Indian Institute of Handloom Technology for 12th Plan

A. Weavers Service Centers

Sl no	Detailed of actions		2012-13	2013-14	2014-15	2015-16	2016-17	Total
1	No of Paper designs to be prepared	Computer	2475	2518	2571	2605	2659	12828
		Manual	2837	2864	2826	2842	2894	14263
		Total	**5312**	**5382**	**5397**	**5447**	**5553**	**27091**
2	No of Cloth samples to be developed	Woven	2230	2262	2201	2325	2354	11372
		Printed	1282	1235	1312	1327	1325	6481
		Total	**3512**	**3497**	**3513**	**3652**	**3679**	**17853**
3	No of new shade to be developed	Synthetic	1241	1291	1279	1352	1369	6532
		Natural	711	718	713	741	721	3604
		Total	**1952**	**2009**	**1992**	**2093**	**2090**	**10136**
4	No of persons to be trained	Crashed course	910	937	975	1026	1045	4893
		Training of Trainer	1500	700	600	500	400	3700
		1 yr. special course	100	100	100	100	100	500
		Under IHDS	7047	7462	6833	6684	6400	34426
		Total	**9557**	**9199**	**8508**	**8310**	**7945**	**43519**
5	No of technical assistance to be rendered		3632	3695	3748	3792	3836	18703
6	Workshop/Awareness programmes		300	300	300	300	300	1500
7	No of R & D projects to be undertaken		5	5	5	5	5	25
8	No of languishing handloom craft to be revived		4	4	4	6	6	24
9	Annual show		12	12	12	12	12	60
10	No of exhibitions to be conducted (NHE/SHE/DLE/ATE)		22	22	23	23	24	114

Source: Report of the Working Group on Handloom for 12th Five year Plan (2012-17)

B. Indian Institute of Handloom Technology

Sl. no	Detailed of actions	2012-13	2013-14	2014-15	2015-16	2016-17	Total
1	No of Diploma students to be admitted at Jodhpur, Guwahati and Bargarh	150	150	150	150	150	750
2	No of Degree students to be admitted at Varanasi and Salem	100	100	100	100	100	500
3	No of persons to be trained under 4 month Short Term course	100	100	100	100	100	500
4	No of persons to be trained under ISDS and other schemes	250	250	250	250	2250	1250
5	No of R & D Projects to be undertaken	2	2	2	2	2	10
6	No of workshop/seminar to be conducted	7	7	7	7	7	35
7	No of seminars to be attended	2	2	2	2	2	10

Source: Report of the Working Group on Handloom for 12th Five year Plan (2012-17)

5.6 Proposed outlay for Training, HRD and RandD for 12th Plan

Sl. No.	Name of component	2012-13	2013-14	2014-15	2015-16	2016-17	Total (crore)
1	**Skill development**	**51.00**	**66.00**	**75.00**	**78.00**	**82.50**	**352.50***
2	Strengthening of Existing WSCs/IIHTs						
a	Construction of own building	42.00	40.00	30.00	16.00	22.00	150.00
b	Setting up of new WSCs	7.00	7.00	7.00	7.00	7.00	35.00
c	Infrastructure on machinery	7.50	8.00	7.00	7.00	6.50	36.00
d	New IIHTs under Central Sector	5.00	10.00	20.00	25.00	20.00	80.00
e	IIHTs under State sector	16.00	16.00	16.00	16.00	10.00	74.00
3	NCTD	1.20	1.20	1.20	1.20	1.20	6.00
4	J & K Project	5.00	5.00	5.00	-	-	15.00
5	R & D	1.40	1.40	1.40	1.40	1.40	7.00
6	Orientation Training of WSC/IIHT staff	0.20	0.20	0.20	0.20	0.20	1.00
7	One time assistance for Design and Product development	0.50	1.00	1.00	-	-	2.50
8	Training to Master Trainer & EDP	1.82	1.34	1.28	1.22	1.16	6.82
9	Introduction of Degree course	18.00	18.00	12.00	12.00	10.00	70.00
10	Revival and documentation of languishing handloom crafts	3.50	3.50	3.50	3.50	3.50	17.50
11	Establishment of 5 regional textile museums	10.00	20.00	10.00	10.00	10.00	60.00
12	Innovative ideas like setting up chair in University	2.00	3.00	4.00	5.00	6.00	20.00
13	Other Activities						
i)	Books and periodicals	1.25	1.25	1.25	1.00	1.00	5.75
ii)	Visit to national and international exhibitions	0.40	0.40	0.40	0.50	0.50	2.20
iii)	Workshop/ seminar/ Market research/ website	0.40	0.35	0.35	0.35	0.35	1.80
iv)	Publicity/Annual show/ awareness prog.	3.00	3.00	3.00	3.00	3.00	15.00
	Total	**177.17**	**206.64**	**199.58**	**188.37**	**186.31**	**958.07***

Note: *Rs. 352.5 crore required for skill development will be met from Integrated Skill development Scheme of Ministry of Textiles.. hence net fund requirement is Rs. 605.57 crore.

Annexure - 6

6.1 Communist Party of India (Marxist) Activity

Date/year of Activities	*Movement*
Jan. 23rd 2001	Demanded low price yarn for the weavers
March 31st 2001	Movement focused on the fraudulent act of Co-operative Society. Their demand of import of raw material under Open General License (OGL) was to benefit the owner of the societies
Feb. 12th, 2004	Movement demanding the waiver of loan, providing government facilities to the weavers
April 4th , 2004	,,
April 6th 2004	Demanded the procurement of finished product through handloom corporation, supply of raw materials by govt. on subsidies rate
July 3rd 2004	Demanded: a) procurement of finished product through handloom corporation, b) supply of raw materials by govt. on subsidies rate, c) Loan upto Rs. 50,000 to weavers without interest rate, d) Waiver of all the previous debt, e) Free electricity, f) BPL card to the weavers
Aug. 13th 2004	Movement against the fraudulent in the weavers identity card
Sept. 15th 2004	Movement to implement the policy of Rs. 2 wheat and Rs. 3 rice and on ration card 35 kg ration per family
Jan. 14th 2005	Movement against the weavers' suicide; to keep away the Co-operatives from the cluster program
Feb. 28th 2005	Movement against the administrative drive to chalan weavers for the electricity arrear
Feb. 11th 2006	Letter to Prime Minister of India making them aware of the situation weavers are facing
May 14th 2006	Movement for BPL cards for weavers; waiver of electricity arrear and previous debt; handloom corporation to direct procure the finished product of weaver; providing low costs yarn; minimum of 20 hours electricity supply etc.
Jan. 15th 2007	Demanded 20,000 BPL and 5,000 red card to the poor weavers; Loan on low interest rate; Central Govt. assistance should extend to the individual weavers
Oct. 11th, 2009	Conference of Weaver to articulate their demand
Nov. 16th 2009	First phase of movement against the Electricity bill payment
Nov. 19th 2009	Movement against price rise; BPL cards and end of atrocities in the name of procuring the debt from poor weavers
Nov. 24th 2009	Second phase of movement against the Electricity bill payment
Dec. 2nd 2009	Third phase of movement against the Electricity bill payment

Source: Official record, CPM, District Unit, Banaras

Index

D

E

F

G

H

I

Y

Z